CLEANING UP

Portuguese Women's Fight for Labour Rights in Toronto

Susana P. Miranda
with Franca Iacovetta

Between the Lines
Toronto

Cleaning Up
© 2023 Susana P. Miranda

First published in 2023 by
Between the Lines
401 Richmond Street West, Studio 281
Toronto, Ontario · M5V 3A8 · Canada
1-800-718-7201 · www.btlbooks.com

All rights reserved. No part of this publication may be photocopied, reproduced, stored in a retrieval system, or transmitted in any form or by any means, electronic, mechanical, recording, or otherwise, without the written permission of Between the Lines, or (for copying in Canada only) Access Copyright, 69 Yonge Street, Suite 1100, Toronto, ON M5E 1K3.

Every reasonable effort has been made to identify copyright holders. Between the Lines would be pleased to have any errors or omissions brought to its attention.

Library and Archives Canada Cataloguing in Publication
Title: Cleaning up : Portuguese women's fight for labour rights in Toronto / by Susana P. Miranda with Franca Iacovetta.
Names: Miranda, Susana P., author. | Iacovetta, Franca, 1957- author.
Description: Includes bibliographical references and index.
Identifiers: Canadiana (print) 20220454299 | Canadiana (ebook) 20220454396 | ISBN 9781771136266 (softcover) | ISBN 9781771136273 (EPUB)
Subjects: LCSH: Women cleaning personnel—Ontario—Toronto—History—20th century. | LCSH: Labor movement—Ontario—Toronto—History—20th century. | LCSH: Women immigrants—Ontario—Toronto—History—20th century. | LCSH: Portuguese—Ontario—Toronto—History—20th century. | LCSH: Employee rights—Ontario—Toronto—History—20th century. | LCSH: Working class—Ontario—Toronto—History—20th century. | LCSH: Building cleaning industry—Ontario—Toronto—History—20th century.
Classification: LCC HD6073.C442 C3 2023 | DDC 331.4/816479623097135410945—dc23

Cover art: Expanding Roots / Vhils Studio.
Cover and text design by DEEVE

Printed in Canada

We acknowledge for their financial support of our publishing activities: the Government of Canada; the Canada Council for the Arts; and the Government of Ontario through the Ontario Arts Council, the Ontario Book Publishers Tax Credit program, and Ontario Creates.

We dedicate this book to the strong, brave, intelligent, and proud women who fought for labour rights and respect in Toronto's cleaning industry.

Dedicamos este livro às mulheres valentes, corajosas, inteligentes, e briosas que lutaram pelos seus direitos e o seu respeito na indústria das limpezas em Toronto.

We applaud the committed activists and organizers who supported these workers' struggle for better pay and working conditions and dignity.

"This volume is an outstanding and rich history of the labour struggles and successes of Portuguese immigrant women workers in the cleaning industry in Toronto. Women workers come alive on these pages through deep and poignant analyses of their courage and claims for dignity and self-worth. *Cleaning Up* has vital comparative implications today for those researching migration, gender, and work. If you want to better understand how forms of employment shape the gendered possibilities of resistance, you must read this book."
—Wenona Giles, Fellow of the Royal Society of Canada, professor emerita, Anthropology, York University

"*Cleaning Up* brilliantly documents the strength and determination of Portuguese/Azorean women cleaners of some of the most prestigious office towers in downtown Toronto, fighting for their employment, health, and safety rights during the 1970s and 1980s. As new immigrant women in Canada with limited education and English language skills, they defined sisterhood and solidarity and were undeterred from standing up to their employers to demand respect and dignity as workers. This recounting of their story is an important contribution to working-class history in Toronto."
—Marcie Ponte, executive director, Working Women Community Centre, and Sidney Pratt, founder, Cleaners' Action

"This book tells the inspiring story of the accomplishments of non-English speaking, poorly educated, and low-paid immigrant women who cleaned offices by night and private homes by day. They maintained their dignity as workers and family members, refused to abandon their original values and customs, and challenged their union. Courageously, they provided a model for all immigrant women to identify their rights and to stand up for them."
—Alice Kessler-Harris, author of *Women Have Always Worked: A Concise History*

"This important study of Portuguese women who cleaned homes and corporate offices demonstrates that neither family nor educational constraints, immigration status, or language will prevent women workers from mobilizing and seeking allies when they are faced with workplace exploitation. Their activism will change their family lives. And sometimes they will win their David and Goliath struggles."
—Donna R. Gabaccia, professor emerita, Department of History, University of Toronto

"Deeply and empathically researched and considered, *Cleaning Up* challenges stereotypical views of Portuguese immigrant women as housebound, docile, submissive, and politically apathetic. Instead, Miranda and Iacovetta reveal how the 'earthly womanhood' and 'feisty militancy' of Portuguese women cleaners and their collaboration with left-leaning feminists, unionists, and other community activists, shaped the politicization and Canadianization of women in the second half of the twentieth century. This book is essential reading for anyone interested in the history of women, immigration, or labour."

—Carmela Patrias, professor emerita,
Department of History, Brock University

"This book should be savoured and read slowly to appreciate its insight and energy. Prepare to enter a little-publicized social map of Toronto, where new immigrants adapted to Canadian culture through progressive politics, family solidarity, and feisty public action for justice. It's a terrific book!"

—D'Arcy Martin, co-author of *Educating for a Change*

"In this pioneering book, Miranda and Iacovetta bring a fresh perspective on a little-known movement in the 1970s of a group of recently arrived Portuguese immigrant women who worked as office cleaners. They fought for justice and dignity, dispensing essential services to the city of Toronto, while struggling to adjust to the new land."

—Domingos Marques and Manuela Marujo, co-authors
of *With Hardened Hands: A Pictorial History of Portuguese
Immigration to Canada in the 1950s*

"This is a wonderful book that documents the agency and activism of Portuguese women workers in the office-cleaning sector. It will be of much interest to both labour studies scholars and those engaged with immigration history."

—Mariana Valverde, professor emerita, Centre for Criminology
and Sociolegal Studies, University of Toronto

"*Cleaning Up* is a fascinating and insightful account of Portuguese immigrant women in the 1970s and 1980s. Defying the stereotypes of southern European women as passive and non-political, these women drew upon family, neighbourhood, union, and community ties to become agents of social change, engaging in strikes, demands for legal reforms, and social justice campaigns. Often the main breadwinners when men were seasonal labourers, injured, or unemployed, women cleaners fought exploitation and demanded fair treatment and respect in an increasingly neoliberal context."
—Linda Kealey, professor emerita,
Department of History, University of New Brunswick

"*Cleaning Up* describes the struggles of Portuguese immigrant women doing essential, but invisible, work as cleaners. Capturing their remarkable perseverance in demanding fair wages and decent working conditions, the story highlights the constant effort required when labour laws fail to adequately protect marginalized workers."
—Ester Reiter, professor emerita, School of Gender,
Sexuality and Women's Studies, York University

"This book exposes the history of a group of workers that for too long remained invisible. Through intensive archival research and dozens of in-depth oral histories, Miranda and Iacovetta narrate this untold story with both scholarly care and political passion. *Cleaning Up* documents the long fight these immigrant women waged, against all odds, to win better pay and conditions as well as dignity at work."
—Ruth Milkman, professor of sociology, School of Labor and
Urban Studies, City University of New York

"It is not a secret that hundreds of Portuguese immigrant women worked as cleaners in office towers and private homes in Toronto from the 1970s onward. Less well known are their struggles to keep their jobs, their pay, and their dignity intact. Miranda and Iacovetta have detailed these women's struggles and honoured their courage, using their own words to tell their stories of heartbreaks and victories. *Cleaning Up* is a book with cogent lessons for similar situations in our times."
—John Medeiros, former community organizer

"Miranda and Iacovetta offer a clear-eyed and compelling examination of a group of feisty, strong-willed, and politically astute immigrant working women who are familiar yet strange to most of their fellow Torontonians outside the Portuguese community. This is a fascinating social history of an unexpected and underestimated group of labour activists and their allies, who achieved impressive personal and collective victories and whose militant spirit endures in public memory despite neoliberal rollbacks of their workplace gains."

—Gilberto Fernandes, Department of History and Global Labour Research Centre, York University

"We have waited decades for the struggles and victories of Portuguese immigrant women cleaners to be storied and celebrated in Canadian publishing. In *Cleaning Up*, Miranda and Iacovetta give us an ode to 'feisty womanhood' and the courageous 'labour heroines' who refused to be exploited by government, wealthy corporations, and other bad *bossas*. I am the daughter of a 'Portuguese cleaning lady' activist and thrilled to see my mother in these pages."

—Aida Jordão, York University scholar and Toronto Workers' History Project theatre director

Contents

List of Illustrations	x
Acknowledgements	xi
Preface	xv

Chapter 1
"I have always worked":
Life in Portugal — 1

Chapter 2
Getting Settled — 25

Chapter 3
The Work of Cleaning, Workplace Control, and the Cleaner's Body — 47

Chapter 4
Forging Alliances with Radical Community Workers
in 1970s Toronto — 81

Chapter 5
Battling Corporate Giants: Union Activism in the 1970s — 109

Chapter 6
"We are women and immigrants but we can fight":
First Canadian Place Strike, 1984 — 135

Chapter 7
Fighting Contracting Out in the Workplace and Political Arena — 161

Epilogue — 185

Notes — 199

Index — 237

Illustrations

Young woman poses by the family's field	16
Young women hold fishing nets	18
"Sweep and Say Union"	80
Cleaner's Action logo	101
Cartoon from *Cleaners' Action Newsletter*	102
Azorean immigrant office cleaners become labour heroines	121
Cleaners' Action activist Sidney Pratt with Queen's Park cleaners	122
Cleaners attend a 1979 union meeting with their children	130
A cleaner casts her ballot in 1980	130
Cleaners vote to ratify a two-year collective agreement in 1980	131
A woman on the picket line of the First Canadian Place strike, 1984	152
Boy guards mothers' items during First Canadian Place strike, 1984	153
Striker and her upset young son on First Canadian Place picket line in 1984	154
NDP MP Dan Heap on First Canadian Place picket line	154
FASWOC striker Lucia Ferreira addresses the crowd during victory party in 1984	155
Arminda de Sousa speaks at City Hall	173

Acknowledgements

Susana: My deepest thanks to the various people who have seen me through this project, from dissertation to book. Most importantly, for not giving up on the idea of this book and her continued insistence that it should be published, Franca Iacovetta. I am deeply honoured to be co-authoring this book with Franca—who inspired my choice of thesis topic when I first read her book *Such Hardworking People* in undergraduate studies. This book would never have been possible without Franca's encouragement and then much hard work and insight in getting it to publication. For his support, and astute and thorough comments on my thesis, my sincerest thanks to my dissertation supervisor Roberto Perin. My thanks also to dissertation committee members Craig Heron and Kathryn McPherson, who provided me with sharp comments on my dissertation, as did the members of my examining committee. The Graduate Program in History at York University, the Faculty of Graduate Studies at York University, and the Canadian Union of Public Employees Local 3903 provided much-needed financial support for my research as a graduate student.

I am appreciative of the assistance of helpful archivists at various archives in Canada and one in the United States. Undertaking a research project whose subject matter was relatively recent in history meant that many records had not yet made it to archives. I am indebted to those individuals who allowed me into their homes and offices to access private papers, including David Amow at CAW (now Unifor) Local 40, Domingos Marques, João Medeiros, Wendy Iler, Jean Connon Unda, and Sidney Pratt—who provided primary sources from near, when visiting, and far (Brazil). For permission to use the photos in this book, thank you to David Amow (Unifor Local 40), Domingos Marques, and Maureen Fair at West Neighbourhood House (formerly St. Christopher House).

Oral history was also essential for this project. My deepest thanks go to those community workers, labour and feminist leaders, members of the Portuguese community, and especially cleaners, including my own dear family members, who shared their time, stories, and insights with me. Some of these individuals are no longer with us, and I hope this book bears testament to their dedication and hard work.

I was fortunate to be a part of intellectually stimulating and supportive reading, writing, and social groups in graduate school, including the Women's and Gender History Reading Group at York University, the Toronto Labour Studies Group, the Larkin writing group, and the Toronto Area Women's Canadian History Group. I am lucky to still be close to good friends made in graduate school, including Tarah Brookfield, Samantha Cutrara, Teresa Marques, and Alison Norman, as well as friends from the Portuguese Canadian History Project: Raphael Costa, Emanuel Da Silva, and especially Gilberto Fernandes, whom I pestered with questions while working on this book and who always graciously offered his help and support. Friends outside of academia, you know who you are, have provided many years of devoted friendship and encouragement.

This thesis turned book could not have been completed without the support of my family. My parents provided crucial financial support and encouragement, even if they did not entirely understand what I was up to in the many years of the PhD. Despite my relative lack of income and stability, important values for immigrants who started a new life in Canada with very little, they never questioned my decision to see my studies through, and I know they are proud of me. My brother, Rui, provided much-needed moments of silliness and laughs, and he and my sister-in-law, Misha, have always provided support if needed. My nieces, Sonia and Layla, and god-daughter Julia Marques, bring me much joy and I hope they will be interested in reading about part of their heritage one day. My mother, my best friend, has always been a constant source of amazement for me for her boundless love, generosity, energy, and work ethic. She is the inspiration behind this book and will always be my heroine.

Franca: I would especially like to thank Susana Miranda for giving me the wonderful, enlightening, and humbling opportunity to contribute a little bit of my original research and perspective to the pioneering and eye-opening doctoral work that forms the basis of this study. I am grateful to the friends, colleagues, and comrades who supported my involvement in this collaborative project: Molly Ladd Taylor, Kathryn McPherson, Margaret McPhail, Marcel Martel, Roberto Perin, and Kathy Scardellato. As always, I thank my partner, Ian Radforth, for his critical insights, engaging conversation, helpful editing, and unconditional support and love during yet another project. The interviews I conducted for the Rise Up! a digital archive of feminist activism project, Women Unite: Feminist Activism in Toronto, 1970s–1990s, were not linked to this book project, but they offered me a remarkable opportunity to speak with and learn from feminists who helped to shape the activism that provided an important context for the politicization of the Portuguese cleaners. So, I would like to acknowledge the members of the Women Unite committee—Amy Gottlieb, Meg Luxton, Sue Colley, and Tara Cleveland—and express my immense gratitude to the activists who generously agreed to be interviewed: Judith Ramirez, Barbara Cameron, Holly Kirkconnell, Wendy Cuthbertson, Margaret McPhail, Martha Ocampo, Cenen Bagon, Anita Fortuno, Genoveva (Genie) Policarpio, Beverly Bain, Sidney Pratt, and Marcie Ponte. A special thanks to Sidney and Marcie for sharing their stories and insights about organizing among Portuguese women cleaners and their generosity in responding to the later follow-up questions and requests related to this book.

As our dedication makes clear, this book could not have been written without the willingness of so many to share their stories about this exciting and important but for too long little-known history. We both thank Michael Moir (University Archivist) and Julia Holland with the Clara Thomas Archives and Special Collections at York University for their help in accessing certain photographs in a continuing pandemic. And Lauren Laframboise for solving a mystery. We are grateful to Ian Radforth for the meals and designated recreational periods (for swimming, boat rides, and drinks on the dock) he provided during a particularly intensive period of writing at Franca and Ian's cottage—all while completing his own book. For their generous and helpful reviews of our manuscript, we thank Julia Aguiar, Craig Heron, Julie Guard, Rhonda Hinther, and Meg Luxton. We owe a special debt to Meg, whose thought-provoking questions and detailed commentary helped us to sharpen our analysis and better situate our contributions.

We are both particularly grateful to the artist, Alexandre Farto (Vhils),

Acknowledgements   xiii for permission to use an image of his stunning mural to Portuguese women's labour activism in Toronto for the cover of our book. He could not have known this, but the unveiling of the mural was the spark that propelled us to write this book together. At Between the Lines, editor Amanda Crocker offered the right mix of enthusiastic support and encouragement to finish, and design and production manager Devin Clancy handled the production with care and gave us that wonderful cover. Thanks to Siusan Moffat for the index. And a huge thank you to Tilman Lewis, copy editor par excellence, whose thoughtful questions as well as careful editing made this a better book.

Preface

The Portuguese cleaning lady has been a shadowy yet compelling figure in Toronto's social and cultural landscape. In the second half of the twentieth century, Portuguese women were a common sight on the streets of Toronto, speaking rapidly in their language as they made their way to and from jobs cleaning either the corporate and government buildings in the downtown core or private homes throughout the city. But while the women were visible to some passersby, and to those who encountered the women on the buses, streetcars, and subways of Toronto's public transit system, their labour was largely invisible. For they toiled behind closed doors in the homes of middle-class and rich owners who were away all day, or in the offices of security-protected buildings after the wealthy tenants and staff had gone home for the night.

Between the late 1960s and early 2000s, Portuguese immigrant women carved out and maintained an occupational niche in Toronto's cleaning industry, in the sectors of both nighttime building services and daytime domestic cleaning. The recent unveiling in Toronto's Little Portugal of a stunning mural to Cleaners' Action (est. 1975), a grassroots network where Portuguese office-building cleaners worked with frontline community activists to fight for better rights, offered a tribute to the women's militancy.[1] The mural was created by prominent Portuguese urban artist Vhils (Alexandre Farto). In attendance was eighty-nine-year-old Idalina Azevedo, an Azorean from Pico Island whose portrait dominates the mural. Arriving in Canada in 1969 (initially to Wawa, Ontario), she learned some English. In Toronto, she became a union steward and led a wildcat strike against the Toronto-Dominion Centre, one of the shiny new skyscrapers to occupy the city's financial district. Like the other women whose voices and stories animate *Cleaning Up*, Azevedo defied the stereotype of southern European rural women as docile, apolitical, and hidden in the shadows.[2]

In contrast to the nighttime janitorial cleaners who went on strike and engaged in attention-grabbing picket-line behaviour, the Portuguese women who cleaned the private homes of well-to-do Torontonians for cash were more hidden from public view. As landed immigrants, these domestic workers stood outside the federal government's highly restrictive temporary-worker schemes that recruited racialized women from the Caribbean and the Philippines into ghettoized live-in domestic jobs. As private daytime, or live-out, domestics earning money in the informal economy, Portuguese cleaning ladies negotiated the terms of their labour with individual employers, though as workers who toiled in the underground economy, they could make no claims on the state for benefits.

However, as the stories collected here also make clear, these more isolated cleaners also pursued family-linked strategies of survival and material betterment and they developed effective female networks of information and support. They, too, sought greater control over their work regime and demanded respect for the critical labours they performed. Another striking similarity among the private day cleaners earning cash under the table and the nighttime office cleaners hired on contracts is that their wages, though unjustly low and always vulnerable to being reduced or ripped away, were often the family's main income. With many husbands earning only seasonal wages in the construction industry, nursing injuries from unsafe worksites, or unemployed, these women filled essential roles as family breadwinners.

Still another striking similarity among Toronto's Portuguese house cleaners and janitorial cleaners—and one they shared with other immigrant women workers—was their capacity for hard work and ability to attribute worth to their labouring lives. Women like Joaquina Gomes, an immigrant from the mainland town of Marquiteira in central Portugal who became a lifelong day cleaner, were acutely aware of the social stigma attached to doing the "dirty" immigrant job of cleaning for better-off Canadians. But she also derived a sense of self-worth from a job well done and by keeping her eye on the prize—helping to purchase a family home and ensuring a better future for her two Canadian-born children. Lucia Ferreira offered similar reflections. She was an Azorean immigrant who made ends meet by combining some daytime housecleaning with her main night shift janitorial job at First Canadian Place. Built by Olympia & York Developments, a company owned by the wealthy Reichmann brothers, that towering symbol of corporate capitalism housed the headquarters of the Bank of Montreal as well as other businesses. Ferreira's sense of pride in her work as an office cleaner and family provider, combined with her anger over the exploitative conditions she and her co-workers endured, turned her into a labour activist.[3]

Whether cleaning ladies or janitorial workers, or both, these women also took pride from the fact that their actions increased their control over work regimes in private houses or initiated labour reforms, and changed Toronto in other ways. The stories are also bittersweet. These now elderly women have lived for years with the physical as well as psychological and emotional toll that years of financial worry, strenuous labour, exposure to chemicals in cleaning supplies, workplace exploitation, and anti-immigrant prejudice took on their bodies. All that work and worry may well have cut short the lives of some who are no longer with us.

Cleaning Up tells the largely unknown history of Portuguese immigrant women of mainly rural origins who became workers dispensing essential services to the city of Toronto, and then major agents of social change in Toronto's cleaning industry. More than fifty years after their arrival in Canada after the Second World War, the book gives voice to the struggles, dreams, victories, defeats, and legacies of the women who dominated the domestic- and building-cleaning workplaces of 1970s to early-2000s Toronto. We examine the dramatic changes that occurred in their lives and in the service industry with which they became so closely associated. The book highlights the stories and strategies of non-English-speaking immigrant women who spearheaded social change by transforming the conditions of their paid daytime domestic labour and by fighting for workers' rights. In doing so, it replaces the conventional passive portrait of the immigrant cleaning lady with that of the engaged woman worker and militant labour activist.[4]

Drawing on interviews, newspapers, social agency and union records, and other sources, the book traces the women's transition from labouring in Portugal's impoverished farming and fishing villages and towns to becoming waged workers in Toronto. Born mostly in the 1940s and early 1950s, the women's pre-migration experiences often included some participation in waged labour or encounters with urban markets or districts beyond the village. Our narrators recall the sacrifices made as young immigrant mothers juggling the demands of wage earning and child rearing in an unfamiliar city. They highlight the dense networks of

Preface   xvii female relatives, co-villagers, and neighbours who helped them find jobs or negotiate with employers or join a union drive. Daytime house cleaners quickly embraced their new identity as women workers and purposefully sought to reshape the "servant" experience of domestic work into a skilled or "professional" occupation. By demanding higher wages and shorter workdays and cultivating an occupational expertise, they created more equitable, but never fully egalitarian, relations with the mostly female Canadian employers whose homes they cleaned. Acting as female immigrant workers and family breadwinners, the office cleaners' struggle for justice and dignity in Toronto's building workplaces offered an impressive example of rank-and-file labour mobilization.[5] By pressuring unions and politicians to respond to their concerns as low-paid immigrant workers in the service sector, these janitorial cleaners played a role in (temporarily) reforming labour law in Ontario. They also earned the respect of the labour movement. In sum, by shaping the sectors of both live-out domestic cleaning and building cleaning for the better and influencing the community work agenda of social service agencies, the actions of Portuguese house and office cleaners in Toronto had an effect on the wider Canadian society.

While daytime private cleaners toiled in isolation and enjoyed few state-sanctioned labour protections, the nighttime cleaners hired on precarious contracts to clean buildings faced the daunting challenges associated with the neoliberalism of the 1970s and 1980s. Neoliberalism, premised on the pro-business argument that "human well-being" is best achieved by "liberating individual entrepreneurial freedoms and skills" in a free-market and free-trade context, views the role of the state as one that mainly facilitates these conditions.[6] One of the most pernicious practices embraced by profit-thirsty building owners who advanced a neoliberal agenda was the outsourcing—or contracting out—of cleaning services to far-less-capitalized subcontractors who competed fiercely for contracts, bringing down the price. Corporate building owners actively undermined workers' hard-fought union rights by awarding contracts to cleaning companies that issued unrealistically low bids. The corporate owners were then freed of the legal responsibility of being an employer while the contractor, deemed the employer under labour law, found ways to cut costs. For their part, government institutions used contracting-out measures in order to cut the costs of cleaning their public buildings. Since labour was the single most costly item in a cleaning contract, the workers' wages, unions, and jobs were constantly endangered.[7]

xviii

Cleaning Up

With a passion still evident many years later, office cleaners who faced these assaults reflect on how they overcame their fear, lack of English, and other obstacles to protest contracting out and to save their livelihood by forging links with community and social justice activists, joining unions, striking, and lobbying politicians to act in their interests. In shedding light on the centrality of contracting out as a profit-making strategy for capital and a cost-cutting one for governments, the book also documents the economic vagaries and injustice wrought by neoliberalism.

The support that striking Portuguese office cleaners received from husbands and children underscores the critical importance of family-linked strategies of survival, and challenges southern European stereotypes of overbearing patriarchs and submissive wives. To be sure, many women carried the burden of the double day, and the fear or experience of domestic violence was part of the grim reality of their lives.[8] In writing about Toronto's Portuguese women, anthropologist Wenona Giles insightfully notes the paradox of women who resisted workplace exploitation not overtly challenging the unequal division of labour in the home. But our research suggests Giles draws too sharp a contrast. Many of these women compelled husbands to take on child minding and other domestic chores, and otherwise effected change in their families.[9]

The nighttime cleaners who took on big capital and pro-business government ministries, spoke out at press conferences, railed against indifferent elites ensconced in their favourite upscale restaurants, and shaped picket-line culture in distinctive ways arguably deserve recognition as labour heroines, even as we acknowledge the mixed and ambiguous legacy of that activism. Most everyone—journalists, union leaders, and the corporate owners, government ministers, and cleaning contractors who expected docile workers—was astonished by the militancy of the Portuguese women who led union drives, sustained strikes, and lobbied the state for better protections. Highlighting both their successes and their disappointments, we trace the women's transformation from non-political actors under Portugal's Estado Novo (New State) dictatorship—which repressed women and harassed and imprisoned unionists and radicals—into labour militants in Toronto. Apart from a tiny left-wing element and some sympathetic priests, the Portuguese community and its male elites showed no interest in these plebeian women. This was particularly true for the Azorean islanders who stood on the margins of a (still emerging) organized immigrant community made up mainly of

Preface   xix

mainlanders.[10] Aided by the efforts of activists radicalized by 1960s-era social movements, the politicization of Toronto's female cleaners took shape amid the insurgence and resurgence of multiple radicalisms in the 1970s and 1980s. Born out of a contracting-out crisis, one successful grassroots experiment was Cleaners' Action, the subject of Vhils's mural. The cleaners' stories of turning for support to radical community organizers, social justice activists, and labour feminists reveal their determination to acquire the tools needed, including a knowledge of unions and labour legislation, to improve their lives and bring about social change.[11]

Interviews with the mostly female activists who worked closely with the nighttime cleaners, as well as documentary and media sources, reveal a fascinating mix of New Left, feminist, and liberation ideologies, Freire-inspired pedagogies, and pragmatism. This loose coalition of allies included US-born and Portuguese-speaking Sidney Pratt and Azorean immigrant Marcie Ponte, both of Cleaners' Action and other initiatives, feminist labour lawyer Michelle Swenarchuk, and union organizer Wendy Iler, as well as prominent New Democratic Party politicians like Dan Heap. An examination of their strategies and actions sheds light on the radicalization of Portuguese immigrant cleaners in late-twentieth-century Toronto. That the Portuguese cleaning woman became a symbol of the new era of assaults by big business and the state on working people also helps to explain the support these workers received from the labour and feminist movements and the NDP, as well as from community activists.[12]

Men were also involved in cleaners' activism, but the women proved more militant. In assessing Portuguese women's wider contribution to Toronto's labour movement, we raise broader questions about researching and commemorating non-English-speaking immigrant women's still understudied role in the expanding service sector and in labour activism in postwar Canada.[13] We note some of the similarities and differences between the Portuguese working women and the Italian and Greek women who arrived earlier and to whom they were frequently compared. We offer some comparisons between Portuguese daytime house cleaners, who arrived as landed immigrants from Europe, and the racialized Caribbean and Filipina women who arrived under the highly restrictive domestic guest-worker schemes.[14] We draw some comparisons as well between the Portuguese immigrant office cleaners who became politically active in 1970s and 1980s Toronto and the Latina/o im/migrant cleaners who participated in the Justice for Janitors (J4J) campaigns in the United States.[15] The relationship that Portuguese women cleaners forged with union organizers, community activists, and other allies in Toronto also speaks to a pattern of acculturation rarely addressed in studies of immigrant adaptation, namely that grassroots organizations and progressive unions can provide an alternative, more bottom-up, and more radical path to integration into the host society than that offered by middle-class gatekeepers promoting bourgeois models. Furthermore, it points to a strong case for the importance of union organizing that starts with the concerns and knowledge of the workers involved and is linked by coalitions with other activist groups.[16]

Our analysis of Portuguese women's labour militancy diverges from feminist labour histories whose concepts of working-class femininity, female respectability, and militancy derive mainly from research on dominant-majority women, such as Anglo-Canadian workers in heavily Protestant Ontario. We highlight the more earthy and proletarian culture of southern European women that drew on their capacity and pride in performing demanding physical labour, their "sharp tongues," and the close link between their protest strategies and their commitments to family obligations.[17] Finally, we discuss why these women's stories and experiences remain important to present-day immigrant cleaners and other workers who, in the 2020s, face the intensification of neoliberal measures like contracting out. Our historical research, the epilogue also suggests, offers some insights, even lessons, for present-day labour struggles.[18]

A Feminist Collaboration

As co-authors, we have moved in organic fashion towards this collaborative project. The book's origins lie in Miranda's 2010 doctoral dissertation on Portuguese immigrant women in Toronto's cleaning industry. That thesis built upon the growing body of work in immigrant working women's history produced by feminist scholars, including, by the mid-1980s, Iacovetta, who initially focused on southern Italians in post-1945 Toronto.[19] Iacovetta's subsequent research trajectory involved archival research on Portuguese working women, while her political work with Rise Up! a digital archive of feminist activism involved interviewing labour and community activists, including Pratt and Ponte.[20]

We are trained historians, and the book is rooted in plenty of archival research and fifty interviews with cleaners, labour leaders, feminist activists, community organizers, and cleaning company employees.

Preface   xxi

Within the context of feminist standpoint theory—which might be characterized as rejecting male (and elite and bourgeois) defined modes of knowledge presented as universal truths in favour of the (often divergent) knowledge generated from the material realities and everyday life experiences of women and other historically marginalized groups[21]—we note our personal and political motives for completing this project in immigrant women's labour history. As a Portuguese Canadian whose mother, aunts, and neighbours were domestic cleaners, Miranda knew that the widely shared assumption that most Portuguese immigrant women were homemakers was patently false. And she had heard enough stories about the cleaners' strikes as well as day cleaners' interactions with employers to know that neither did they fit the docile workers' profile that other outsiders held of them. Two decades earlier, Iacovetta's research on southern Italian working women in Toronto had been motivated by similar reasons (her mother was a laundry worker) and challenged the same stereotypes.[22]

Oral History

Given the importance of women's stories in this book, some further commentary on our oral history sources is in order. During the period 2006–9, Miranda conducted forty-one in-depth interviews; the sample includes eighteen cleaners, twenty-one community and union organizers, and two male employees of cleaning companies. As part of Women Unite: Feminist Activism in Toronto, 1970s–1990s, a project undertaken by Rise Up! a digital archive of feminist activism, Iacovetta conducted seven interviews with a total of twelve community, union, and feminist activists, including Pratt and Ponte, during 2020–22. In addition, we both carried out follow-up conversations via email or phone, and consulted other relevant Women Unite interviews, all of which are posted on the Rise Up! website. We also discussed Miranda's interviews in detail and consulted the transcripts, most of which Miranda had translated from the original Portuguese to English. When drawing on the in-depth interviews, the use of a pseudonym or actual name reflects the choice of our narrator (interviewee). When drawing on confidential social agency records, the client's name is avoided or fictionalized. We do identify individuals (strikers, managers, public figures) who appear in archival documents, were quoted in newspapers, or delivered speeches that we attended by their actual names. In a few instances, the source itself provided only a woman's first name.

Like other feminist practitioners of oral history, we want to "tell stories that matter," particularly about historically marginalized subjects who left behind few records because they were illiterate, did not have the time to write, or did not think their stories worth telling. (All of these reasons applied to most of the Portuguese women cleaners interviewed for this project.) Insofar as this is a work of historical recovery, oral history is also here a feminist methodology to uncover and assess the courage and militancy of non-English-speaking immigrant women who barely appear in mainstream histories, and to challenge damaging stereotypes and renarrate conventional histories. As the editors of a recent volume in feminist oral history put it, "We know, too, that the telling of those stories—the processes by which they are generated and recorded, and the contexts in which they are shared and interpreted—also matters—a lot."[23]

Almost half a century ago, pioneering feminist historians such as Sherna Berger Gluck used oral history to validate and highlight the rhythms of women's lives, and to negotiate the dynamics of authority and power that shape what Luisa Passerini, another ground-breaking scholar, calls the "social relationship that is the interview." Across many disciplines, feminist practitioners were motivated by a desire to share knowledge about women and other historically marginalized subjects, and to disrupt understandings of the past as well as of the present. They sought to write impactful histories that could empower women and contribute to meaningful social change. Over the past five decades, many important stories have been narrated and analyzed, and the methods by which they were collected and shared subjected to critical reflection. Certainly, the self-reflexive turn in the field has in some cases degenerated into navel-gazing, but there is today an impressive body of research, theory, and debate that not only features more subjects but also seeks to decolonize knowledge and decentre knowledge rooted in heteronormativity, patriarchy, and capitalism.[24]

This book is neither primarily an engagement with theory-and-method debates in oral history nor an exercise in self-reflexivity, but some key insights certainly informed the interviews and our interpretation of them. Put baldly, the interview is no less a mediated source than the fragmentary records preserved in the archives. Just as we must understand the written record's provenance and the possible motives of its author, we must be attentive to how our narrators tell their stories as well as the historical context about which they speak. We are labour feminists, but our approach eschews a polarized dichotomy between a

Preface

naively empiricist view that assumes the interview tells us what actually happened in the past and the postmodern stance that relegates every interview, like every archival document, to the record maker's fiction. As with other types of sources, in interpreting the interviews, we have been attuned to both the material and the discursive.

We understand "the material" in the first instance as our responsibility as social historians to be informed interviewers who understand the historical context about which our narrators speak. In the second, to be attentive to the material realities that circumscribed women's lives and to appreciate that their stories not only bear some resemblance to their past—including their efforts to make their own history amid challenging circumstances—but also shed light on those past experiences. As regards "the discursive," we appreciate that (retrospective) interviews, like archival records, are mediated sources that require careful interpretation. In addition, unlike other historical sources, the historian/interviewer plays a role in creating this record, and so must be aware of their relationship to their narrator and how their position as an insider (Miranda) or outsider (Iacovetta) affects the dynamics of the interview.[25] And, of course, the interviewer may be both an insider and outsider.[26]

Interpreting the interview requires us to appreciate that interviews are memory sources shaped by the narrator's present as well as their past. And to pay attention to how the women told their stories. The repetitive phrases, multiple and/or competing narratives, as well as the silences can be equally revealing of how a narrator understands their own history. We draw on the analytical insights of different approaches that help us best understand the women's complex lives and how they understand and give meaning to them. In telling their stories, we have been sensitive to the range of factors just described.[27]

Finally, this book is not only an intellectual and political project, but also a labour of love. Our analysis points to the tensions between, on the one hand, the women's courage and achievements and, on the other, the stinging defeats and ambiguous legacy of their labour struggles. Our social position as the Canadian-born daughters of rural southern European women who became lifelong workers in Canada has shaped our appreciation for the sacrifices they made and influenced the pride we take in their accomplishments. We hope that we have done justice to their stories and to those of their allies.

Chapter 1

"I have always worked":
Life in Portugal

When Carolina Soares, an immigrant to Toronto from a rural village in the Estremadura region in central Portugal, was asked whether she expected to enter the workforce in Canada, she said yes. But she also seemed a bit offended. "I always thought I would work [in Toronto]," she explained; "I have always worked—so there." She added, "Life was like that" in Portugal; "working from a young age . . . I knew I was going to work here too."[1] In Toronto, Soares picked vegetables on a farm outside the city outskirts and then worked in a laundry before becoming a daytime cleaning lady, earning cash by cleaning private homes. Azorean-born Idalina Azevedo also cleaned for wages in Toronto, but mostly in the formal (officially recorded) workforce. A nighttime janitorial worker who cleaned downtown corporate offices, she would become a union steward.[2]

Soares's observation about having "always worked" applies to the tens of thousands of other women who left their villages in mainland Portugal and the Azores for Canada after the Second World War. While of mainly rural origins, many of these women had held a variety of jobs and interacted with "outsiders" before settling in Toronto. Like Soares and Azevedo, most had migrated to Canada as members of young families, and their strategies were informed by family goals, a transplanted family work ethic, and obligations to relatives both near and afar. Compelled to leave Portugal because of threats to the livelihood of their struggling farming (and fishing) families, these women had also been denied a decent education and full political rights by a long-standing dictatorship. Far from being simply insular and backward peasants, however, many of them had participated, albeit modestly, in the growing consumerism as well as the expanding urban female job market that obtained in Portugal by the 1960s. Nor were they a homogenous group. Their homeland experiences differed depending upon various factors, including age, family finances, proximity to cities, and the timing of their emigration.

Soares and Azevedo were among the millions of people who over the course of the twentieth century left Portugal for locales around the globe. Until 1974, when the Portuguese military overthrew the long-reigning right-wing Estado Novo regime, Portugal lagged well behind other western European countries that had undergone significant, if uneven, degrees of industrialization and urbanization. Its economy remained rooted in small-scale production. "The rural and village world," notes political scientist António Costa Pinto, "dominated Portuguese society" well into the twentieth century.[3]

As late as 1960, 77 percent of the population was still rural, though thereafter the pace of urban and industrial growth picked up.[4] Yet even as improved housing and city jobs increased after 1960, people left in large numbers for Canada and other countries, including France, the United States, and Brazil. In migrating, they left an authoritarian regime, first under António Salazar (1932–68) and then under Marcello Caetano (1968–74), that had regulated and constrained their lives. To better understand the lives of Portuguese immigrant women like Soares and Azevedo, we need first to better understand life in their homeland and why they left.

Portugal: Politics

Once an imperial power, Portugal by the nineteenth century was a relatively poor nation. Having lost some of its colonies, including Brazil, the nation's ruling classes continued to live off diminishing colonial returns and the exploitation of rural labour rather than investing in domestic industrial production. The republican coalition that ousted Portugal's constitutional monarchy in 1910 introduced a range of modest reforms and invested in some industry. It also exploited the African colonies (which included the Cape Verde Islands, Guinea-Bissau, São Tome, Angola, and Mozambique) for their resources and oversaw a tiny export sector of wine, cork, canned fish, and textiles. It endorsed universal suffrage (at least initially), anti-clericalism, and an anti-British nationalism in defence of Portugal's empire, which also included holdings in India, Macau, and Timor.[5]

The political instability of the republican government—which faced opposition from the Catholic Church, monarchists, and the landed elites, as well as a large national debt and labour strife—undermined its efforts to build a civic political culture. Living off subsistence agriculture, politically inactive, and strongly Catholic, the populace offered no surge of support "from below" for the Republic. In 1917, the fascist-leaning Sidónio Pais seized power and appointed himself president-dictator, but the Republic was reinstated a year later following his assassination.[6]

The inability of the military dictatorship that overthrew the republican government in 1926 to take a firm hold on power set the stage for the União Nacional (National Union). A proto-fascist party led by generals, the União Nacional seized the reins of government in 1930 while making concessions to the far-right extremists. The result was a single-party dictatorship headed by an appointed prime minister and a national assembly deprived of any real power. The 1933 constitution then established the Estado Novo.

António Salazar, the former minister of finance in both the military dictatorship and the União Nacional government, served as the Estado Novo's head of state until 1968. A pious conservative Catholic of rural origins who became a university professor of economics, Salazar's political doctrine was rooted in far-right social Catholicism. Like Mussolini and Hitler, he opposed liberal democracy and violently repressed opponents, though unlike his charismatic counterparts, he avoided public speeches. The state's repressive machinery was bolstered by strict censorship laws, the control of the courts, the banning of political parties, and myriad laws curtailing any social organization that might inspire dissent. There was also the secret police, PIDE (Polícia Internacional e de Defesa do Estado, or International and State Defence Police). Aided by spies and informants, PIDE's torture and murder of dissidents, real and imagined, both in Portugal and overseas, kept people in a perpetual state of fear.[7]

Some scholars argue that the regime's lengthy tenure—four decades—owed something as well to its ability to cultivate "an external image of a benign and aging authoritarianism that stood as an anti-communist bulwark of Western civilization."[8] Canadian officialdom, at least, was not easily duped by such actions as permitting the United States to build an air force base on the strategically located Azorean islands. "Portugal, one must remember," cautioned an External Affairs official in 1958, "is a dictatorship, however benevolent it may seem."[9]

Like other dictatorships, the Estado Novo endorsed a common form of state corporatism, by which a ruling party assumes the role of mediator between the workers, capitalists, church, and other important state interests by institutionally incorporating them into its apparatus.

Dismissing liberal democracy and capitalism as the cause of class conflict and cutthroat competition in the pursuit of selfish personal interests, Salazar spoke of corporate bodies that would encourage class harmony, but as sociologist Diamantino P. Machado notes, that harmony was in fact manufactured through coercive state measures. And the nation's wealth was produced on the backs of exploited peasants and workers, both urban and rural.[10]

The 1933 statute that institutionalized state corporatism (*Estatuto do Trabalho Nacional*) ensured government control of the labour unions. All unions outside state control, along with strikes, sit-ins, and lockouts, were outlawed. The primary units comprising the corporate structure—such as the trade or industry-specific guilds, *casas do povo* (rural unions of employers and workers), and *casas dos pescadores* (fishermen's associations), were organized into larger regional or national federations. But most people rarely if ever interacted with these bodies or with politics in general, making a mockery of claims about equal representation.[11] The hypocrisy was not lost on a Canadian embassy official in Lisbon, who noted that the directors of these institutions were "handpicked from the Prime Minister's National Union Party." "The Corporative State," he opined, was a "façade to mask Dr. Salazar's dictatorship."[12]

Assessing the regime's mantra of *Deus, Pátria, e Família* (God, country, and family) reveals more hypocrisy. Theoretically, families, as the primary social unit, could exercise their voice through the *freguesia* (a unit of local government), but there was in fact no popular participation in government. Through its docile ally, the Church, the state maintained long-standing inequities by fostering the quiescence of the poor and prohibiting the formation of working-class organizations.[13] Such political realities would affect the immigrants' worldview in Canada, manifested by a suspicion of state authorities and a reluctance to engage with formal politics in general. Emigration itself can be a political act, however, and many families left Portugal to avoid the drafting of sons into the military and the colonial wars. The decline of Portugal's empire began in 1961, when the Indian army reclaimed its Indian territories, including Goa. Then, in what were known as wars of liberation in the former African colonies, Portugal conscripted hundreds of thousands of young men to fight in an ultimately unsuccessful set of campaigns to defeat nationalist movements in Angola, Portuguese Guinea (Guinea-Bissau), and Mozambique between 1961 and 1974.[14] Overall, though, economic suffering, more than politics, drove emigration.

Education

The extremely limited educational opportunities available in authoritarian Portugal are illustrated by the fact that in 1970 fully half of the population was illiterate.[15] The Estado Novo had no interest in modernizing education, as limiting schooling was itself a form of non-violent social control. Compulsory education came only in 1956, at four years for boys and three for girls (upped to four in the 1960s), but the shortage of teachers and facilities in rural areas meant many children never attended school. In addition, parents needed children to start supporting the family at a young age, usually ten or eleven. And even if a working-class family could spare a child's labour, the cost of high school and university was prohibitive. One way for poor, rural boys to pursue a higher education was to join the seminary, which was always eager to mould young boys into priests. Salazar, though not poor, went this route.[16]

Strict teachers and the use of corporal punishment undoubtedly kept other students away. Canadian immigrant Maria Vasconcelos recalled, "The teachers would hit us with rulers on our fingers, when we didn't know how to do the math."[17] The ideologically laden curriculum taught students the conservative values of resignation and obedience, the centrality of the family, and Christianity.[18] Some of Canada's Portuguese immigrants, particularly the earliest arrivals, were illiterate, but after 1960, a majority of them had literacy skills. Women exhibited higher levels of illiteracy than men. Grappling with illiteracy, even in their own language, would make the task of earning a living in Canada even more challenging for them.

Society

Under the Estado Novo, Portugal was deeply divided along class lines and economic power was heavily concentrated. The very small upper class was composed of large landowners, financiers, industrialists and businessmen, the officer corps, the Catholic hierarchy, and prominent professionals. A modest middle class consisted of small-scale entrepreneurs; civil servants and academics, most of them men; and less prestigious professionals such as teachers. The working class comprised the largest segment of the population, with a substantially lower standard of living than the classes above them. Between 1950 and 1970, working-class people made up 75 percent of the economically active population.[19] Largely agrarian, the working class included small landowners and rural labourers who sometimes engaged in other forms of wage labour. The small urban working class grew larger in the 1950s and 1960s.

The upper classes demanded strict deference and obedience from those under them. Class differences informed codes of speech: an elite person used the familiar *tu* (you) with a social inferior, while the latter addressed their superiors by *o senhor/senhora* or *senhor doutor* (not necessarily a doctor). A middle-class housewife would call her domestic by her first name (as in Maria) while she addressed her employer of the same name as Dona Maria.[20] In Canada, many Portuguese immigrants would reject these practices of subjugation, partly in the belief that it was a more egalitarian society. This class inheritance would also inform the efforts of immigrant women who became cleaners to transform their relations with their private homeowning employers or to resist exploitative management practices.

Economy

In the 1950s, Portugal was still Western Europe's poorest nation, but some progress had been made over the course of the dictatorship's lengthy rule. During the Second World War, the great demand in neutral Portugal's traditional exports (minerals, tinned fish, textiles, and wine) led to an increase in the number of factories, particularly around Lisbon and Oporto. In the 1960s, Portugal's membership in various European and international economic arrangements and institutions signalled an opening up of its economy and the emergence of a "modern" middle class. Still, efforts to industrialize without abolishing the corporative system, or allowing greater democratization, stymied economic development.[21]

Despite the stresses of the colonial wars, the Portuguese economy generally expanded during the 1960s and early 1970s. But the wars in Africa absorbed almost half of the nation's annual budget,[22] as the regime subordinated the nation's socio-economic development to support them. Measures like increasing income tax to help subsidize the military effort hit the poorest workers the hardest.[23] A Canadian official insightfully observed that "the whole tax structure, like the whole economic machinery, tends to weigh against the little man—the small entrepreneur and wage-earner."[24] But war also brought some economic benefits. The cost of maintaining the empire forced the regime to open up the country to foreign investment, and the army's growing demand for consumer goods and military equipment stimulated production. The manufacturing and service sectors increased significantly, while agriculture and fishing stagnated. With increased industrialization came increased urbanization.[25]

Nonetheless, Portugal remained sharply divided between a tiny minority of the rich and well-to-do bourgeoisie and the great majority of the people, who faced varying degrees of poverty. Dismissing "the picture of well-being and prosperity" drawn by Portuguese diplomats, another insightful Canadian official reported that "the economic reality" in 1960 Portugal "is that life is hard" and "the standard of living is pitifully low."[26] As regards immigrants, Canadian officials (and their industry allies) were mainly interested in Portuguese men as cheap labour, but some understanding of people's difficult lives and the many applications received from prospective emigrants did play a role in Canada's decision to open the doors to Portugal.[27]

Estado Novo ideology embraced rurality as an almost sacred way of life and demonized cities, but the regime never initiated agrarian reforms. Portuguese agriculture was characterized by a strong predominance of small farms in the north and large farms in the south. Since the regime limited farmers' access to the capital resources necessary for modernization, outdated farming techniques contributed to poor performance. In the south, wealthy absentee landlords who profited by exploiting cheap rural labour chose not to purchase modern machinery or use modern farming methods. Scarce agricultural investments led to a low proportion of irrigated land relative to need and potential, as well as inadequate supplies of farm machinery and fertilizer.[28] A Canadian official travelling through the southern province of Alentejo in 1958 wrote about the "rows of reapers working not even with scythes but with sickles as in Biblical times."[29]

Furthermore, increases in the income earned through farming products generally lagged behind increases in the price of farm machinery or fertilizers. Official pricing policies sought to keep food costs artificially low rather than providing incentives to farmers. As a result, the rural sector saw an exodus of workers and the increased importation of agricultural products. But the emerging industry could not absorb the rural exodus, and Portuguese industrial workers were the worst paid in Western Europe. Facing such poor prospects, "the Portuguese worker was forced at best to emigrate and at worst to live at a bare subsistence level."[30]

Like Carolina Soares and Idalina Azevedo, most Portuguese immigrants to Canada came from rural villages. These typically consisted of a cluster of houses, a parish church, a school, and possibly a general store that doubled as a café or tavern. Families walked, sometimes long distances, to their fields beyond the village. Before the late 1960s, one-storey, red-roofed, and white-washed houses made of stone and clay predominated in the central regions and the Azores. Houses made of the large stones available in the more mountainous region were the norm in northern Portugal. Furniture was minimal; it included beds, nightstands, dressers or trunks, and a kitchen table and cabinet.

Most families raised chickens, rabbits, pigs, and other small animals meant largely for a family's consumption, but the animals were also sold for extra income. It was a common practice to butcher one or two pigs a year; the meat was an important source of food in the winter months. Cows were also common, particularly in northern Portugal and the Azores. People travelled to larger towns to buy shoes, textiles to make clothes, or other goods. Television sets appeared by the early 1960s, not in individual households, but at a local store or café where villagers gathered to watch shows.

The needy had few avenues for aid outside of charity. Better-off individuals might provide alms to the poor, a practice ingrained in this Catholic society. The father of Maria Martins, who later immigrated from Castelo do Neiva, a village in northern Portugal, to Canada (initially Sudbury) in 1972, donated a small plot of land to a landless family (the poorest of all) so they could build a house. As eldest daughter, Martins's own contribution to her large family was significant: she worked in the fields and, having learned to sew at age thirteen, made clothes for her parents and siblings.[31] Individual families might donate food and clothing to the local parish for distribution to the poor. The *casas do povo* and *casas dos pescadores* provided some unemployment benefits and medical care, but many poor families could not afford the monthly membership dues.[32] Receiving government assistance was still more rare. The immigrants' use of social services to buttress struggling family incomes in Canadian locales like Toronto would thus mark a rupture from their homeland experience. Or, put differently, the social welfare state created opportunities to develop new strategies of survival.

As with most migration streams of economic migrants (as distinguished from refugees), neither the destitute nor affluent left Portugal in large numbers. Rather, it was small landholders and underemployed workers that most often sought to improve their status through migration. Between 1926 and 1967, over one million workers left Portugal.

Persistent emigration during the 1960s actually led to a drop in Portugal's overall population, with the northern and Azorean regions being the most heavily depopulated. Indeed, in terms of scale and impact of emigration, Portugal is second in Europe only to Ireland.[33]

Before the Second World War, Portuguese migrants favoured the United States and South America, particularly Brazil and Argentina. By the 1960s, Western Europe, particularly France and West Germany, as well as North America were the primary destinations.[34] Approximately 17,000 Portuguese migrants came to Canada in the 1950s and then 140,000 in the 1960s and 1970s, half of whom were women.[35] Emigrants from Portugal were leaving from the industrial as well as agricultural sectors. Certain industrial employers tried to stem the flow of workers by raising wages and improving benefits, but the Portuguese state generally relied on emigration to solve the problem of unemployment and underemployment. The Emigration Junta created in 1947 (a time of high unemployment) to regulate and oversee emigration developed a quota system based on a familiar safety-valve principle: export the excess labour and restrict departure for those in occupations deemed important for the nation's economic development.[36] Also, emigrant remittances became an important source of financial aid to the country. In 1972–73 alone, they totalled US$1.1 billion, or 10 percent of Portugal's national income.[37]

Local Scenarios

Portugal is not a large country, but it does have distinct geographic and socio-economic regions. Specific regional and local conditions motivated emigrants' departure from the various regions. In the north, emigration was largely triggered by two interrelated factors. First was the excessive fragmentation of the land into increasingly smaller and less productive farm plots. The problem reflected the practice of partible inheritance, by which all children inherited a part of their parents' land.[38] Second, the region's weak industrial and service sectors could not absorb the supply of workers leaving the farms in search of jobs. Rita Ramos's recollection of farming as a young woman in northern Portugal before she left for Toronto in 1971 captured part of the dilemma. To feed themselves, her family used every inch of their small farm plots, but overcrowding the plots with corn, pumpkins, and other crops made it difficult to plant or gather certain crops without damaging others. No one, she said, talked about modernizing agriculture until the 1974 Carnation Revolution that toppled the regime. In response to the greater yields that resulted from the introduction of crop specialization, modern technology, and fertilizers, she added, an uncle had sadly lamented all the time wasted in his life "doing work the wrong way."[39]

The central region of Portugal, which includes the capital city of Lisbon, was more densely populated because of its comparatively more developed industrial and service sectors. Both on the small farms that predominated in the north and the larger farms that tended to be based in the south, families supplemented their farm income with fishing, an important activity along the coast of the entire country. (Everywhere, however, the fishing industry was handicapped by antiquated techniques and equipment and undercapitalization.) Overall, however, most farms were too small to provide full-time employment or an adequate livelihood for families, while wages in industry and the trades remained too low to provide a decent standard of living. As is so often the case, emigration was a rational response to people's difficult and worsening situation.[40]

In the middle of the Atlantic, the archipelago of nine islands that comprise the Azores produced the largest number of Canada's postwar Portuguese immigrants. Here, people combined farming, the primary way of life, with some participation in the fishing and dairy industries. No significant industrial sector existed. The large landowners and their hired labourers tended to be concentrated on the largest island of São Miguel, while small holders dominated the other islands. The rising demographic pressures in an underdeveloped area with limited land and few industrial prospects led people to emigrate. The vast majority of them headed to North America, where a chain of migration, at least to the United States, had existed since the mid-nineteenth century. By the 1980s, more than 60 percent of Portuguese immigrants in Canada came from the Azores, though "mainlanders" figure significantly in more recent migration streams.[41]

Conversely, many postwar mainland Portuguese migrated to other European countries such as France, which was a relatively quick train or car ride away.[42] Venezuela was the preferred destination of those who emigrated from Madeira, the largest of the group of islands located off the northwest coast of Africa, but a modest number of those who left the densely populated island and its small-scale cottage industries (embroidery, wicker furniture) came to Canada.[43]

Some scholars partly attribute the 1974 democratic revolution that overthrew the Estado Novo to Portugal's transition from a peasant to a post-industrial society. The rise of a new urban middle class, increased emigration, a tourist boom, and emigrant remittances, they note, accelerated the pace of socio-economic change. When emigrants returned home on holidays, they showed off new cars and built houses made of concrete on family plots.[44] The tensions created by an official ideology of ruralism and the signs of urban emigrant wealth were exacerbated by people's weariness over the string of unsuccessful colonial wars.[45]

Still, Portugal never witnessed a mass mobilization against the dictatorship, though there was a small but active—and mostly Communist, urban, and male—underground resistance, as well as some (harshly repressed) labour and student strikes.[46] Instead, the Portuguese military seized power in a virtually bloodless coup. Nursing professional grievances, increasingly aware that the wars in Africa were unwinnable, and conscious of the plight of the country's own agrarian poor, military captains led soldiers into Lisbon on 25 April 1974 and liberated the country from the Estado Novo.[47] But since most Portuguese immigrants to Canada left before 1974, they arrived with little experience (unless they had migrated elsewhere first) of a democratic society.

Women

Like other dictatorships, the Estado Novo endorsed the patriarchal family and an ideology of "Women for the Home" rooted in the notion, endorsed by the Catholic Church, that women by nature were best suited to stay at home, bear children, and serve their husbands. The laws passed reinforced the authority of the husband-father and the subordinate status of women, who were stripped of the few rights gained under the republican government. The republicans had instituted mandatory education for young girls and boys, legalized divorce with equal treatment of both sexes, introduced a two-month maternity leave even for single women, and created some new jobs. The constitution of 1933 reduced the maternity leave, curtailed divorce, ended co-education, and gave husbands the right to force wives to stay at home. Without a husband's consent, a woman could not leave the country (until 1969) or open a business or enter into a contract.[48] The Civil Code of 1967 went further still by legally requiring women to perform the family's domestic labour. Officially dubbed undesirable, women's paid work outside the home was considered acceptable only in the lowest orders. The use of contraception was illegal, and women caught having an abortion faced up to eight years of imprisonment.[49]

The high rate of infant mortality under the Estado Novo regime (50 percent) reflected women's malnutrition and their physically ravaged bodies, and their pronounced illiteracy (64 percent in 1970) exposed the pitifully low priority placed on educating them. And yet, there was no major mobilization around women's rights during the Estado Novo. According to feminist scholars such as Virgínia Ferreira, women's overwhelmingly rural existence precluded their emancipation. Poor levels of education and minimal experience with urban consumerism constrained the freedoms of women, who remained tied to their families. Of course, with the ongoing labour required to make a living from small-scale farming, rural parents wanted at least some daughters to stay at home. Women who landed urban jobs, adds Ferreira, were constrained by the lack of state social supports, so they would rely on family for child care and other forms of aid.[50] The climate of fear created by repressive state agencies like PIDE also stifled women's activism.

But nor did rural women live static lives. Even the wives of husbands who migrated internationally underwent change as they took over the family farm in Portugal and performed other important economic roles. Beginning in the 1960s, women's participation in the labour market increased for various reasons, including the depletion of male workers due to the colonial wars and emigration.[51] Also, employment opportunities expanded with industrialization. Portugal's accession to international economic organizations increased industrial policies focused on the export of consumer goods, such as textiles, in which female labour was important. The coastal urban centres that supplied the internal markets also grew, thereby stimulating the growth of service industries that hired women. The feminization of the active labour force thus increased from 18 to 26 percent during this decade.[52]

By 1970, women's wage earning had become decisive. The female rate of participation in the formal labour force varied by region: for example, it was 23 percent on the mainland, 29 percent in Madeira (with its local embroidery industry), and 8 percent in the Azores (because of minimal industrialization). Overall, 30 percent more women held jobs in factories and other workplaces in 1970 than in 1960. The figure for the service sector was 47 percent. Conversely, the proportion of women working in agriculture declined.[53] Still, women entered the manufacturing and service sectors largely through unskilled and poorly paid jobs. The worst off was the *criada* (servant or maid), who in 1961 earned an hourly wage of 2.5 escudos (US$0.09). For a monthly income of 300 escudos (US$10.50), a live-in maid worked twelve-hour days, seven days a week. "Typically a country woman," notes Machado, "the *criada* was the most exploited worker in Portugal until 1974."[54]

Out of the Shadows

Without denying institutionalized sexism, feminist scholars have challenged the reductionist claim that women's lives in Catholic, patriarchal Portugal have historically been marked solely by subordination. Anthropologists have done so for the post-1945 era by studying women's everyday lives in various locales. In a pioneering study of peasant women in a central Portuguese village in the early 1960s, Joyce Riegelhaupt shows that while legal codes excluded the majority of married women from participating in political life and limited their economic activities, women played an active role in family decision-making and economic life.[55] Emilio Willems's study of family structure in Portugal during the 1950s reveals that women in working-class families were not subjected to the seclusion practices that applied to the women of the bourgeoisie. Noting that the harsh economic realities led women, both married and single, to become family breadwinners to a significant extent, he goes so far as to argue that women's full participation in breadwinning activities precluded male dominance.[56]

Based on her extensive analysis of women in northern Portugal, Caroline Brettell issues a caution akin to that made by feminist scholars of other southern European rural women. Namely, that we need to juxtapose the legal and religious codes subordinating women to men with the socio-economic realities of women's lives. Examining Portuguese women's lived experiences, she shows how they were situated at a complex nexus of subordination and agency.[57]

Women's Labour

A focus on women's everyday lives, and the labour they performed, offers valuable insight into the oppression-agency nexus. Women were central to their family economies in Portugal through both their unpaid and paid labour. Evidence from oral interviews and from case files from the International Institute of Metropolitan Toronto, a social agency that served immigrants, documents women's varied work backgrounds in Portugal. "Housewife" is commonly listed, but so, too, is farm, garment, domestic, and factory work. As in rural Italy and Greece, the term housewife itself can be misleading, as it often encompassed a wide range of activities. The household was a site of women's work, but outside it, there were few tasks (including fieldwork) that were not habitually performed by both men and women.[58]

As youthful immigrants, many Portuguese immigrant women had very recent experience as daughters and young wives supplementing the family income in various ways. This was especially true of later arrivals, as Portugal's economy diversified over the 1960s. Like Carolina Soares, they came to Canada intending to secure paid work. Economic need was a major motivating factor, though they were not, as earlier scholars of Canada's Portuguese claimed, "forced" to work for wages.[59] (The same was true for women who left villages for cities within Portugal.) Paid work in Canada was not a significant rupture with women's experience in Portugal, particularly by the mid to late 1960s and into the 1970s.

Just as rural families who migrated to cities within Portugal continued with a family-centred economy that involved women working in factory and service jobs,[60] Portuguese women's activities in Toronto were informed by a collective work ethic transplanted from their rural villages and towns. As in other rural societies, the nuclear household was the primary form of economic and social organization, and families relied on every member, including children, to do their part. When children married, they created their own households and were no longer expected to support their parents, though they were supposed to care for them in their old age. Grandparents often watched small children while parents worked. From a young age, daughters were trained to become efficient household workers. In a period when domestic labour was onerous, household chores—baking bread, cooking, making clothes, doing the laundry, cleaning—were time-consuming tasks. As families were typically large, this reproductive labour was an especially important component of the family economy.

Modern home comforts emerged slowly in Portugal, but in the 1960s and 1970s many homes began to transform, albeit unevenly. Electricity was available before indoor plumbing. Women's pre-migration domestic worlds depended on their family's economic means as well as time of migration. Those who left for Canada earlier, in the 1950s and early 1960s, had lived in more rudimentary homes than those who came later and thus made a greater leap in terms of living conditions through migration. When Mariana Batista came to Canada in 1961, her family home in the rural fishing village of Ribamar in central Portugal had neither electricity nor running water. As a girl and young woman in the

1940s and 1950s, she fetched water from a natural spring near her village or collected rain water in barrels. Women washed laundry by hand at a communal site near a natural spring that villagers called *rio do povo* (river of the people). Batista's father eventually installed a wash basin outside the family home, and later a well. Petroleum lamps were used for light. Women cooked food over firewood in the kitchen's fireplace-like oven. Just before Batista left in 1961, the family got an indoor bathroom when a toilet and hand basin were installed in the house. But they still fetched water from the well for bathing.[61]

Depending upon the location, the floors of these village houses were generally made of ceramic, cement, or unvarnished wood. Women scrubbed floors on their hands and knees with a brush and a bar of soap, and sometimes applied bleach in powdered form to whiten them. As our narrators recalled these scenes in interviews, some shook their heads in sadness, saying, "See how backwards things were" or "It was a disgrace." Such commentary also "speaks from the present," to quote prominent oral historian Luisa Passerini, meaning in this case that it reflects in part the home comforts they later enjoyed in Canada. The women's recollections are filtered as well through their experiences as immigrant workers cleaning houses or offices in Toronto.[62]

The later-arriving immigrants in particular included many women who had experienced a transformation in living conditions at home before leaving for Canada. Some of those who had married in Portugal before migrating had built more modern houses made of bricks and cement and had enjoyed indoor conveniences. For them, an engagement with growing consumerism began in Portugal, not Canada. The daughters of better-off families had similar experiences. This was true of Joaquina Gomes, a 1970s-era arrival from the central mainland village of Marquiteira who became a cleaning lady in Toronto. Gomes's father made a good living in fishing, and by the time she left for Canada in 1972, she had spent a dozen years living in a "new" modern family house with electricity, indoor plumbing in the bathroom, and a gas stove. But even so, they still fetched well-water for kitchen use.[63]

Married and living with her husband in their home in Peniche, a fishing town in central Portugal, Joana Soares had enjoyed the benefits of indoor plumbing for a number of years before migrating to Canada in 1972. Her story about the doctor who visited in 1965 to check on her newborn son offers a revealing insight into class relations in Portugal. Upon entering the house, the doctor was shocked to find an indoor bathroom (with toilet, sink with running water, a bidet, and full shower). With obvious pride, Soares remarked that "it was probably one of the first bathrooms of poor people like us."[64]

Sewing or embroidering was another economic activity centred in the home. Many married women made clothes for their own family, but also some items for extra income. This is how Lucia Ferreira, who later left São Miguel for Toronto in 1972, supplemented her family's income.[65] The files of the International Institute of Toronto cite hand sewing, machine sewing, clothing repair, embroidery, dressmaking, seam-stressing, and needle work, as well as "sewing factory" and "dress factory," as women's former occupations in Portugal. Textiles for clothing were no longer made by hand by this period, but some women made bed coverings from the purchased raw cotton they spun on a home loom.[66] Many women had used sewing machines powered by a foot pedal, but they would still have to learn to operate the new industrial machines in factories in Toronto.

Portuguese women performed plenty of agricultural labour. In addition to farming their own land, farm families might rent parcels of land for cultivation, earn wages by working for larger landowners,

Dressed in her Sunday best, a young woman who later became a cleaner in Toronto poses by the family's field in the late 1960s. The outline of the town, located in central Portugal, is visible at the top of the terraced hill. Susana Miranda collection.

or earn some cash by selling crops. All family members participated in these activities. In the Soares family, two sons and three daughters grew potatoes, carrots, grapes, and other crops on their farmland, while their mother sold "excess" produce at the local market. The mother also supplemented the family income through sewing.[67] The selling of goods at the markets in nearby towns or cities was gendered. Women generally sold produce, eggs, and small animals, whereas men sold large animals (such as cows and bulls) and wine. On Pico Island, Idalina Azevedo would make and take breakfast to her father and brothers working on the family plot and then work with them. Her mother did not do so, only because their large family of six children kept her extremely busy completing time-consuming household tasks.[68] But many other wives and mothers worked in the fields alongside the men.

Many women earned much-needed wages for their cash-starved farm families by working for other landowners, both small and big. In summer and fall, they picked fruit on neighbouring farms. Those hired by the large commercial farms that supplied Lisbon merchants sorted the fruit and wrapped it up for selling.[69] Hardly exceptional, women made up a large portion of the paid agricultural labour force because, as Brettell noted, they could be paid less than men. Often, women were concentrated in agricultural labour, while men pursued trades such as masonry or embarked on temporary sojourns.[70] As Rita Ramos recalled the physically demanding nature of agricultural labour—she remembered never sleeping enough after a hard day's work because she had to get up very early to milk the cows—she quipped, "I lived at the wrong time."[71] But agricultural work could also be a time of socializing. Maria Martins, who hailed from a rural village near Viana do Castelo in the north, recounted how local families would help each other gather cereal crops such as corn or wheat. In a wistful tone, she remembered, too, how they sang together as they worked.[72]

Women also played gender-specific roles in the fishing industry, an activity that usually combined with some agriculture for many families. Several of our interviewees had assisted their fishermen fathers by repairing the fishing nets, usually as unpaid labour. But women might also earn a wage by fixing nets for other fishing families, as Celia Filipe did after her father quit the industry.[73] Women as well as men collected seaweed to use as fertilizer on the family's land or sold it for cash; men did so from the ocean, while women stayed on shore and used a sieve-like tool to collect the seaweed at the water's edge.

"I have always worked"

Young women hold fishing nets in a religious procession where the town residents present the fruits of their labour to the community, thus highlighting the important role of daughters who repaired their fathers' nets in the economy of families that combined fishing and agriculture. Central Portugal, c.1965. Susana Miranda collection.

The growing number of women who entered Portugal's formal labour force after 1960 toiled in various workplaces. Immigrants to Toronto had worked in shoe, biscuit, glass, canning, jewellery, cigarette, button, paper, cork, and garment factories in Portugal. Most of these factories would have been on the mainland, where industrial activity was concentrated. Daughters financed the all-important trousseau with these wages. Instead of parents siphoning what little family cash there was for a trousseau, the daughter paid for her linens, towels, china, and glassware through factory work, though it did mean the family lost her valuable unpaid farm labour.

During the mid-1960s, sisters Carolina and Joana Soares, who lived near the fishing town of Peniche, worked at a fish-canning factory from their mid to late teens. Along with about eighty other women, they organized and cleaned the freshly caught fish, while their male co-workers ran the ovens and packed the fish for delivery. "That factory," declared Carolina Soares, "was a godsend in our area at that time," the "first thing we had then that was not agriculture." Soares preferred the factory not only for the income, but also because she enjoyed socializing with the other women. At home, she had worked only with her parents. One of the twenty or so married women employed at the plant, Soares continued to work there for a year after getting married, while her husband worked in France. They left for Canada in 1968. Soares's factory had a syndicate that collected workers' complaints, but as she noted, it was sympathetic to management. So nothing was done regarding employees' complaints about not being paid for the time spent waiting (sometimes for hours) for the fish delivery. But the syndicate did ensure that they received some income during the winter slack period.[74]

Born in Batalha, a small town in central Portugal, Emilia Silva had worked at a sweater factory from the young age of twelve. The adults, she recounted, operated the big knitting machines, while the children earned a few pennies each day unravelling the sweaters with defects so the knitters could reuse the yarn.[75] Rosa Moreira's work experiences point to opportunities created by women's growing engagement with the commercial economy. She left her small village, also in central Portugal, to live with an older, married sister in the nearby town of Lourinhã, where she worked as a salesperson in a home appliances store. Like many wage-earning daughters, Moreira sent money home, where her parents and four other sisters continued to farm under inhospitable conditions.[76] As Joana Soares's story illustrates, income-earning opportunities opened up in the service industry too. After getting married, she and her carpenter husband bought a café. She and one employee ran the café while her husband practised his trade (just as he later would in Canada).[77]

In Europe and elsewhere, rural families commonly placed daughters in service to perform domestic work in other people's homes, some located nearby and others far away. Postwar Portugal was no exception.[78] Sent into *servir* by her parents, who lived in the central Portuguese fishing village of Ribamar, Mariana Batista worked for several families in the region. She performed every household chore, from cleaning, washing, and cooking to minding the older children after a mother gave birth. She also spent two years as a maternity nurse's assistant at the local hospital. She then immigrated to Canada with her husband in 1961.[79] Natalia Vilela cleaned and did the laundry for the teachers who came in from Lisbon to teach at the local school in the small village of Marquiteira; a co-villager worked for the parish priest.[80]

Domestic jobs were typically found through personal connections and word of mouth, as was the case for Joaquina Gomes from central

Portugal. From age thirteen, she served as nanny and cleaner for two different families based in larger cities (Aveiro and Caldas da Rainha) located quite a distance from her hometown of Marquiteira. Personal networks help explain why one of these family employers urged her to take night classes while working for them so she could keep up with her education. Gomes's sister went as far as France to find work; she first joined a village couple who had moved there and then landed work as a nanny. Both sisters returned home after a few years to tend to their father's fishing nets and then both married. One of them, Joaquina, later left for Canada. The sisters' experiences in service underscore Riegelhaupt's point that, for all of its exploitative features, there were certain positive advantages to paid domestic work. In contrast to family-based farming, women working in the cities could more easily make wider contacts with the outside world. Their contact with more affluent and modern homes could be transformative, at least culturally. As teenagers in the mid-1960s, Gomes and the two sisters closest to her in age (the family had five girls and two boys) were the first women in their village to wear pants.[81]

The lack of industrial activity on the islands made service a particularly common occupation among Azorean women. Family size and age could also determine who entered paid domestic work. The parents of Fernanda Correia, the second-eldest of four daughters, kept her at home to assist her overtaxed mother, whose household included four men, and sent her sisters to clean houses in Ponta Delgada, the capital of São Miguel.[82] In addition to agricultural labour, Idalina Azevedo cleaned houses for wealthy families on Pico Island before marrying and migrating to Canada in 1962.[83] The files of the International Institute of Toronto record Azorean women who had kept house for elite professionals (doctors, professors) and Americans connected to the US army base on Terceira Island.

Sofia Bettencourt's story well illustrates how Portugal's class system and Cold War realities shaped the experiences of Azorean women. Bettencourt grew up very poor but, at age four, her paternal grandfather, who had sojourned in Brazil and acquired some larger knowledge of the world, hired a neighbour to teach her to read. Noting that she "didn't want, in any way . . . to be ignorant," Bettencourt wished to continue with her education, but her parents could not afford it. Her father's employer, however, had a cousin who was a doctor with two young children, one of them a daughter Bettencourt's age. The doctor's family hired her as their daughter's playmate and supervisor and allowed her to attend secondary school. In short, her parents' ability to form a relationship of patronage with a well-to-do family allowed Bettencourt to escape a life of poverty.[84]

But when the doctor's family fled Portugal for political reasons, Bettencourt lost her support system and had to give up her dream of becoming a schoolteacher. Instead, at age sixteen, she held service-sector jobs such as kitchen help in a restaurant and a nighttime caregiver to a widow. Then, through her sister—who, like many Azorean women, worked at the US army base on Terceira Island—Bettencourt, now nineteen, became a nanny for an American family. (The family's cleaning lady was also Portuguese.) Like some other Azorean women, Bettencourt's sister eventually married an American soldier and moved to the United States. Bettencourt instead married a Portuguese carpenter. The couple lived in a modernized home on São Miguel Island until 1966, when they left for Canada with their two children.[85]

Across Portugal, women faced limited educational opportunities, but the most disadvantaged were Azorean women, because they lived so far from the higher-level schools. Like the woman from São Miguel who "wanted to take a course to be a midwife," the isolation could kill dreams. "My parents," this woman wrote years later in a life story, "did not give me permission to study because I would have to go to the mainland. . . . I was sad for a long time."[86] Joaquina Gomes's father would not let her train as a nurse because it required her to work at night, which he thought was not respectable. Nor did he want to spend the money for her keep in Lisbon.[87] Clever enough to have "skipped" grade two, Maria Martins also wanted to pursue an education beyond the elementary system, which ended at grade four. But because her parents could not afford to send all their children to school, they chose to send none of them.[88] Their own dreams crushed, many women, when deciding to emigrate to Canada, considered the better opportunities that might exist for their children there.

Emigration

Fifty years after feminist scholars began to "disaggregate the family"— namely, to view it not as an indistinguishable unit but instead an arena of negotiation among members with unequal power—much light has been shed on the decision to emigrate. Despite their subordinate position, many (though not all) women influenced decision-making in their families. This was equally true of Portuguese women.[89]

The first Portuguese migrants were men, many of whom left behind wives who joined them later. Some single men, like Mariana Batista's husband, returned to Portugal after sojourns in Canada (or elsewhere), got married, and later sponsored their wife's arrival in the country. Having married a man who had left for Canada single five years earlier, Batista became in 1961 the first woman from her central Portuguese village to settle in Canada. Indeed, her home in Toronto became a reception area and temporary boarding house for newly arrived Portuguese immigrants.[90] While men were the earliest migrants, the family-sponsored chain migration through which many Portuguese arrived in Canada both drew on and elevated the importance of women's kin networks. It enabled a woman like Celia Filipe of Ribamar, whose parents had paid her to repair the family fishing nets so she could build up a trousseau, to confidently tell her prospective husband that she would not marry him unless he agreed to emigrate to Canada. It was 1977 and, shortly after marrying him when she was twenty-one, they left for Toronto.[91]

Shared objectives also mattered. Whether they migrated through male or female kin networks, couples generally decided together on whether migration was the best strategy for improving their family's standard of living. When Sofia Bettencourt's husband heard from a friend that "Queen Elizabeth" wanted workers in Canada, he told Bettencourt, and they agreed to take the plunge. Emilia Silva's interest in migrating was influenced by a sister already in Canada who reported that making money there was easy. The sister had reinforced the point during holiday visits to Portugal, when she came bearing so many clothes that relatives thought everyone in Canada was rich. "We had the illusion that when you arrived in Canada," recalled Bettencourt, "there would be a tree . . . with dollars falling from it."[92]

The return of immigrants to Portugal helped to spur further migration, though Canadian social workers who worried about ill-prepared rural villagers flooding into Toronto probably exaggerated the naïvité particularly of young men who sailed for Canada expecting to make a quick fortune and return home rich. Most Portuguese immigrants knew that they would have to work hard in Canada. Then, too, some migrants left for political reasons, the growing anxiety over sons being drafted into the military to fight in Africa prompting a number of families to relocate permanently to Canada.[93]

Conclusion

Given the central role that work of all types played in working-class girls' and women's lives in Portugal, Carolina Soares had good reason to assume that she would not only keep house in Toronto but also earn an income. In Portugal, her life, like that of Idalina Azevedo and the other women whose stories appear in this book, had been heavily shaped by a weak economy, the lack of job and educational opportunities, rigid class inequities, institutionalized patriarchy, and an authoritarian regime that instilled fear in its population.

Still, it would be a mistake to pathologize them as submissive women toiling in the shadows of patriarchs in primitive rural households and cut off from the wider society. As critical contributors to a family economy that marshalled the labour of every family member in order to manage, Portuguese women arrived in Toronto having already juggled a variety of economic activities, from domestic and field chores to waged work on farms and in factories and domestic service. They were accustomed to performing physically demanding work even as that work already had taken some toll on their bodies. Many of them had some experience with the growing consumerism and expanding economic opportunities of a changing post-1960 Portugal. In choosing to emigrate, women like Soares and Azevedo were not only part of a long history of emigration from Portugal to locales around the world. They were also among the first generation of Portuguese immigrants to settle in Canada; unlike the post-1945 Italians and Greeks, there were no pre-existing Portuguese communities in Canada who might have offered them support. Portuguese women, especially those from the Azorean islands located that much farther from continental Europe, would have to contend with stereotypes of southern Europeans as backward rural folk with a "sluggish" work ethic. Finally, in contrast to Canadian assumptions that these family-sponsored dependants of husbands and fathers would never really contribute to Canada's economy,[94] thousands of these women arrived in Toronto ready, if not fully equipped, to confront new realities—including industrial restructuring—by drawing on and modifying old strategies of survival and developing new ones.

Chapter 2

Getting Settled

In May 1961, a home visitor with the International Institute of Metropolitan Toronto, a local United Appeal immigrant aid agency, visited the Faria family to assess their need for assistance. Having arrived from Portugal a few years earlier, the Farias were sharing a small two-storey house with the Lopes family. The women in the two families were sisters and the Farias had sponsored the Lopeses' arrival a year earlier. Counting the five Faria and six Lopes children, fifteen people lived in the house in Kensington Market, the west-end neighbourhood that would attract many Portuguese. The visitor's notes shed some light on how two immigrant families connected by kinship were getting adjusted to life in Canada. Despite their low incomes, the sponsoring couple—Mr. Faria (whose part-time job earned $38 weekly) and Mrs. Faria (who made $14 a week cleaning two houses)—were covering the monthly rent ($100). In addition to taking care of their own family, the Farias were supporting the Lopes family while that couple looked for work.

A volunteer recruited through one of the middle-class women's organizations that supported its work, the International Institute visitor commented on how the families were managing. "The morale" was "high," she noted, "even though they are poor." The house, she added, "was clean, but furniture sparse" and "the children were well cared for; clean, hair shining and combed and plainly but warmly dressed." With a mix of sensitivity and paternalism, she described the two mothers as "clean, but strained, worn and shabbily dressed; as if they gave their all for the sake of the children." The visitor, who would have received some on-the-job social work training from the institute's counselling staff, recommended donations of furniture (including beds), pots, and dishes, as well as clothes, shoes, and toys. At Mrs. Faria's request, the household also received donations of food (including macaroni, eggs, Mazzola oil,

25

cheese, and *bacalhau*, or cod) and household products (soap, detergent, and toilet paper).[1]

The visitor's recorded observations were, of course, filtered through her privileged social position and her admittedly rudimentary training. But they also capture some key features of the immigrant experience of Portuguese women and their families in Canada. These include the family and kin networks that initiated and sustained chain migration, the practice of mutual assistance among extended families, the use of community agencies to secure social supports in times of need, and women's significant roles in both paid and reproductive labour. Although not explicitly stated, the two families may have doubled up to save money not only to meet immediate needs but also as part of a strategy of homeownership that also mobilized kin networks. As with Italian and Greek immigrants, this strategy offered low-income Portuguese newcomers, who had been greatly disadvantaged by inequitable landowning systems in their homeland, a way of attaining a modicum of security in their new hostland. It also required high levels of wage earning, including among women and youths, and heroic levels of saving.

Women's pursuit of family goals pressed into service a transplanted family work ethic that was adapted to Toronto, where a mixed economy offered plenty of low-income "female" jobs in manufacturing and service. Portuguese women and their husbands drew on familiar survival strategies, such as marshalling the labour of each member to ensure a livelihood, as well as new ones, such as turning to outside agencies for support. As newcomers, they encountered gatekeepers such as employment officials, social workers, and volunteers. Sometimes, the immigrants sought out these outsiders; other times, they were visited upon. In their quest for economic stability, Portuguese working women resisted the negative labels placed on them and asserted family strategies that included high levels of wage earning among married and single adult women as well as among teenagers. But they also faced the burdens of the double day of paid and unpaid work, even when husbands helped with child care.

By 1981, the number of ethnic Portuguese in Metropolitan Toronto, the single most popular destination among Canada's Portuguese immigrants, would reach 88,885 people.[2] Particularly for the early Portuguese arrivals of the 1950s, however, the challenge of settling into Toronto was compounded by the absence of an existing ethnic community that might have provided some support in the form of charities or immigrant aid agencies. Lacking access to such resources, Portuguese immigrants turned to familiar institutions, such as the newly established Portuguese parishes, and new ones, namely the community organizations of the wider society.

As the city's west-end Catholic churches, such as St. Mary's and St. Agnes, attracted Portuguese priests and began offering mass in Portuguese, they served important social and devotional roles for the immigrants. Hence, the popularity of the picnics, fairs, and dances that, to the chagrin of Anglo-Torontonians who dubbed them "Portuguese beer-drinking brawls," were part of the summer religious festivals held in Trinity Bellwoods Park.[3] For women denied access to other avenues of social activity, such as the pool halls the men frequented, parishes became important social centres. And both men and women tapped the parish-sponsored Portuguese service centres that offered practical aid to newcomers.[4]

The outside agencies that attracted Portuguese immigrants included the International Institute of Toronto, which for much of its history was based in the heavily immigrant west end. By the late 1960s, the Portuguese were the institute's largest single clientele, prompting the hiring of Portuguese-speaking counsellors. The 1960s-era projects aimed at improving the access of southern European immigrants to health and welfare resources and skills training programs also hired Portuguese fieldworkers. St. Christopher House, a long-standing settlement house in the west end, drew a growing number of the Portuguese moving into the neighbourhood; later, in the 1970s, it would become a critical site of cleaners' activism.[5] Whether initiating or drawn into these social welfare encounters, Portuguese women used social agencies selectively. In many cases, they requested material and practical support but rejected the counselling advice that accompanied the support; in other cases, they adapted that advice to their customary norms.

Missing Live-in Domestics

Portuguese women would become important wage earners in Canadian cities like Toronto. They held a range of jobs within the manufacturing and service sectors, but became most closely associated with cleaning work. They were not, however, among the earliest arrivals. Nor were they directly recruited as domestics for Canada, as was true of some Italian women (under 100) and many Greek women (10,000). The first Portuguese immigrants were men who arrived in the 1950s through the government-assisted labour schemes (or "bulk orders") that were initially designed to recruit refugees, and then immigrants from West Germany and elsewhere, to fill labour shortages mainly in agriculture, mining, and railway building and repair. Like other male recruits, the Portuguese men, who were placed mainly in farm and railway work, later sponsored wives and children.[6]

The Portuguese bulk orders, like the Italian and Greek schemes, reflected Canadian assumptions about southern Europeans performing a primarily labouring role in the nation's economy. A Canadian official's description of the Portuguese as "religious, patriarchal, honest, kind, courteous, courageous, disciplined, hard working, happily disposed, with limited initiative but intelligence within their own confines" referenced attributes that would make them suitable for low-skilled labour.[7] It bears stressing, however, that, like other Europeans recruited on labour contracts, these Portuguese recruits arrived in Canada as landed immigrants with certain rights, not as guest workers. The latter was the status of the Caribbean and other racialized domestics and farm workers recruited later through temporary-worker schemes. Canadian officials hoped to recruit some professionals and engineers from Portugal, but the country's authoritarian regime prohibited the men who belonged to its small professional and skilled class from leaving. In that regard, the Estado Novo played a decisive role in ensuring the working-class profile of Portuguese migration to Canada.

During the 1961 selection of male recruits, who submitted to the usual medical tests and security screenings, pathological portraits of Portuguese abound. In the same unashamed manner with which many behind-the-scenes officials spoke of lazy, devious, high-strung or otherwise unsuitable southern European candidates from Italy and Greece, the Canadian medical officer sent to the Azores explicitly referred to the intelligence tests weeding out the many expected Portuguese "mental retardation" cases caused by illiteracy and poverty.[8] That same year, however, the Canadian psychiatrist sent to Lisbon to examine "illiterate Portuguese migrants" adopted the comparatively more enlightened position of delaying judgment until they saw how the men fared in Canada.[9] Like earlier European recruits, many Portuguese men filled their one-year contract, but many others abandoned the isolated farms and work camps in which they were placed and "disappeared" into the cities looking for better jobs. In response, the officials again threatened stricter selection criteria and stiff penalties but did nothing, in this case because, like the earlier Italians, Portuguese men were filling the demand for construction workers in Toronto and elsewhere. The small number of skilled men in the Portuguese schemes sought trade jobs as bricklayers and carpenters or mechanics and electricians.[10]

By rejecting Canada's requests for female domestics, the Estado Novo also shaped early Portuguese migration to Canada as male. Facing a continuing demand for live-in domestics at home and "dwindling supplies" of preferred Europeans abroad, in 1953 Ottawa issued an order of one hundred female domestics from Portugal. The proposal resembled the earlier European female-domestic schemes, including with respect to the double moral standard. Canadian officials wanted single, able-bodied women of good moral character, and they promised to guard the women's virtue during the voyage and initial housing by hiring chaperones. (No chaperones accompanied male recruits.) Quietly, they expressed doubts about recruiting "any great numbers" of Portuguese domestics on the erroneous grounds that "the females remained in the home and did not migrate." Portugal's official response—that no women were available—reflected not women's opposition to migration but state restrictions on their movement. Invoking a paternalism common to authoritarian leaders, Salazar declared that "migrating alone" would endanger the morals of "unattached" women.

Under Portugal's tight rules, only married women could obtain passports, at their husband's direction. Denied access to a passport until 1969, single women could emigrate only by being sponsored by a close relative already in the country in question. With so few Portuguese in Canada in 1953, this was not a viable option for most prospective immigrants. Consequently, many families surely would have taken seriously the domestic-scheme option because, once in Canada, the daughter, as a landed immigrant, could sponsor the rest of them. After all, the Greek women who entered Canada as domestic recruits between 1951 and 1963 sponsored parents, siblings, and in some cases, husbands, though many other Greek women arrived as family-sponsored immigrants.[11]

Certainly, most Portuguese women came to Canada through the family sponsorship system. Although the legal dependants of sponsoring husbands or fathers—or, as in this chapter's opening story, sisters—many of them immediately or soon sought employment. Significantly, all but some of the most economically vulnerable among them rejected the option of live-in domestic service in Canada. Even women who had held live-in positions in Portugal refused them in Toronto, much to the consternation of agency staff who kept rosters of well-to-do Torontonians keen to hire a live-in maid.

The women typically rejected live-in service on the grounds that they preferred to live with family. This was true even of single adult women like the thirty-five-year-old Portuguese woman who told her counsellor at the International Institute of Toronto that "she would rather live with her relatives."[12] Having failed to convince her Portuguese client, a twenty-nine-year-old single woman, to accept a live-in domestic job by emphasizing its positive features—the opportunity to learn English and Canadian customs more quickly—a frustrated institute counsellor exclaimed: "There is no way to get them [to] understand that."[13] In rejecting live-in work, Portuguese women, like other European recruits who abandoned their domestic contracts, were asserting their own strategies, even if living with one's family was not necessarily more liberating.[14]

The main exceptions to this pattern were widows and single mothers who had migrated independently and those with a weak family-support system. Examples from Toronto's International Institute files include a young Portuguese widow with an eight-year-old daughter who was sponsored by her sister in 1969. She accepted a live-in position with an employer who allowed her daughter to live with her in the woman's home because it gave her a form of support that her sister could not provide.[15] Other "lone" women included a former accountant and mother who was separated from her husband, and a single mother who applied for admission to Canada while in the country on a visitor's visa. (This was legal until November 1973.) Having no doubt faced stigma in Catholic Portugal for their unconventional status, and lacking family in Canada, both women likely saw the live-in arrangement as providing some family-like support for their child, as well as an income.[16] Much like Finnish women experienced in early-twentieth-century Canada, or Mexican women in contemporary California, live-in work, though exploitative, potentially offered lone Portuguese women a place to work and live, some security, and a chance to learn English.[17] As Wenona Giles observes, while in the minority, the women who arrived as independent immigrants and/or worked and lived outside their families challenge the exclusive emphasis on women's dependency found in the older scholarship on Portuguese immigration to Canada.[18]

Looking for Work

As their own stories underscore, newly arrived Portuguese women in Toronto often found jobs through family and friends. Some of these stories also involve getting lost on the streetcar on the way home after the first day of work, usually because they got off at the wrong stop and then walked and walked in search of their street and house. The following narratives show, too, that other women—sisters, sisters-in-law, cousins, neighbours—played key roles in helping them find their first and even second and third jobs. Having moved from Edmonton to Toronto in 1966, Mariana Batista, like many others, wanted a job cleaning houses rather than factory work: it meant she could get home to her four children in the late afternoon rather than in the evening (see chapter 3). A sister-in-law who already worked as a cleaning lady got Batista her first house to clean. With her foot in the door, Batista secured additional jobs through word of mouth with employers and other Portuguese women.

The sister who sponsored Emilia Silva along with her husband and young daughter in 1974 found Silva her first job doing what she (and other Portuguese) arrivals did: picking worms (destined for live bait suppliers) between 9 p.m. and 5 a.m. (Those who did this low-paid stoop labour were taken in vans to the fields at night and, with a flashlight strapped to their forehead and a tin can attached to each ankle, picked as many worms as they could.) In a common scenario involving night-time building cleaners like Silva, her husband, who came home from work in the evenings, watched their daughter while she worked. Like the two sisters of this chapter's opening story, Silva and her sister and their respective husbands saved to buy a house. Keen to help pay off the mortgage, Silva asked a Portuguese female neighbour who worked on the nighttime janitorial staff of the recently completed First Canadian Place complex about getting cleaning work there. At the neighbour's suggestion, Silva visited the supervisor of the cleaning company contracted to clean the complex, who gave her a job. For years, she cleaned at First Canadian Place, but she also became a union activist.[19]

When the ethnic networks failed them, some women, like men, might turn to the National Employment Service (later the Department of Manpower). Others did not bother because relatives said they offered little help.[20] As the acknowledged head of the family, men had greater access than women to the government-sponsored skills training or upgrading courses and English as a second language (ESL) classes. But they, too, faced insensitive staff who spouted bureaucratic rules and treated them like simple villagers. More cut off from such services because of their legal status as dependants, women were relegated to very low paying jobs mostly in service and factory work, though these incomes proved critical to their families.[21]

Usually on the advice of relatives who had earlier received assistance, Portuguese newcomers gravitated more towards St. Christopher House, which hired Edith Clarke, a Portuguese-speaking worker, in 1962, and the International Institute of Toronto, with its multilingual staff. But the job hunt was often a family affair. Couples appeared at the institute with their children, wanting a job for each of them. As participants in transnational family economies, already employed immigrants asked for an extra part-time job in order to send money to close relatives still in Portugal.[22] Some families arrived together at a job meant for one of them. The owner of a garment factory to which her institute counsellor had sent Elsa Carvalho was so annoyed that her husband and four children also came that he did not hire her. The counsellor's reply? To "advise the people to go on their own, or with an interpreter—but not the whole crowd!"[23] Some married couples, including the Rochas, preferred to work together; they were hired by the same cleaning company. Another couple were told to consider posts as caretakers at the same school.[24] Overall, thousands of Portuguese found work through the institute, though the jobs were mostly low-skilled ones.

While appreciative of such assistance, the Portuguese were not passive clients but instead pursued their own goals, even when that drew criticism. Looking to maximize their earnings in order to increase the combined family income, many balked at dead-end jobs such as picking worms or, in the men's case, handing out flyers or dishwashing in restaurants. In response, counsellors sometimes labelled them "uncooperative" or "very difficult." Some clients could be equally blunt in rejecting advice. When an International Institute counsellor phoned one woman to recommend enrolment in an industrial sewing course being offered in conjunction with a government training program, her husband, who had picked up the phone, said she was cleaning houses. Insisting that a power-sewing factory job would earn more than cleaning private houses, the counsellor asked after the wife's current earnings only to be told to mind her own business.[25]

Institute counsellors understood that men's inability to earn a family wage largely explained why many wives entered the workforce, though they underestimated women's income earning in Portugal (see chapter 1).

32 Cleaning Up

Women dominated the wave of Portuguese immigrants of adult working age who entered Canada between 1962 and 1982. Perceptive social workers like Edith Ferguson correctly predicted that, like their Italian and Greek counterparts, many Portuguese women would become lifelong workers who moved in and out of the workforce for mostly family reasons. She had learned a lot about these southern European women while heading the International Institute's health and occupational training projects in the 1960s. At the same time, institute counsellors often adhered to the era's middle-class gender ideal of the breadwinning husband and homemaker wife.[26]

Cases involving Portuguese mothers of young children looking for work suggest how such seemingly contradictory positions might inform the advice meted out. Counsellors regularly advised young Portuguese (and other) mothers to forgo waged work if they felt the husband was earning enough to support them. Most women rejected the advice, however, as they were as committed as their husbands to paying off debts incurred through migration or homeownership or for other reasons (such as expensive medical operations). When a counsellor urged Evangelina Ribeiro to stay at home with her baby and toddler on the grounds that her husband would earn "fairly good pay" working full-time on a farm located on the city outskirts, Ribeiro insisted that they had "to pay off their flight fare to Canada." The counsellor also failed to persuade her that, if she stayed at home and took English classes, she would later land a better job, and the children, being "a little older . . . wouldn't suffer as much" by her absence. Given similar advice, another Portuguese client told her counsellor that she had to work because she had a large family (five children) and a mortgage.[27]

Family-based goals with an emphasis on earning money *now* also explain women's reluctance to enrol in the ESL classes that sponsored wives could attend. Canadian service personnel considered English classes a training in good citizenship as well as a means to a better-paying job, but their female clients often replied that they had bills to pay and no time for classes. A thirty-three-year-old client of the International Institute offered an additional reason: she was too old to return to school. Since many of these women had only attended school for a few years as very young children (and some, not at all), this, too, was a reasonable response. But it prompted some annoyed counsellors to call the women "stupid," stubborn, or ill-informed even though they themselves knew that other factors, including the lack of bilingual (English/Portuguese)

Getting Settled

33

instructors, also contributed to the problem. Conversely, a good student like Fernanda Oliveira received plenty of praise. Her counsellor noted that she had "persevered so well with her English" that she deserved a reward, but we do not know if she received one.[28]

Female respectability among Portugal's working classes was not shaped by the trickle-down effect of bourgeois female codes of genteel and demure behaviour. But the notion of being a good wife and mother was tightly bound up, in the eyes of one's neighbours and community, with keeping a clean and orderly house. This gender ideology crossed the ocean with the women. At one point, the female members of an ESL class used their new English skills to convey the point. Noting that "every week we change the beds, dust the furniture, wash the bathrooms, clean the stove and the oven, wash the floors, vacuum the carpets, wash the clothes and sweep and wash the veranda and backyard," their narrative concludes: "We are proud when we finish cleaning our houses because our houses look fresh, shining and new."[29] Such declarations lend support to the paradox identified by Giles between Portuguese women's resistance to the exploitative conditions of their paid labour and their failure to overtly challenge the unequal division of labour in the home. Still, our evidence, which includes other kinds of ESL narratives, oral interviews, and newspaper coverage of cleaners' strikes, suggests a less sharply drawn contrast.[30]

Social Welfare Encounters

To say that immigrants sought to use outside agencies in pragmatic and selective ways is not to suggest that the social welfare encounter involved an egalitarian relationship. The counselling staff wielded power over clients in these local sites. They could refuse them help or jeopardize their support from a government department or a different social agency by writing critical reports. But they never exercised full control. As previously noted, the clients exercised their agency in these encounters by, for example, demanding practical help and rejecting unwanted advice. They might apply pressure on counsellors through repeat visits or, alternatively, cut things off entirely by refusing to return. The mediated glimpses into the interactions offered by the International Institute case files show, too, that the social welfare encounter was an uneven and messy process. There was plenty of negotiation and frustration on both sides, but also evidence of a sympathetic counsellor or home visitor and an appreciative client.[31]

The context also mattered. When the request involved specific and temporary support, the clients might better control the terms of the interaction or set limits on outside intrusion into their lives. Many new and expectant mothers who asked for baby layettes, for example, secured the modest but timely support without further intervention. As did new fathers like the thirty-one-year-old man whose wife had given birth to twins, their fifth and sixth child. He admitted to what working wives and social workers already knew: a husband on a labourer's income "has a hard time" supporting his family. The counsellor gave him two layettes, and urged him to send his wife once she felt better so they could give her clothing for the children.[32] By contrast, as we will see, child-care and child-rearing matters involved far more complicated negotiations.

So, too, did cases involving psychological and emotional fallout. International Institute counsellors encountered clients of every background who displayed symptoms of acute anxiety or depression caused by the stress of experiencing a decline in their living conditions.[33] Increasingly concentrated in construction—a highly seasonal and injury-prone sector—unemployed and injured Portuguese men showed up distraught because they could not fulfill their role as family breadwinner. Usually, we do not know whether these men saw a doctor or psychiatrist, but, taken together, such cases indicate both instances of mental ill health and social workers' efforts to facilitate more substantial interventions into the lives of frustrated immigrants.[34]

Women, too, struggled with acute anxiety and depression that was often linked to fears of not being able to support their children. They also faced the additional stresses caused by pregnancy and childbirth, especially when there were other children to care for and very little money on hand. Institute counsellors or home visitors might learn about distressed women through the hospital staff who asked them to interpret for a crying or disoriented woman or provide follow-up support after she was released. At times, the cause of the ill health seemed pretty obvious, as with the immigrant from Madeira who told her institute visitor that she was expecting her ninth child.[35] Of course, childbirth in an alien hospital could itself be a harrowing experience for non-English-speaking immigrant women, who were familiar with home births delivered by midwives in the company of other women. In her contribution to a 1984 collection of stories written by the members of an ESL class, Lourdes, a Portuguese woman who gave birth in a Toronto hospital in the 1960s, highlights the abusive behaviour of Canadian hospital staff. The nursing

Getting Settled

35

assistant who came with a wheelchair to take her to the delivery room kicked Lourdes's legs and then barked, "Sit properly, stupid" when Lourdes found it too painful to bend her knees. Lourdes did understand the nurse's damaging words and actions, but she was in too much pain and spoke too little English to say anything. Many years later, however, the experience still rankled.[36]

In strife-ridden families, women were more vulnerable than men to desertion. On occasion, International Institute counsellors, usually through third parties (such as the family court or other social agencies) encountered a woman who walked out on her family. In one of the very few Portuguese cases uncovered by our respective research on the International Institute, the deserted husband was referred to the institute by Father Cunha of St. Mary's parish. Cunha explained that the wife left her husband, a parishioner, and their three children, because she could no longer endure his rants against Canada and his almost daily fits of crying. Like in a few other non-Portuguese cases of this type, the husband's inability to care for the children and the lack of family help led to the children ending up in foster care.[37]

The cases of wife desertion were more common, however. One Portuguese case from the early 1960s involved Belmira Mata, a mother of four children. With the help of Catholic Family Services, she took her husband to family court for non-support and won. But it was Mata, then renting a house with another Portuguese family, who had to provide for her children when the husband failed to pay. Her nighttime cleaning wage ($35 weekly) was not enough. The counsellor, who praised her as "really willing to work and do her best for her children," found her a private house to clean on Saturdays, for $7, and approved her for a donation of children's clothing.[38] By contrast, the advice some counsellors offered men who admitted to thoughts of abandoning their family was not particularly helpful. One counsellor told a seriously injured Portuguese construction worker who said that, even with his wife and one child working, the financial troubles were so great that he wanted "to desert his family," to register for English classes as it would give him "less time ... to worry."[39]

Daycare and Drawing a Line

Outside agencies like the International Institute most commonly helped Portuguese women to manage their family economies through job searches. The institute's aim to promote cultural diversity among

Canadians and to facilitate immigrant integration into the mainstream, as well as its multilingual staff, distinguished it from other agencies serving the city's immigrants. The institute promoted cultural pluralism by mounting folk fairs and multicultural festivals that showcased the immigrants' cultural contributions (or "gifts") to the city and nation. If such cultural events offered a therapeutic multiculturalism that kept immigrant misery at bay, the industrial sewing classes created for Portuguese (and Italian) women sought to improve the immigrants' material lives.[40]

While clearly anti-assimilationists, International Institute personnel did ultimately hope to Canadianize the immigrants and turn them into modern citizens. In their view, southern European "rural villagers" like the Portuguese required intensified efforts at socialization because of the bigger-than-usual gap between their lifeways and those of modern urban Canadians. To that end, they ran mothers' classes on child rearing and ESL classes that taught Canadian content and values. An interest in Canadianization also informed St. Christopher House programs, but the arrival in the 1970s and 1980s of radical community organizers on its staff would transform the organization's relationship with the working Portuguese women of the neighbourhood (see chapter 4).

Portuguese women who sought practical assistance from the International Institute or St. Christopher House simultaneously resisted the pressure to shed their customary practices and conform to Canadian models of behaviour. One site of conflict was child care, a responsibility that fell most heavily on mothers. Like Manuela Pacheco, a cleaner in a downtown office building, some women shared child-care duties with husbands by seeking alternative work shifts, though this arrangement might leave the children alone for a period of time when the parents' jobs overlapped. Pacheco's infant son slept alone for an hour and a half between the time she left for her shift at 4:30 p.m. (it ended at 11 p.m.) and her husband got home from his construction job at 6 p.m.[41] But this couple, like others who chose alternate jobs, likely did so because they could not afford to pay for child care. Those who could took their children to a babysitter, usually a neighbour, for the short period before their husbands finished work.[42]

In a familiar child-care strategy transplanted from Portugal, women showed a preference for having family members rather than acquaintances watch their children. But with many female relatives also in the workforce, it could be difficult to secure familial child minders. Still,

Getting Settled 37

child-caring duties were most often shared among female kin and neighbours. Sisters, sisters-in-law, and cousins chose alternate workdays in order to cover the child-care needs of families within the same kin network. One International Institute client asked her counsellor for a nighttime cleaning job so she could alternate child care with a sister-in-law who worked during the day. Another wanted to clean on the three weekdays that her sister-in-law did not work.[43] An additional strategy was to put daughters in charge of younger siblings. As in the case of Maria Fernandes's fourteen-year-old daughter, who watched her two younger siblings in the evenings while her mother worked, the sitter might not be much older than her charges.[44] A daytime hotel cleaner convinced her sister in the Azores to join her in Toronto and help with her two children.[45]

Grandmothers were also pressed into service. A typical scenario involved a woman convincing her mother in Portugal to join her in Toronto. One International Institute counsellor recorded a client's plans thus: "She was waiting for her mother to arrive from Portugal to take care of her household while she was at work." It was also less expensive to sponsor one's mother than to hire a babysitter or pay for daycare. Even so, family arrangements did not necessarily prevent mothers from feeling guilty or sad about their choices. A daytime house cleaner whose mother was her live-in babysitter, Mariana Batista sadly recounted that her two children always liked the grandmother with whom they spent most of their time better than they liked Batista herself. Even when she was at home, Batista was too busy with housework to spend much time with the children.[46]

Still others had to look outside their kin networks. Some of these women paid for informal child care, such as unlicensed landladies or neighbourhood-based child caregivers. Many of them were Portuguese, but others were Italians, chosen on account of their cultural and religious similarities and because communication could be managed between the two languages.[47] Others responded much like Canadian working mothers and left their children in regulated daycare centres. In 1964, St. Christopher House started a Foster Day Care Project in part because, as Clarke put it, "a large number" of the local Portuguese working mothers were "not making use of the existing excellent Day Care Centres for children over two," but instead leaving children with relatives and neighbours who might even leave them unsupervised for much of the day. Also, the staff believed that, if more Portuguese parents knew about existing daycare services, and Portuguese workers were hired to bridge the linguistic and cultural divide, they would be more willing to use the services.[48] There was some truth in this claim, as evidenced by the actions of the Luso-Canadian Association, a Portuguese community group that approached St. Christopher House about providing daycare services for Portuguese families. Some mothers signed up.

The disapproval of St. Christopher's pre-1970 staff of Portuguese women who prioritized "the desire to make and save money" over their children's interests and chose inadequate caregivers also affected relations with the community. Not surprisingly, then, the mothers did not flock to the daycare. The fees were also an issue. St. Christopher subsidized the cost but required proof of income from parents. The weekly charge for one couple was $6; most parents demanded a lower fee while refusing to expose their income to outsiders.[49] A report that complained about "these people" not being "forthcoming" with "financial matters" revealed the staff's broader concern with socializing the children in Canadian ways. Or as the report negatively put it, "The parents' attitude represents the cultural blocking of Portuguese people [regarding] Canadians."[50] Nevertheless, the staff enjoyed some success in attracting Portuguese mothers. Among them was Margarida Rocha, who explained that she was happy that her children were being cared for by trained and qualified professionals. She also saw value in the daycare's role in the children's socialization, though she articulated the matter somewhat differently than the staff. "Being in contact with others of the same age, with economic problems or different personalities," she told a reporter with the recently founded progressive Portuguese-language newspaper *Comunidade*, the children "get used to confronting the world more realistically."[51]

Also located in Kensington Market, St. Stephen's Community House opened a daycare in 1964. Founded by the Anglican diocese in 1962, initially as a Christian settlement house to provide services mainly to youth, St. Stephen's now offered a wider range of programs, including ESL classes, counselling and employment services, and electronics and woodworking workshops for youth. (A decade later, St. Stephen's became an independent, United Appeal–supported charitable organization.)[52] Significantly, given the emphasis among social service personnel on immigrant rejection of such services, the daycare appears to have been established in response to the growing calls of local families as well as community groups, such as the Portuguese Parents Association, for more daycare programs.[53]

Getting Settled

Once opened, the majority of the children in the new daycare program were Portuguese (75 percent); the remainder were of Canadian, Chinese, "Spanish" (likely Latin American), Caribbean, and Asian Indian origins.[54] One St. Stephen's staffer attributed the success largely to their ability to break through to the parents who assumed that, like the municipal daycare centres, St. Stephen's would give preference to single parents and require two-parent families to submit to a rigorous means test. Another reason was the cost, which was much lower than the $30 a week that some private daycare centres charged. The report added that daycare services eliminated a disruptive effect of family-based arrangements that had parents working alternate shifts, namely, the couple seldom saw each other.[55]

Like the mothers' clubs and baby clinics, the daycare services provided by outside community agencies aimed to socialize both the children and their mothers in Canadian ways. The goal of their various house programs, noted a 1967 St. Christopher report, was "to educate Portuguese mothers" in "the areas of nutrition, child care and up-bringing, laws and regulations etc."[56] St. Christopher records do not detail how the mothers responded to their initiatives, but St. Stephen's records, which do, reveal sources of tension between the social workers and the Portuguese mothers. They also shed light on the line beyond which mothers were not willing to tolerate outside interventions. One such line concerned the punishment of children.

The conflict itself requires some context. By the 1970s, the St. Stephen's Community House daycare program was more progressive than others in that it aimed not to "preach" to mothers but to develop a co-operative relationship with them. To that end, the staff held parent-staff meetings so that parents could voice their opinions, and encouraged parent participation in the committees that made decisions about the daycare program. At the meetings, topics such as nutrition, discipline, and the philosophy of early childhood education were discussed. One of the guest speakers invited to speak to the mothers was a staff member of the Clarke Institute, a psychiatric facility, who discussed positive ways of dealing with children. During subsequent discussions, the issue of discipline sparked debate. Presenting themselves as modern experts, St. Stephen's staff emphasized that spanking children was not only not condoned but against the law. The Portuguese mothers, who were raised with corporal punishment, thought spanking a valid way to discipline a child and resented being told otherwise. They expressed their hurt feelings at a party held for them by the daycare staff—who had even hired Portuguese cooks to produce a buffet that included traditional Portuguese fare such as cod cakes—by refusing to touch the food. As Brenda Duncombe, one of the daycare workers, recalled, they got the message: the mothers had "showed they were displeased." She also found the whole incident "so sad" because they "were trying so hard." Soon enough, however, Duncombe would be involved in many ESL and other projects involving Portuguese cleaners (see chapter 4).[57]

Portuguese mothers also drew the line at using food as a tool of Canadianization. A 1963 St. Christopher report identified food habits as well as a lack of English as major barriers to the Portuguese becoming "good Canadians." The lack of English, it noted, made it difficult to get better jobs or to access government health services. As for the second barrier, the report singled out for special blame the mothers and their supposed "lack of desire to adopt better eating and health habits." Even sympathetic Canadian nutritionists and pluralist-minded social service personnel who encouraged Canadian mothers to experiment with (usually modified) "ethnic" meals endorsed certain transformations in immigrant mothers' shopping and cooking regimes as necessary for modernizing their behaviour and improving family diets. In the context of a 1963 Family Life project, St. Christopher House staff identified the need to convince Portuguese mothers to use less fat and carbohydrates in their meals and more milk and vitamins. The emphasis on nutrition was fair enough, though here too, assumptions about backward southern Europeans and modern urban North Americans operated.[58] More insidious, however, were the efforts by fashion makers and profit-minded companies to encourage rural immigrant mothers to shop in modern supermarkets rather than in old-fashioned ethnic shops or in the open-air Kensington Market, with its animal stalls and loud bartering. In the face of the resistance from Portuguese women, who, as a 1965 St. Christopher House report negatively put it, "feel they must preserve their own culture as much as possible," St. Christopher workers in that decade derided the women as backward. The women themselves, however, stood firm on the matter. True, over time, the food customs of Portuguese (and other immigrant) women would be modified, but the persistence of Portuguese (and other ethnic) food traditions in Toronto had as much to do with the women's fierce determination to maintain valued foodways in the hostland as to the practices of ethnic entrepreneurs serving an expanding immigrant market or liberal promoters of multiculturalism.[59]

Working Teens

Another major source of conflict between front-line personnel and southern European immigrants like the Portuguese was the latter's decision to send their teenaged children out to work. Children were just as important to the family economy in Canada as they were in Portugal (see chapter 1), and many of them left school in their teens to help with family finances. The International Institute counsellors criticized these parents for disrupting their children's education and socialization in Canadian ways. The mandatory school age in Ontario at this time was sixteen, but some parents were able to secure the early release of children as young as fourteen on the grounds of economic need.

The specific reasons that triggered a teen's wage earning could vary, but they included a father's illness, workplace injury, or even prolonged disability with inadequate award of compensation. The government-run health insurance plan only started in 1969; before that time, illness or injury could bring major expenses to families. The wife and sixteen-year-old daughter of an injured Portuguese construction worker came to the International Institute in 1962 wanting help in finding work. He was recovering from a chest injury caused by a workplace accident involving some Italian co-workers who did not understand his English, but he accompanied the women. Convinced that the man alone was responsible for sending the daughter to work and keeping the wife out of English classes, the counsellor wrote that he cared "only about making his family work to earn money."[60]

Another common, and highly contentious, reason for turning teens into wage earners was homeownership. Again, insightful social workers like Ferguson appreciated that former land-hungry peasants with few marketable skills would be preoccupied with attaining financial security through kin-linked homeownership strategies that involved families doubling and tripling up, taking in boarders, assuming mortgages, and years of saving and making do without. Yet she, too, conjured up stereotypical images of rural villagers as unaccustomed to electrical appliances, indoor plumbing, telephones, and modern banks. The parents, went a familiar argument, were insufficiently engaged with modernity to realize that putting their teens to work undermined their chances for a better future. By the latter, experts like the institute counsellors who encountered these teens usually meant white-collar office jobs for the girls and the trades for boys, both of which required a high-school education (grade ten) and some additional training.[61]

In their case file entries, International Institute counsellors expressed frustration with parents like the Portuguese cleaner and mother who showed up wanting a job for her teenaged daughter. When the counsellor urged her instead to keep the girl in school, the mother replied that the family had bought a house and her daughter must help pay for it. The counsellor's observation that the mother "is a bit tired of hard work and thinks that it is only right that the daughter should start to earn her living" hints at the toll that physically demanding work took on mothers.[62] Only a few of the teens expressed an opinion about, for example, liking or disliking school. Instead, most adopted a matter-of-fact tone when asked why they were leaving school to work. The replies consisted of variations of "I have to help my big family" and "I have to help pay for the house."[63]

Of course, Portuguese and other working-class immigrant parents were not entirely to blame for their children's high dropout rates from school. As numerous studies have documented, the school system was streaming Portuguese children as well as Italian, African Canadian, and Caribbean children into technical schools and manual occupations, not university. Ironically, the children whom educators considered intellectually limited served critical roles as family interpreters for parents dealing with English-speaking government staff, employers, and the visitors who knocked on their door.[64] By the 1970s, the streaming of immigrant children would get attention from progressive members within the Portuguese community as well as progressive politicians, including those who would provide support to women's labour activism.

Conclusion

In adapting to life in postwar Toronto, Portuguese women drew on both customary and new strategies of family survival. The transplanted networks of female kin in Toronto facilitated women's search for work and shared child-care arrangements. Pregnancy, childbirth, and personal or family crisis frequently interrupted their wage earning and kept them in low-income jobs when they returned to the labour force, but these women would become lifelong workers. Committed to a homeownership strategy that drew on family networks and was informed by pre-migration experiences as well as new realities, women, like men, adopted new social arrangements, such as living in multiple (as opposed to nuclear) family households, that also required adaptation. While exceptions existed, women appeared as willing as their husbands to turn their teenaged children into family income earners.

However, a collectivist family economy in which couples shared the same goals and even certain responsibilities did not necessarily produce egalitarian households. True, the willingness of some, even many, husbands to share child-care duties with their working wives is noteworthy. It also represents a departure from life in Portugal. The men's support also enabled nighttime cleaners to participate in union campaigns and spearhead militant labour activism (see chapters 5–7). But women, including working wives, still did the bulk of the household labour, and men exercised their patriarchal privilege in various ways. The gendered division of household labour in Portugal was strict, and there was significant continuity in this realm in Canada.

With the exception of the parishes, before 1970, Portuguese immigrants sought practical assistance from outside rather than from within the Portuguese community. The local Portuguese community was underdeveloped and lacked the resources required to provide the support services offered by host society agencies such as the International Institute of Toronto, St. Christopher House, and St. Stephen's Community House. The later arrival of better educated and more prosperous Portuguese did not significantly alter matters, because the class divisions of Portuguese society perpetuated themselves in Toronto. The immigrants used the services provided by the largely male Portuguese shopkeepers, real estate agents, and travel agents who profited from their role as middlemen between newer arrivals and Canadian society, but these were paid-for transactions. Nor did "ordinary" immigrants get much support from the elite strata of businessmen, managers, and professionals, most of them also mainland Portuguese, who built community organizations and institutions. With the exception of the leftist Portuguese Canadian Democratic Association, Portuguese community leaders neglected their working-class counterparts, especially the women.

It was not until the 1970s, and particularly after the Portuguese Revolution of 1974, that a progressive faction of Portuguese emerged to help immigrants with their most pressing needs. These individuals immersed themselves in the concerns of the working class and associated with the NDP. They also started their own left-wing newspaper,

Comunidade, the first newspaper to discuss class, gender, and immigrant adjustment issues. By that point, a number of non-Portuguese grassroots activists, many of them women, also emerged and became critical allies to the Portuguese immigrant women who cleaned up the city.[65]

Chapter 3

The Work of Cleaning, Workplace Control, and the Cleaner's Body

By the 1970s, Portuguese immigrant women had become crucial workers in Toronto's expanding postwar service sector. They would occupy an occupational niche in the city's cleaning industry until the early 2000s. Their predominance in the 1970s and 1980s among both the daytime domestics who cleaned the private homes of better-off Torontonians and the janitorial workers who cleaned the city's government and corporate buildings at night gave rise to the singular stereotype of the Portuguese cleaning lady. A Labour Day episode of CBC Radio's *Identities* program in 1972 invoked this trope alongside such other familiar ones as the Ukrainian farmer, Chinese laundryman, Greek restaurateur, Jewish businessman, and Japanese gardener. Equally revealing is the story told in the *Toronto Star* by Mario Silva, who in 2004 became the first Portuguese Canadian member of Parliament. During the years he spent on Toronto City Council and then working for Liberal MP Aideen Nicholson, Silva met constituents looking for a lead on a cleaning lady. One woman actually asked him whether his mother might be available to clean her house. That she correctly guessed that Silva's mother was a cleaning lady reflects both the power of stereotypes and that stereotypes might be grounded in some truth.[1]

Yet, more than half a century after these women began carving out a niche in Toronto's house- and building-cleaning sectors, their labouring lives still remain largely hidden. Whether captured in the historical record or recounted in interviews years later, these women's stories and experiences shed important light on the similar as well as differing dynamics in the two cleaning sectors. Their stories offer critical insight into how non-English-speaking immigrant women of mainly rural origins who cleaned up the homes and office towers of a major metropolis derived dignity from their labour even as it wreaked havoc on their bodies. In contrast to patronizing images one might hold of foreign women who toiled silently in the shadows of the host society, these women fairly quickly embraced a working-class identity in Toronto. They led rich and complex lives that were marked by exploitation and hard physical labour, but also framed by pride, tenacity, and everyday resistance. Their stories underscore the heavily circumscribed contexts in which they lived as well as the different strategies they pursued. In contrast to their office-cleaning female compatriots, who joined unions and struck for better pay and working conditions, and to the Caribbean and Filipina live-in domestics on temporary work visas, who organized with feminist allies to lobby the state for basic rights, Toronto's Portuguese private daytime house cleaners neither led nor joined union or lobby campaigns. But they, too, adopted albeit informal collective strategies of empowerment. Tapping into their extensive kin- and neighbour-linked female networks of information and support, they sought to more effectively negotiate the terms of their labour with their employers, and to cultivate a status as skilled, even professional, workers deserving of greater respect.

Choosing Housecleaning or Building Cleaning

Although some Canadians thought so, Portuguese immigrant women were neither innately nor culturally predisposed to cleaning work in postwar Toronto—or anywhere else. When house cleaner Beatrice Pinto recalled that some employers treated her like a "servant" because "they thought we did this job because of what we are," she spoke eloquently to the self-interested assumptions of bourgeois Torontonians who perceived of the cleaning of their toilets and floors as somehow "natural" work for foreign working-class women.[2] As with other clusters of immigrant workers in a given industry,[3] various economic and social factors account for the Portuguese concentration in the daytime housecleaning and nighttime building-cleaning workforce. The postwar economic boom fuelled the building of corporate skyscrapers that needed cleaning, as well as the expansion in white-collar jobs filled by Canadian women who then wanted their own homes cleaned. The structure of the local economy (including the availability of female jobs) and a labour market segmented along class, gender, and racial-ethnic lines mattered too. So, too, did long-standing sexist definitions of skill, the timing of the women's arrival in Toronto, and the dense female kin networks that facilitated their entry into certain types of cleaning work.

As non-English-speaking newcomers whose capacity for household labour was not recognized as a skill, Portuguese women were relegated to low-paying jobs in manufacturing and service. But they did exercise some choice over where they worked. Within the cleaning sector, women had reasons for preferring daytime housecleaning jobs in the informal economy (where economic activity is not taxed or monitored by government) or nighttime office-cleaning jobs.

Keen to maximize their income, and to balance the demands of paid work and family duties, the women who considered domestic day cleaning a viable option did so because, being paid in cash without tax deductions, they could make more money than low-skilled factory workers while working shorter days, leaving more time to care for their families.[4] Some could take their children with them to an employer's house on school holidays. Those caring for elderly parents or in-laws could alternate between days devoted to unpaid elder care and wage-earning housecleaning days. Women like Celia Filipe were also attracted to what they considered the independent qualities of day cleaning compared to factory work. "Not having a punch card," she said, "made work less stressful."[5]

Since they didn't pay income tax on the cash they earned under the table, private cleaning ladies could also make no claim on the state for benefits. But if they hid, in a sense, from the state, state actors like the Women's Bureau of the Ontario Department of Labour (renamed, in 1972, Ministry of Labour) understood that house cleaners did not want employers to deduct money for benefits from their pay because "they do not plan to declare their income for tax purposes."[6] By not requiring employers to contribute to Canada Pension Plan or unemployment insurance premiums, or vacation pay and so on, the state also ensured that better-off Canadian families could tap into a labour pool of casual domestics. (A similar pattern applies in the United States with respect to undocumented migrants.) Nor did government officials want the administrative headaches or costs that would attach to regulating multiple workplaces and employers.

Besides, the state has always resisted enforcing workplace standards in private homes. In Ontario, apart from a brief period in the 1990s under the NDP government, domestic workers (defined as such because they work in private households, whether as nannies, elder-care workers, or cleaners) have been excluded from the legislation that in the 1940s

The Work of Cleaning

49

legitimized workers' right to collective bargaining in the province. Whether live-in or live-out, the isolation of domestic workers in individual homes has historically made them very difficult to organize.[7]

The Portuguese women who chose building over domestic cleaning in Toronto rejected the insecurity of private cleaning, with its lack of benefits such as sick pay. A minority of these women worked on the ethnically diverse janitorial staff of Toronto hospitals and downtown hotels. The latter included luxury hotels such as the Four Seasons, Sutton Place, and Inn on the Park, as well as more moderate ones like the Waldorf Astoria and Lord Simcoe. But their numbers remained comparatively small for several reasons. A staff preference for workers with enough English to read written instructions or to understand hotel guests who approached them hurt the chances of newly arrived immigrants to land jobs in these workplaces. So, too, did the tendency of hospital cleaning jobs to be higher paid and the workers more likely to be unionized, along with nurses and nurses' aides. But Portuguese women also rejected these jobs, usually because of the weekend shifts. As in Portugal, they considered the weekend a time for family, church (at least "sometimes on Sundays," as one woman put it[8]), and rest. Others quit their hotel jobs because they found it too difficult to clean so many rooms during one shift.[9] Women's vulnerability to sexual harassment or assault in the hotel rooms they cleaned also made these jobs unpopular with many women and their husbands.[10]

Managing child-care arrangements was another reason for choosing office cleaning. Like Piedade Silva, many cleaners explained that they worked at night because their husband was home "to look after the children," making them supper and putting them to bed.[11] These arrangements are evidence that some Portuguese men took on more domestic labour in Canada than they had in Portugal, however limited it might have been, and signals an adaptive strategy of women to cope with balancing household duties and paid work. Building cleaning also offered an opportunity for couples to work together or with a larger network of family and friends. Conversely, some women rejected the sector because of the low pay (which, as detailed below, hovered around the minimum wage) and the heaviness of the work. And those who had other child-care arrangements preferred to work during the day.[12]

Regional origin also influenced job choice: Azoreans tended to concentrate in building cleaning and mainlanders in housecleaning. The pattern reflected in part the fact that while mainland families migrated more often with the intention of later returning to Portugal, the Azorean families who left a more economically depressed region more often chose permanent migration. Expecting to stay put in Toronto, Azoreans chose work that offered long-term benefits, such as a pension, even if it paid less. In choosing housecleaning because it offered short-term rewards in the form of higher immediate income, mainland women acted like "sojourners" (that is, although landed immigrants, they assumed they would return home after building up a nest egg to secure a more comfortable life there). Even as many mainland women eventually realized they would not permanently return to Portugal, many of them remained in domestic work because of the higher short-term wages, as well as the narrowing of options in other economic sectors, such as manufacturing, due to globalization.[13]

Daytime Housecleaning and Nighttime Building Cleaning

While the clandestine nature of live-out domestic work precludes precise estimates of the number of employers or workers, it was an important sector in Toronto's larger economy. The demand for day cleaners remained high during the period under review, the 1960s to early 2000s. The growing number of married Canadian women entering the workforce by the 1960s increased the demand for domestic help. A 1967 article in *Chatelaine* cited the "enormous need" for domestics particularly among professional women, working wives, single mothers, and hard-pressed or ill young mothers at home.[14] As working wives still responsible for the household labour looked to other women to take it up, it became more common for middle-class households with two wage earners to employ house cleaners, something once associated with a greater class privilege.

These and other changes affected the nature of the job. In the 1950s and 1960s, middle- and upper-class Canadian women hired cleaning ladies on the recommendation of friends, or through specialized employment agencies that issued newspaper advertisements. By the early 1960s, an immigrant agency like the International Institute of Metropolitan Toronto was doing a brisk business finding immigrant cleaners for wealthy Torontonians, particularly those who lived in heavily Anglo-Canadian Rosedale and heavily Jewish Canadian Forest Hill.[15] Day cleaners reflected the city's immigrant makeup at the time, and included eastern and southern Europeans.

By the late 1960s and early 1970s, Portuguese women comprised the majority of the daytime cleaning workforce. Partly this reflected the fact

The Work of Cleaning

that, by the time they arrived in Toronto in large numbers, other immigrants had their own occupational niches, such as Italian women in manufacturing, particularly in the textile and garment industries.[16] Also, the first generation of other immigrant cleaners who had preceded the Portuguese—such as German, Hungarian, and Yugoslavian women—were aging and leaving the workforce. Certain immigrant women, including Italians, rejected live-out domestic work.[17] So, too, did Black Caribbean women, who, in the years before Canada's introduction of a racist guest-worker system in the early 1970s, were landed immigrants who (like the European immigrants arriving on labour contracts) could remain in the country after completing their live-in domestic contract. Given a choice, Caribbean immigrant women reportedly preferred factory over cleaning jobs. The information came from a female counsellor with the Services for Working People (SFWP) agency, who attributed the women's dislike for housecleaning to the job's association with servility and their own negative experiences as live-in domestics. But racism also kept Black women out of daytime cleaning. The International Institute's jobs register records the comments of Canadian women who said they would hire anyone but Jamaicans and that they did not want "coloured girls."[18] Southern Europeans did not possess an uncontested whiteness, but in the realm of domestic work, they were racially privileged. In addition, as the SFWP counsellor also noted, Portuguese women "do not feel" that cleaning "is below their dignity."[19] In the mid-1960s, employers who used the International Institute routinely requested Portuguese cleaning ladies; in the early 1970s, Portuguese women dominated some of the institute's lists of requests.[20]

As migration from Portugal increased markedly, already employed cleaning ladies played a key role in initiating and directing an ever-widening network of female relatives, co-villagers, and neighbours in Toronto into domestic cleaning. Drawing on family and kin connections, Portuguese women actively created their own ethnic networks to help them find work. By the early 1960s, International Institute counsellors who called to offer a Portuguese client a housecleaning job often learned that a sister or sister-in-law had already found her houses to clean. Oral histories with cleaners bear this out. Interviews conducted with thirteen women who were still cleaning houses full-time in the early 2000s, or who had previously done so, revealed that none of these late-1960s and early-1970s arrivals had to contact an agency to find work. All but one of them found work through family and friends. The one exception was

Irene Sousa, who, like other janitorial workers in the building sector, got some day work from the tenants of the building she cleaned at night.[21] Thanks to the arrangements made particularly by female kin already in Toronto, Portuguese women increasingly arrived with housecleaning jobs waiting for them.

Toronto public transit also emerged as a key site for the exchange of information and support. As Portuguese cleaners traversed the city to and from jobs, they met each other on the subway or bus or streetcar. Their conversations often began with "Do you know someone who needs a cleaning lady?" or "My employer has a friend who wants a cleaning lady." And these conversations often led to employment.

The relationship between the usually female employer and cleaner was hardly egalitarian, but in the initial encounter, each party did evaluate the other and decide whether to proceed with the unwritten contract. Some cleaners immediately or soon left an employer because they thought her too demanding ("telling me to do this, do that, all the time"), or her house too messy. Others quit because they felt cheated, as when an employer paid them less than promised and one streetcar fare instead of the return fare. Especially insulting was the action of employers who tested the cleaning lady's honesty by leaving cash in semi-obscure places, such as under the sofa or between the cushions, to see what happened. In response, some women directly confronted the employer, saying that if the employer did it again they would quit. Others were less confrontational but delivered the same message by leaving the money on full display in the spot where the employer left their payment. Still others quit after putting up with the behaviour a second or even a third time. Another reason for rejecting jobs was the location: women avoided long or underserviced public transit routes and houses that involved a very long and exhausting walk.[22]

Employers had their own reasons for hiring or firing a cleaning lady. Plenty of them dismissed women whose cleaning they thought not quite up to snuff ("didn't work hard enough" or "wants a stronger worker"). Others rejected women they thought too "fat" or too thin or frail-looking for the job. "Bad" manners ("she doesn't do what she is told") could also get a cleaner fired.[23]

As these examples suggest, the well-to-do women (and families) who hired cleaning ladies often held what Michelle Johnson, writing about a different national context, describes as "clear visions about the quintessential working bodies" they wanted. Those who did not meet their ideal of the strong, agile, clean, and efficient body were rejected.[24] In one such example from April 1963, an employer fired Josefa Pereira, who had been sent to the house by the International Institute, because she "smelled." Pereira immediately returned to her institute counsellor, who wrote that she was a "very clean appearing woman" and that they detected only a "very slight musty odour as if clothing had been packed in a damp place."[25] If Pereira did "smell" on the day she cleaned this home, it was likely because the strenuous manual labour involved made her sweat. Employers also tried to avoid pregnant women on the grounds that they would soon be out of commission, though they may have also felt uncomfortable or guilty about a pregnant woman doing manual labour in their home. The behaviour speaks volumes on the uncomfortable disjuncture between feminine vulnerability embodied in pregnancy, and the strain and stresses that the manual labour of domestic work would heap on this same body.

International Institute counsellors acted similarly, recommending "clean" and "healthy" women for domestic jobs and discouraging "older" (over forty) or weak-looking bodies from accepting cleaning work.[26] A counsellor's assumption that women with "very fine white hands" were "more suitable for factory work than housecleaning" is absurd, given the harsh conditions of factory work, but the preference for (presumably) red, rough, or hardened hands nevertheless informed classed, gendered, and cultural notions about who should perform domestic work. In short, bourgeois notions of femininity precluded difficult manual labour. In a rare exception, a counsellor did think the woman who fired a Portuguese client for being a "poor" ironer was probably "very fussy."[27] Overall, the paradox identified by Johnson in relation to domestic workers in Jamaica applies here too. Insofar as they were being hired to perform domestic labour, Portuguese immigrant women were "perceived of as (gendered) women," but "the bodies that were needed to complete that labour were (masculinised) strong bodies."[28] These women navigated a terrain where Canadian employers and intermediaries considered domestic labour appropriate for ethnicized or racialized women with strong and clean (odourless) bodies.

Just as married Canadian women's entry into the workforce created job opportunities for Portuguese immigrant women in private housecleaning, the rapid expansion of the financial and public sector opened up cleaning jobs in buildings. As municipal and provincial governments grew in size, and Toronto assumed its new position as Canada's leading financial centre, the construction of downtown office buildings and skyscrapers proliferated. New government buildings included New City Hall, inaugurated in 1965, its modernist architecture making a distinctive mark on the city's landscape. The Queen's Park office complex, which was located east of the Ontario Legislature, included four new office towers occupying close to two city blocks. Over the course of the late 1960s and the 1970s, glitzy corporate skyscrapers truly transformed Toronto's skyline. For three decades, the thirty-four-storey Canadian (Imperial) Bank of Commerce Building (Commerce Court North) had dominated that skyline. But in 1967, the new Toronto-Dominion Centre, with its fifty-six-storey tower, became the tallest building—and a symbol of Toronto's new economic power. By 1974, the TD Centre consisted of three office towers and a pavilion. The 1970s also ushered in Commerce Court West (1972), First Canadian Place (1975), and Royal Bank Plaza (1979). These "glass towers" of big capital would become sites of class conflict.[29]

The workforce hired to clean these buildings, which became more centralized as well as bigger workplaces, expanded accordingly. A 1974 union report estimated that the national workforce had more than tripled in a decade.[30] The building-cleaning workforce had always been immigrant based, including British immigrants before the Second World War. By the 1950s and 1960s, it was increasingly eastern and southern Europeans. The same processes that led to Portuguese women's concentration in domestic cleaning occurred here. As earlier-arriving Europeans left the workforce or clustered in their own occupational niches, newer groups, in particular the Portuguese, formed a niche by the late 1960s in a rapidly expanding janitorial sector.

As with housecleaning, family and female ethnic networks bolstered the Portuguese presence among office-building cleaners. Again, sisters, in-laws, and cousins found each other work. The stories told by Emilia Silva and Arminda de Sousa underscore the importance of Portuguese neighbourhoods more generally as sites of job information: they landed jobs with First Canadian Place and Metro Police Headquarters, respectively, through female neighbours. Employers also established networks within the Portuguese community. The supervisors with companies contracted to clean large office buildings—such as Modern Building Cleaning at the Queen's Park complex in the mid-1970s—asked their hardworking employees to bring them other women from their village. (Modern also registered with the International Institute as a company that employed Portuguese workers.[31]) Or, when approached, supervisors

The Work of Cleaning

55

agreed to take on a reliable employee's female relatives. Cleaning companies also hired Portuguese recruiters who sought out women in the Portuguese neighbourhoods who wanted work. A van would pick up the women at home and take them to work, but also charge them for the trip.[32] Estimates of the size of this workforce vary: the most cited figure is twenty thousand for the 1980s, though a 1975 *Toronto Star* article cited over thirty-six thousand cleaners, char-workers, and janitors in Toronto. But there is general agreement that the Portuguese comprised a majority of Toronto's janitors from the 1970s to the early 2000s.[33]

Wages

The wages of house and building cleaners differed considerably; house cleaners were paid more, although they had none of the benefits that building cleaners enjoyed. However, janitorial workers had to contend with the competitive contracting-out process that kept wages low and with the gendered pay rates that disadvantaged women. In the early 1960s, house cleaners earned $1 an hour for a standard seven-hour workday (9 a.m. to 4 p.m.), plus public transit fare. Wages increased steadily over time, a growth that reflected inflation, but also cleaners' refusal to accept especially low-paying jobs. By March 1965, the daily wages increased to $10, but with the hourly minimum wage in Ontario set at $1, cleaners' wages stood only slightly above minimum wage levels. In 1974, the wages for a now six-hour day (9 a.m. to 3 p.m.) jumped to $18, and in 1976 to at least $20 a day ($3.30 an hour), when Ontario's hourly minimum wage was $2.65. Given that a junior female typist or office clerk then earned about $26 a day, a house cleaner's earnings fell somewhere between minimum wage manual labour and low-level female white-collar work.[34]

Oral interviews with former cleaning ladies tell us more. Women recall having earned a day rate of $40 by the mid-1960s and $60 a decade later. The jump in wages by the mid-1970s, to a rate well above minimum wage, no doubt coincided with a dramatic increase in demand among Canadian women for house cleaners, particularly as growing numbers of baby boomers entered the job market.[35] Portuguese women took advantage of the potential labour market scarcity in cleaning ladies to demand better wages.

The change at this time from hour-based wages to a flat cash rate reflected the broader shift within the occupation from a personal and maternalistic to a more contractual working arrangement between employer and cleaner. But an unwritten contract also had negative wage-related implications. If, for instance, the employer asked the cleaner not to work because they were going on vacation, the cleaner was not paid for the loss of work. If the cleaner was too sick to work, she again lost her pay. And there was certainly no paid maternity leave or access to unemployment insurance. Thus, while cleaners could negotiate higher wages, the unregulated nature of the working relationships offered no wage protection.

The cleaners themselves helped to bring about the changes that reinforced the (to them preferred) shift from a more personal to more contractual relationship. Take the case of lunch. In the 1960s, employers still factored into the wage their provision of lunch—a vestige of an older maternalistic relationship where employers acted as caring, "motherly" employers to their grateful employees. The cleaners' dissatisfaction with the lunches they were served reveals class tensions as well as ethnocultural differences between the Portuguese cleaners and their employers. Some women, including Elisabete Almeida, quit employers who served them lunch very late in the day (3 p.m.) and then only provided a light soup with no coffee. Middle-class women might sustain themselves on low-calorie soups, but women performing manual labour needed more. As for the missing coffee, it was a common drink in Portuguese culture and a familiar break ritual for workers, as well as a necessary pick-me-up. So cleaners read its absence as an insult.[36]

Another item to drop from the unwritten wage contract by the 1970s was the public transit fare to get to and from work. The eventual disappearance of this practice (with its maternalistic connotations) from the wage similarly reflected the growing contractual working relationship in private cleaning. Also, while the early 1960s generally saw a standard wage for all homes, by the 1970s there were variable standard wages based on the size of the house to clean. The change indicates that cleaners were now labouring in a wider variety of homes, and that they expected the owners of large houses to pay more than those of small homes. The higher rates were based not on working more hours, but instead on the fact that cleaners had to work faster and harder in larger homes to get everything accomplished within their regular working day. Again, the cleaners' informal female networks of friends and family helped them to gauge whether they were being paid fairly. Conversations in which a cleaner was told "you're crazy" to accept "so little money" from an employer, or that explained how someone else had demanded a raise, propelled many

The Work of Cleaning

a cleaner to ask for more.[37] This point is important because domestic cleaners are often portrayed as isolated workers who cannot act collectively. While labouring in individual homes, Portuguese women also exhibited a collective worker culture, one embedded in informal female networks of kin, village, and neighbourhood, that enabled them to make demands of their employers.

Many cleaners effectively supplemented their wages with their employers' donations of second-hand goods such as clothing, toys, small appliances, and furniture. The donations hearken back to the maternalistic relationships that historically marked live-in domestic work, but such items did prove very useful. Unlike the im/migrant and racialized "maids in the USA" who resented the "gift" of used clothing made in lieu of wage increases, Toronto's Portuguese house cleaners found the items helpful in supporting their families, particularly in the early years. They especially valued children's clothes, since children quickly outgrew them. One resourceful cleaner, Sofia Bettencourt, recalled transforming an employer's clothing into outfits for herself and her daughter. As immigrant workers who supported transnational as well as local family economies, women also sent donated clothes to Portugal. Joaquina Gomes sent many large shipments of clothes to her home village of Marquiteira during the 1970s and 1980s; the arrival of a bundle was the occasion for a *festa* (celebration) for her large extended family, who gathered to select what they wanted.[38]

Women's wages in janitorial cleaning are complicated by gender discrimination. The majority of the Toronto (and Canadian) building cleaning workforce—at least 80 percent—was and remains female.[39] Women are categorized as light-duty cleaners while the men are categorized as heavy-duty cleaners, for which they earn a higher wage. Light-duty cleaning includes picking up litter, emptying and cleaning ashtrays, emptying wastepaper baskets, cleaning and dusting furniture, mopping with a twelve-ounce mop, vacuuming, and cleaning washrooms. While women tend to work horizontally (and are assigned to specific floors), men tend to work vertically through the building. Heavy-duty cleaning is more often performed in the building's public spaces, such as lobbies, and includes emptying and cleaning heavy waste receptacles, washing and scrubbing floors, mopping with a twenty-four-ounce mop, removing and applying floor finishes, washing walls and ceilings, cleaning and replacing light fixtures, operating powered cleaning and sanitation equipment, shovelling snow, and cutting grass. The historical association of men with outside domestic chores and women with inside ones shapes these work assignments. Further, men's jobs are perceived as heavier because they work with more machines, such as floor buffers. In fact, many of the tasks (cleaning floors, vacuuming) are the same for both types of cleaners, but the designations imply an easier (or unskilled) "feminine" job versus a more labour intensive (or skilled) "masculine" job.

In the early 1960s, the National Employment Service and the only cleaning union in the industry at the time, the Service Employees International Union (SEIU), believed that men would eventually outnumber women in the industry, partly because of increasing automation. But newfangled devices like the kelk broom designed to replace the vacuum cleaner, or the offensively named "papoose," a cleaning apparatus strapped to the back, never caught on.[40] The longevity of relatively unsophisticated cleaning methods involving traditional vacuums, mops, soaps, and rags largely accounts for the feminization of the building-cleaning workforce.[41] The comments of the cleaning contractor who in 1962 claimed that "nothing will replace a woman's neat touch with an executive desk" indicates as well the persistence of gendered perceptions of women as meticulous cleaners.[42] Indeed, women's skills are denigrated in the cleaning workplace because of their association with the "natural" women's work that most women are taught to perform early in their lives. Cleaning, then, is socially constructed as unskilled work. Women's skill in maintaining clean offices, particularly as night cleaners, is thus rendered invisible.

The economic reasons for hiring women, who have always been paid less than men, also contributed to the continued feminization of the building-cleaning sector. Collective agreements from the 1960s show that job classifications were then, and before, explicitly divided into "male" and "female" cleaning jobs, and that it was a common practice to pay women less than men. In the 1970s—an era when the women's movement was challenging the inferior position of women in the workforce—these classifications were changed to light duty and heavy duty to make the gender discrimination less explicit. Modern Building Cleaning, for example, renamed its job categories in 1971 following the passage of the Women's Equal Employment Opportunity Act in Ontario. But this hardly changed gender segregation and discriminatory wages in the industry. Since the company allowed women to apply for heavy-duty cleaning only if they were deemed physically strong enough, these jobs continued to be filled mainly by men.[43]

Above all, however, it is the highly competitive contracting-out practice in the building-cleaning industry that acts as a downward pressure on wages, which have historically hovered around minimum wage, particularly for women, even when unionized. Often at the direct encouragement of the building-owning capitalists who most benefited from the situation, smaller-scale cleaning companies offered absurdly low bids to win a contract to clean a given skyscraper and then had to cut costs by reducing labour costs. Indeed, the profit margins for cleaning companies declined over the period under review, because of increasing competition in the industry.[44] Just before 1944, when the SEIU first appeared in Toronto, women made 25 cents an hour and men 40 cents. There was no sick leave, hospital insurance, or holiday pay.[45] The table of Wages for Building Cleaners (on the next page) shows wages for the general period and companies investigated in this book.

Some unions made some gains above minimum wage by the 1980s, but these were eroded by high inflation rates. Given that the Ontario government never meant the (provincially set) minimum standard to seriously affect employers or significantly alleviate poverty, female cleaners' wages arguably stood at poverty level.[46] They were also disadvantaged in terms of working hours. Men worked on a full-time schedule, often during the day, but women were mainly employed part-time, in the evenings. With many part-time workers, cleaning contractors avoided paying extra benefits, such as paid breaks.

The broadly based Equal Pay Coalition of Ontario that emerged in the mid-1970s did not ignore female janitorial workers. In a public forum on the subject in Toronto in 1975, Ontario NDP leader Stephen Lewis declared that "the sole difference" between the male cleaners who, on an annual basis, earned between $1,372 and $1,456 more than women "in the same job" was "the mop size and how many rungs of a ladder have to be climbed."[47] That same year, the Ontario government responded to pressure from the Civil Service Association of Ontario and other groups to end salary discrimination within provincial government buildings first by denying it, and then by instituting a fair wage policy for government contractors who provided janitorial (and security) services. The wage rates were set according to going rates in contract cleaning, but did not apply to those cleaners who worked directly for the government and made higher wages. At a time when the minimum hourly wage was $2.40, a light-duty cleaner was to make not less than $2.76 and a heavy-duty cleaner, $3.56. In comparison, non-contract government cleaners

Wages for Building Cleaners, 1967 to 1987			
	TD Centre	Queen's Park	First Canadian Place	Minimum Wage
1967	Light $1.35 Heavy $1.80 (SEIU—Modern Building Cleaning)			$1.00
1975	Light $2.85 Heavy $3.74 (SEIU—Modern)	Light $2.40 Heavy $3.15 (SEIU—Modern)		$2.40
1976	Light $3.26 Heavy $4.26 (SEIU—Modern)	Light $2.90 Heavy $3.40 (SEIU— Consolidated Maintenance Services)		$2.40/$2.65
1979	Light $4.32 Heavy $5.27 (CUPE—Modern)	Light $3.90 Heavy $4.40		$3.00
1980		Light $4.60 Heavy $5.10	Light $4.40 Heavy $5.45 (FASWOC— Federated Building Maintenance)	$3.00
1984			Light $5.83 Heavy $6.97 (FASWOC— Federated)	$3.85
1987	Light $7.05 Heavy $8.12 (CUPE—Empire Building Maintenance)	Light $8.53 Heavy $9.41 (SEIU—Concorde Maintenance Ltd.)	Light $6.78 Heavy $7.73 (FASWOC— Federated)	$4.35

CUPE: Canadian Union of Public Employees; FASWOC: Food and Service Workers of Canada; SEIU: Service Employees International Union. Source: Company-Union Agreements, RG 7-33, Archives of Ontario; City of Toronto Archives.

doing light and heavy duties made \$3.74 and \$4.43, respectively. Despite the constraints on negotiating higher wages, unions were able to make some other gains for workers, particularly around benefits such as paid sick and holiday leaves, and some working conditions, such as overtime and breaks.[48]

A landmark bill, Ontario's Pay Equity Act of 1987 applied to both the public and private sectors, but cleaners remained disadvantaged in the realm of equal pay. Some unions made significant gains for women, but the legislation benefited those already in the best-paid female jobs: mainly white, unionized women who worked for larger employers, such as teachers, nurses, and clerical workers. The Act did not cover the many smaller (under 100 workers) and non-unionized buildings.[49] Even if cleaners could secure equal wages in a particular workplace, the rise in wages would likely lead to the loss of the cleaning contract and, with it, the loss of the union (see chapters 5–7).[50] So, although the unions were aware of gender discrimination in wages, or were now more willing to publicly acknowledge the problem thanks to the work of feminist activists, they were in a weak position to fight for equal pay for building cleaners in the contracting-out system. Then, too, certain contractors wanting to institute pay equity were "shocked" that some women voted against it because their husbands, who worked in the same building, thought it offensive. This reflected patriarchal relations within Portuguese families, though the women did try to reduce the gender differential by fighting for across-the-board, rather than percentage, increases in wages in union contracts.[51]

Workplace Control

Popular depictions of paid housecleaning in postwar Canada—like the *Chatelaine* article that speaks of two parties "engaged in a business proposition, the buying and selling of services, with a contract that can and should be terminated by either side if there's any dissatisfaction"—glossed over serious class inequities.[52] Still, by the early 1960s, Portuguese house cleaners were entering an occupation that was already somewhat contractual: employers and cleaners together negotiated the nature and expectations of live-out domestic work. Despite vestiges of maternalism, daytime housecleaning entailed a relatively more balanced exchange between cleaner and employer compared to live-in domestic work, where maids were legally tied to their employers and dependent on them for shelter.[53]

Poverty, debt, and prejudice offer women poor choices, but as landed immigrants who lived with family and opted to clean private homes, Toronto's Portuguese private house cleaners were in a comparatively better position than the racialized Caribbean and Filipina women who, beginning in 1973, arrived in Canada under temporary work visas that tied them to one private employer, often as a family's live-in nanny. By 1979, these live-in domestics, as well as those from the United Kingdom, organized with feminist allies to found INTERCEDE (International Coalition to End Domestics' Exploitation). The advocacy group's wide-ranging agenda was partially captured in the slogan "Good enough to work, Good enough to stay." Various lobbying efforts and then a national campaign resulted in the passing of federal legislation in 1982 that created a pathway to landed status (after two years) for thousands of women. For INTERCEDE activists like Martha Ocampo (Toronto) and Cenen Bagon (Vancouver)—who were also active in the international coalition against Philippine dictator Ferdinand Marcos—the 1982 legislation was only a partial victory for many reasons, including the continuation of a state-sanctioned system of semi-indentured foreign domestics and the absence of collective bargaining rights.[54] INTERCEDE and its feminist and labour allies won another partial victory in Ontario in 1993, when, as noted, the NDP government legally recognized domestic workers' right to collective bargaining, only to have the policy reversed two years later by the right-wing Progressive Conservative government of Mike Harris.[55]

Portuguese day (or live-out) cleaners in Toronto did not join INTERCEDE, nor were they approached by a union aiming to organize them.[56] While hardly overprivileged workers, their superior status (compared to live-in foreign domestics) as landed immigrants or Canadian citizens not legally bound to any employer offered greater leverage to negotiate wages and work regimes with their employers. Drawing on their dense female networks of information and support, they negotiated new or improved arrangements that reinforced the occupation's contractual character and aligned with their values of hard work, skill, and dignity. Through their collective networks, they defined the boundaries of acceptable and unacceptable tasks and pursued strategies that standardized the occupation. Through such informal collective means, they were able to overcome some of the challenges posed by their isolated workplaces and lack of state support and even to redefine the terms of their work regimes.[57]

The Work of Cleaning

Take, for example, the end of the employer-provided lunch in the 1970s. The change partly reflected the fact that employers were less often at home during the day to prepare these meals, but the women's resistance to the arrangement also played a role. Preferring food that was familiar and culturally important to them, cleaners like Joana Soares, who disliked her employer's sandwiches, began to pack and eat their own lunches. Soares "would only make coffee at their house."[58] Others, like Joana's sister Carolina, were insulted by the stale bread they were served, and attributed the bad manners to the ignorance of employers who "didn't know what we ate at home" and "that we ate better than them."[59] To the extent that the disappearance of lunch from the working arrangement reflected major changes in the roles of both middle-class and working-class women, this was arguably a reciprocal process of change based on the needs and desires of both parties. But it was the concrete actions of the immigrant cleaners that sealed the deal.

The daytime absence of female homeowners, who themselves went out to work, facilitated the growing independence of immigrant day cleaners. Giving cleaners the house keys may have been a necessity, but it meant placing far more trust in them than in the past. Left to develop their work routines without their employers' supervision or interference, cleaners exercised more control over their working hours. Many shortened their workdays so they could devote more time to their children and other family members. Previously, in order to get their money's worth, employers would find extra tasks for cleaners who finished the agreed-upon workload before their scheduled leave time. But as more Portuguese cleaners informed new and continuing employers of their preferred schedule (9 a.m. to 3 p.m.), and cleaning-starved employers agreed, these women workers changed a major defining term of their labour.

Women transformed the conditions of their work in other ways too. The question of which tasks were appropriate for a house cleaner to perform often sparked debate between employers and cleaners. *Chatelaine* acknowledged the tension in its advice to homemakers to "state exactly what you want done," or risk hiring someone who "won't tackle heavy jobs such as floors or walls" or "do laundry."[60] Issued in 1959, the advice partly reflected the fact that cleaning women, even inexperienced "greenhorns," refused to perform certain tasks, such as the outdoor jobs they viewed as men's work.[61] Unlike live-in domestics, daytime house cleaners had more control over what kind of tasks would fill their workdays. Basic tasks such as dusting, vacuuming, or cleaning a washroom were a given, but other tasks fell into a grey area of negotiation between employer and cleaner. The negotiations produced varied job descriptions.

As cleaners who once did whatever employers asked of them, including moving heavy furniture, grew more assertive in rejecting certain tasks, they increasingly structured their workdays as they wished. Carolina Soares's account of her changing relationship with her employers offers insight into how these immigrant women embraced and asserted their identity as women workers. Initially, she said, her employers "thought we were stupid" because "we didn't know . . . English" and "we [did] whatever they wanted." But as she learned English and developed a sense of what constituted exploitative work, she became more confident about telling her employers, who themselves began treating her differently as her English improved, what she would not do.[62]

Another way of asserting greater workplace control was to standardize a cleaning regime across the five or six houses that one usually cleaned. As cleaners compared the duties performed in the different houses they cleaned and exchanged information with each other, the women came to collectively identify what constituted suitable and unsuitable tasks. The women worked in individual homes, but the dense and overlapping ethnic, kin, and occupational networks they nurtured as more women arrived from Portugal and entered the field provided a key source of commentary on the nature and expectations of the job. Women shared stories and opinions about their work regimes with family and friends at home and in the neighbourhood, and at festivals, community clubs, church, and again, on public transit. Far from idle chatter, women's gossip networks identified overly demanding employers (though individual cleaners might make concessions to certain "picky" employers). They reported on the workplace victories of individual cleaners, however small, which in turn emboldened other women to act. Learning about women who, for example, had successfully eliminated a certain task or tasks from their work routine led others to confront their employers. As Carolina Soares recalled, these conversations were informal but illuminating, and for her, empowering. "We talked to each other," she said, "and I say how I did this or that, or ironed or something. And then someone would say, 'You're not supposed to do that work in these houses,' and then I [saw] . . . that I shouldn't . . . and then I start saying no, that I won't do it."[63] As a result, more "personal service" tasks like laundry and ironing became less common. So, too, did those tasks viewed as heavy or dangerous, such as climbing ladders to clean chandeliers or windows.

The Work of Cleaning

Cleaners sought as well to exert control over the tools of a job that they increasingly redefined as a skilled, even professional, occupation. Like all immigrant domestics, newcomers came up against well-heeled employers who scolded or fired them for such mistakes as using abrasives to clean silverware or mishandling an appliance.[64] Some of the specific skills they requested—like the employer who asked the International Institute to supply a woman who could hand-wash, iron, and carefully fold king-sized bed sheets and pillowcases—underscore their bourgeois privilege. In recommending "a good Portuguese [as] they are experienced with hand washing and ironing," the counsellor also confirmed that the task required certain skills. More common were requests for women who could operate vacuum cleaners, floor polishers, and other "modern" electrical equipment. Or who had "Canadian experience," a common employer concern in a sector that historically employed immigrant women and a common conundrum for money-starved newcomers keen to gain the experience.[65]

Training programs for im/migrant domestics in "Canadian" household methods have existed since at least the early twentieth century. Even if not formally trained in institutions, immigrant domestics, who often hailed from impoverished rural or urban backgrounds, or were refugees of atrocities and war, quickly had to learn domestic skills on the job.[66] Portuguese women also went through a learning period as they adjusted to the material and technological realities of domestic work in post-1960 Canada. By the early 1960s, when many if not most homes in Canadian cities were modernized, modern home comforts were only just beginning to emerge in Portugal (see chapter 1). Upon arrival, noted Carolina Soares, "the only thing [she] knew how to do, like they did here [in Canada,] was ironing."[67] Skill, then, was culturally constructed, but the constructions themselves reflected differing material realities.

Many of the women who left Portugal for Canada in the 1960s and 1970s would have witnessed the installation of electricity into their homes, but very few families could have afforded expensive electrical appliances like vacuum cleaners and washing machines. Women's experience at doing laundry varied depending upon locale and timing of emigration as well as age. As she recounted the old-fashioned way that the women in her northern Portuguese village near Viana do Castelo were still washing clothes in the early 1960s, Rita Ramos laughed at the memory of how it took all week. On Monday, they scrubbed the clothes with a bar of soap and soaked them overnight, and then scrubbed them again the next day. They then laid out the whites on the grass in the sun to bleach and hung the dark items to dry right away. At midweek, they flipped over the whites, occasionally spraying them with water to keep them damp, and later still, rewashed them and hung them to dry.[68] By contrast, wringer washers were used widely in Canada at this time, though automatic washing machines were still rare. (Not until 1966 did sales of the latter pass those of the former.) As for cleansers, the increasing availability of products such as *cloreto* (powdered bleach) and Tide (detergent) in parts of Portugal meant that other female emigrants already had been spending less time on laundry.[69] The one small "modern" appliance that many women could afford by the time they left Portugal was an electric iron, which replaced the old coal-heated iron.

Still, the general lack of availability and cost of modern cleaning products kept cleaning in Portugal pretty rudimentary. Products that were commonplace in Canada in the 1960s and 1970s, such as Windex, furniture polishers like Pledge, and oven and bathroom cleansers were not yet common in Portugal. With rags made from old clothing, women in Portugal used water for dusting, and water and vinegar for washing windows. They occasionally applied wax or oil to the furniture or wood floors. But an ethos of cleanliness, one that associated a clean house with a good wife and mother, also prevailed. The reality of their poverty even enhanced its importance. When women like Natalia Vilela insisted that, though poor, their house was always clean, they were articulating a gendered work ethic from which poor women attained a sense of dignity and respectability. And they carried this code with them to Canada.[70]

Once in Canada, however, they had to quickly adapt to the technology and cleaning products in the middle- and upper-class homes they cleaned. In their own homes, the prohibitive cost of many appliances and products made for a more gradual adjustment. Unable to read instructions or labels printed in English, newcomers who were employed within days or weeks of arriving in Toronto turned to more experienced female relatives for a crash course on cleaning products. Many employers provided on-the-job training on using a vacuum cleaner and dishwasher, while some cleaners recall asking their employers about the purpose of each cleaning product in the house. No doubt, the frustration of having to invest time and effort into training "greenhorn" cleaners explains why some of the employers who registered with the International Institute requested experienced cleaners.[71]

The cleaning products and tools themselves changed dramatically in this period. Before items such as Windex, Comet, Ajax, and Mr. Clean became common home products in Canada in the 1950s and 1960s, women might have used vinegar and water, bleach, ammonia, baking soda, or bars of soap to clean surfaces.[72] While domestic cleaning continued to involve difficult manual labour, new technology and products did make the job easier in some respects. By the 1970s, the physically difficult task of waxing and buffing wood floors largely disappeared with the widespread use of urethane wood-floor finishes. Much later, lighter vacuum cleaners replaced cumbersome ones, making it easier to carry them up and down stairs.[73] The appearance of self-cleaning ovens made another task less cumbersome. Cleaning products also improved: the arrival of Fantastik (good for grease) and Tilex (for bathroom mildew), noted Gomes, made her job easier.[74]

As women learned which machines and products worked best, and asked their employers to provide them—whether by leaving notes or clipped ads of the items—they were not simply embracing Canadian ways. Like establishing their own work routines, persuading employers to purchase their items of choice increased their independence within the occupation. Cleaning ladies cultivated a status as skilled workers, even professionals, through their expertise in cleaning tools, products, and methods. An important achievement was to have all the homes they cleaned equipped with the same set of materials. Getting employers to replace their clunky old vacuum cleaner with a better model bolstered their claims to skilled professionalism. It also points to the role of immigrant workers in changing, even transforming, the households of better-off Canadians and, later, middle-class immigrants.

These workers' aspirations for greater workplace control and respect did not simply involve abandoning the old for the new. Rather, the women incorporated some of the skills, tools, and methods used in Portugal into their new jobs, producing a hybrid system of cleaning. Cleaners insisted on using rags for dusting, rather than the paper towels or dusters that employers supplied. If the employers did not provide rags (made from old clothing or towels), they brought their own. Forgoing mops, some cleaners washed floors as they had in Portugal—on their hands and knees using soap and plenty of elbow grease—because they believed it produced a better result. When an employer advised Joana Soares to use a mop instead, she explained that "the mop doesn't get to the corners." In a noteworthy example of Canadian adaptation, many cleaners came to recommend to employers the modern appliances that, through trial and error, they came to prefer. One insistent cleaner even brought her own vacuum cleaner to work until the employer bought an acceptable one. The creation of hybrid cleaning regimes, where customary cleaning routines existed alongside modern appliances and applications, speaks to the ability of Portuguese immigrant women to reshape an occupation they had come to dominate. But we should not exaggerate the point, for these women toiled at the bottom ranks of the labour market.[75]

Janitorial staff who cleaned office buildings had less control over their work than domestic cleaners in part because their employers determined the cleaning tools and products used. As employers with contracts to clean company and government office buildings intensified the work process over the 1970s and 1980s in order to cut costs, these workers faced even greater pressure and less control on the job than did domestic cleaners. Lucia Ferreira noted that by the 1990s, the 1970s-era ratio of two cleaners per floor at First Canadian Place was cut to one, while working hours either remained the same or decreased. When Consolidated Maintenance Services replaced Modern Building Cleaning at the Queen's Park complex in 1975, its management cut the light-duty cleaners' night shift from six to five hours, with no reduction in the assigned tasks. Supervisors told cleaners who complained about the extra workload sabotaging their allotted fifteen-minute break that they were easily replaced by someone who would work harder and faster. When asked about cleaning the towers of the TD Centre in the 1970s, Idalina Azevedo replied, "I found that it was like slavery, to tell you the truth."[76]

Spouting claims about greater productivity helping everyone, employers intensified work in an effort to maximize profits in an industry where labour costs make up 80 to 85 percent of the operating budget. The managers of cleaning companies, for example, claimed that cleaning more square footage per hour was both entirely "within people's capability" and achieved a collective good, namely improved productivity.[77] In truth, the cost-cutting practices born of the contracting-out system forced workers to work more and work faster and often for less pay. Unions could not stop the trend, precisely because the employers controlled the labour process. Toiling under heavy management control, building cleaners were less able than private house cleaners to exercise some control over workplace conditions. Some staffers with the Department of Labour warned against encouraging "sweat-shop" conditions in government buildings, but the Ontario government never really

The Work of Cleaning

acted on the matter.[78] As workers committed to doing "a good job" tried to maintain a certain standard of "cleanliness" under these conditions, their physical and mental health suffered.[79] One cleaner told a reporter that, since she found it too upsetting to "leave anything undone," she had to keep working faster and faster. Ferreira recalled the enormous stress caused by her inability to clean "everything" as well as she once did at First Canadian Place, because it was just too much work.[80]

Janitorial cleaners' actions in the workplace were more heavily circumscribed compared to those of house cleaners. They were prohibited from taking a break or a meal in tenant space or using tenant phones or office supplies.[81] While resourceful domestic workers took items they considered useful from the garbage of their better-off employers, janitors who salvaged items from the trash of billion-dollar corporations risked serious penalty. Insofar as retrieving still-functioning lamps and paper saved cleaning ladies the cost of buying such items, bourgeois "garbage" could supplement workers' wages.

But corporate greed was very much on display when a "janitress" who retrieved some paper and desk pads, a broken kettle, and a discarded microphone and tape from the garbage bins at First Canadian Place was fired by the building's contracted cleaner, Federated Building Maintenance, for "theft of Bank property." She left the building with the items in full view, but security guards made a show of apprehending the would-be thief. During a subsequent arbitration hearing between Federated and the union, the Food and Service Workers of Canada (FASWOC), a co-worker who testified on the woman's behalf said the company threw out a remarkable volume of useful stuff. But the chief of security for the building owner, Olympia & York, insisted that the garbage remained the owner's property. The arbitrator sided with the woman on the grounds that she had never tried to conceal the items and the bank had never clearly indicated (through messages on their waste containers or memos to their employees) that it retained property rights over its trash. The woman also got her job back. But the episode discouraged others from salvaging useful items from the garbage. The union itself warned its members, "Protect yourself from unjust accusations—get permission before you take anything out of the building, even garbage."[82]

This 1979 case notwithstanding, theft did occur in the industry, but it is better understood as a form of workers' informal resistance against class exploitation than a crime.[83] Within the cleaning industry, the point is underscored by the fact that, while cleaning ladies in private homes were often given access to their employer's coffee, janitorial workers who helped themselves to a cup of the building tenants' coffee were accused of theft.[84] Then as now, when workers steal paper or cleaning supplies from a corporate building they clean, or soap and towels from the hotel they clean, they are not just acting badly or trying to get something for nothing. They are enacting a type of workers' justice that involves taking a greater share of the profits that employers make from their labour, however small.[85]

Relations with Employers

In domestic cleaning, the most historically prevalent form of relationship has been maternalism. In the classic model of live-in domestic work, the "caring" mistress nurtures her employee but also expects in return the servant's loyalty, deference, and gratitude. Scholars differ, however, in their assessment of what happens with the shift to live-out domestic work. Mary Romero argues that her interviews with Latina maids in the United States reveal their rejection of personal relations with employers. The maids strove instead to negotiate a businesslike relationship with employers in an effort to eliminate exploitation stemming from race, class, and gender hierarchies.[86] By contrast, Pierrette Hondagneu-Sotelo asserts that her interviews with more recent Mexican and Central American domestic workers in Los Angeles document a rise in what she calls personalism—or more positive relationships in which the two parties view each other not solely in terms of their economic role, but as persons embedded in a unique set of social relations. Noting that her interviewees saw non-personalistic employers as potentially more exploitative, because it often meant they failed to see the cleaner as a person, Hondagneu-Sotelo attributes the rise of personalism to the absence of female employers in the home, and the cleaners' greater ability to exert more control over their labour and thus resist "servanthood." For them, an employer's show of concern for their personal well-being signalled dignity and respect.[87]

Oral interviews with Portuguese immigrant domestics in Toronto indicate that personal relationships with employers improved as the occupation became more contractual over the 1970s and 1980s. The women valued being treated with respect and kindness. Some expressed appreciation for employers who asked rather than demanded they perform a given task or who complimented them for a job well done. Or who showed an interest in their personal lives. Joaquina Gomes fondly recalled the employer who asked her to bring her children with her on school holidays so she, the employer, could visit with them. Employers who shared intimate details about their own lives similarly elicited praise. For these cleaners, the shift from a formal mode of address (where they addressed employers by their surnames but were called by their first) to a more casual one (first names all around) signalled a power shift in the working relationship.[88] Besides the absence of employers from the home being cleaned, the workers' improved English, and the more contractual nature of live-out cleaning, these changes reflected as well the growing awareness among middle-class Canadian women of the increasing diversity of their society and the importance of showing class and cultural tolerance. As in the United States, the women's movement in Canada, which led women to consider the value of housework and to appreciate the "personal is political" mantra, played a role as well. Canadian culture in general also became more informal, and the employers' own experiences in the workforce no doubt influenced how they treated their employees.[89]

Some cleaners developed personal relations with employers that extended beyond the workplace. Carolina Soares, for example, attended the baptisms, bar mitzvahs, and weddings of some of her employers' children and grandchildren. And one of her employers attended her daughter's wedding. Two of Mariana Batista's employers attended her son's funeral. Other cleaners had employers visit their home for a social call. Ferreira, a cleaner who worked in both sectors, recalled that in contrast to the cleaning company that exploited her, her private employers treated her "like family" and she forged long-lasting relationships with them. But these were the exceptions rather than the norm. Class and ethnic differences and the employer/employee dynamic generally impeded the development of full friendships. There were also cleaners who, like Rosa Moreira, rejected personalism. Much like the domestics that Romero interviewed, she kept her distance from her employers lest they expect her to perform extra tasks without extra pay. And there were employers who took no personal interest in their employees.[90]

While some scholars position personalism in opposition to maternalistic relationships within domestic work, the concept of paternalism as used by labour historians usefully includes aspects of both maternalism and paternalism. A familiar example of employer paternalism is the company strategy of showing kindness or affection towards employees—whether through the provision of health care, housing, or social

72   Cleaning Up

activities—in order to nurture their individual loyalty and prevent the emergence of a collective worker identity. (Company paternalism could also exist alongside severe repression of worker activism.)[91] Similarly, private employers of cleaning women might act in a maternal manner in order to get more work out of their cleaners and elicit their loyalty. Still, in daytime housecleaning work, interactions were not as grounded in stark unequal power relationships. Day cleaners were not tied to one specific employer and had no legally binding contract. Workers who lost their jobs did not lose health or housing benefits attached to that job, as there were none. To make the point more baldly, day cleaners were less beholden to their various individual employers than, say, workers in a one-company town were to the all-powerful employer.

Relations with employers in janitorial cleaning were generally more fraught with tension than those in domestic work. Management exercised control over janitorial workers through surveillance techniques. Workers signed in at the front desk and had security passes to get on elevators. There were also security personnel, video cameras, and encoded strip cards that recorded their movements into offices or elevators. They had to carry walkie-talkies.[92] Building owners also exerted technical control. For example, to save money on electrical costs, the computer-controlled lights at First Canadian Place illuminated portions of the premises in a set order. Having to follow a predetermined cleaning pattern gave night workers little discretion or control over their work. They could ask the control centre to turn on the lights in a certain section of the building, but language barriers discouraged such requests. Moving in the darkness also increased the risk of a workplace accident.[93]

The cleaning contractors maintained elaborate managerial systems. At First Canadian Place, a housekeeping manager communicated with the owner of the building. Below him was a day supervisor who managed about twenty-five or thirty employees, and a night supervisor who managed the night shift, when most cleaners worked. The supervisors were also responsible for the general inspection of the building, assigning or reassigning employees to various floors, and making alternative staffing arrangements when employees did not report for work. For each floor, a foreman or forelady ensured that cleaners had sufficient cleaning supplies, but also supervised them and inspected their work.[94] Usually hired from the same ethnic group as the majority of cleaners in order to facilitate communication, forepersons were not members of the bargaining unit and they generally identified with management. The tensions between Portuguese supervisors and Portuguese cleaners reflect the fact that, in this case, class (or status) trumped ethnicity.

Portuguese employees' relations with the supervisors contained elements of homeland practices transplanted to Canada. In Portugal, workers traditionally played roles of subservience and supplication in the hope that employers would treat them fairly. A system of currying favour with supervisors operated in corporate-owned buildings such as the TD Centre and First Canadian Place. Each Christmas, for instance, employees pitched in to buy gifts for their supervisors. The strategy, recalled Emilia Silva, worked for a while, but supervisors eventually returned to their exploitative ways.[95] Other workers, including Idalina Azevedo—who received Christmas gifts from the owners of the houses she cleaned but had to fork out money for gifts for the supervisor of the building she cleaned—saw the latter as yet another example that employers in janitorial cleaning did not appreciate their employees.[96]

Azevedo was not alone in criticizing Portuguese supervisors who lorded it over their Portuguese employees, including by not deigning to talk with them.[97] An owner of a cleaning company recalled that such complaints became serious enough that they began training Portuguese managers in a form of "progressive discipline." This company's investment in training Portuguese supervisors to treat the workers diplomatically offers an example of how immigrant workers compelled their employer to alter its managerial practices.[98] There were also complaints of intimidation and harassment. At First Canadian Place, workers approached their union representative about a forelady who stood by the elevators and made notes on them as they went to their floors. Even if primarily performative, her actions, they said, made them "feel intimidated and harassed." So, too, did supervisors who swore at them. Or who pressured them to finish all the assigned tasks before they left, even when extra work had been assigned without notice. In one such case at First Canadian Place, the "floor lady" insulted Mrs. Sousa, who had been dumped with the extra work of cleaning up after a party held in a conference room, because of the cleaning still to do "so close" to the end of her shift. Her formal complaint noted that she "expects to be treated with respect and in a professional manner."[99]

The Cleaner's Body

The bodies of domestic and janitorial cleaners bear the adverse effects of a lifetime spent in an occupation marked by physically arduous labour and exposure to chemical and other hazardous conditions. From the start, Portuguese immigrant cleaners have been concerned about occupational health. The records of the International Institute of Metropolitan Toronto from the early 1960s show recently arrived women asking for alternative jobs because the detergents and cleaning fluids they used produced eczema on their hands or severe rashes on their arms.[100] The stories of later-arriving women document their daily exposure to a long list of cleansers, including furniture polish, window-and-glass cleaners, all-purpose cleansers (such as Comet and Fantastik), chlorine bleach, drain cleaners, toilet bowl cleaners, tile cleaners, scouring pads, oven cleaners, silver cleansers, and disinfectants, as well as dishwashing and laundry detergents. Inhaling the fumes of ammonia or powder cleansers also made them ill and, though they tried, it was impossible to fully avoid doing so.[101] So, too, for janitorial cleaners, who were exposed to industrial-strength cleaners. Ironically, some of the very products that, by being stronger, made the job easier affected cleaners' health the most.

Another common complaint was joint pain caused by the repetitive movements of cleaning. Washing floors the "traditional" way took a toll on the knees, as did the constant bending and stair climbing. The constant wiping of mirrors and glass caused shoulder pain. Back pain came from repeatedly moving the furniture and bending to clean the baseboards. The frequent wringing of rags and carrying of heavy objects like vacuums damaged hands and wrists. Standing for long periods of time produced varicose veins in the legs, the twisted and enlarged veins causing aching pain and discomfort.

Aggravated joint problems and chronic pain, and stern warnings from doctors who said continuing with such strenuous work could permanently disable them, forced some women to quit cleaning earlier than they wanted.[102] Others tried to heed their doctor's warning to at least avoid the tasks that aggravated their particular ailment, but this was often impossible.[103] Many retired cleaners carried and endured the chronic bodily pain that comes from having performed strenuous labour for twenty or thirty years or more. By the time this immigrant generation of cleaners reached their seventies, some of them no longer cleaned their own floors or climbed ladders to clean their windows, lest their knees permanently give out. Before or after retiring, other cleaners began seeing chiropractors regularly to help manage the pain. Still others have had to rely on other family members to help them, which, given their pride in maintaining clean homes, did and still does cause them emotional pain.

The Work of Cleaning

Cleaners also suffered from the hazardous environment of the workplaces in which they toiled. Some developed lung conditions from constantly cleaning dust and emptying ashtrays. For years, they were susceptible to the perils of cigarette smoke inhalation. Even after smoking was banned in office buildings and many people quit the habit, smokers still smoked at home, creating a hazardous workplace for their cleaners. Some cleaners were so allergic to cats and dogs that they had to refuse to clean any home with pets. The pets also scared some of the cleaners, who never felt totally safe in the animals' company.[104]

Workplace accidents were another reality. While they could not avoid kneeling-and-bending postures and strong cleaning products, some house cleaners tried to avoid accidents by refusing to do certain tasks. As Gomes recounted, "I couldn't go hanging from ladders washing high windows or very high chandeliers" because, "if I fell and broke a leg, who would take care of [me]?" She added, "I automatically resolved to say 'No, I won't do that.'"[105] One employer even told her to be careful because, if injured, she would not be paid for missing work.

Unlike domestic workers, janitorial cleaners could, and did, file claims with the Workers' Compensation Board for injuries and illness.[106] Cleaners were successful enough in claiming workers' compensation that Modern Building Cleaning complained to the union local of "abuse" of sick days and compensation claims.[107] Millions or billions of dollars flowed from the buildings they cleaned, but janitorial workers might have to use faulty equipment that caused electric shocks. When cleaners at First Canadian Place complained about the frayed electrical cords on the vacuum cleaners, their indifferent manager told them to use tape to patch them. The workers then complained to the union, which did force the cleaning company to fix the cords.[108] If construction was being done in buildings, cleaners had to clean up the remnants of the construction, with its attendant dangers (such as disturbed asbestos).[109]

The intensification of work caused not only morale problems, but also an increase in workers' compensation cases, thereby exemplifying one of the cruel ironies of the contracting-out process: it cut labour costs for building owners, but ultimately placed a greater burden on the welfare state. Working harder and faster took its toll on the bodies of cleaners like Delia, who was on workers' compensation for four months in 1988 because of workplace-related lumbosacral (lower back) strain.[110] Unions cited a high level of strain, anxiety, nervousness, and depression among workers from the drive to work faster as hours of work were shortened. Psychological symptoms manifested themselves physically as headaches, sleeplessness, backaches, ulcers, and high blood pressure. Unions like SEIU did try to make health and safety a priority, and provisions made their way into a few collective agreements. But like in other workplaces in this period, an awareness of the issues was a gradual process. In the late 1970s and early 1980s, cleaners' unions became more proactive, including by creating health and safety committees on site. The small but important steps taken included reviews of the soaps, disinfectants, floor sealers, and carpet-cleaning compounds used and the creation of guides for union representatives.[111]

Conclusion

Joaquina Gomes well captured the inequities that shaped her labouring life when she noted that, by hiring someone else to clean, her middle-class female employers "had time for other activities, for going out with their kids, for many things" they considered more important than cleaning.[112] All cleaners had to contend with the social stigma attached to cleaning the dirt, waste, and garbage of more privileged people. Some of the Portuguese women internalized this view and tried to conceal their occupation in various ways. One cleaner kept her job a secret from her father in Portugal because she thought he would be ashamed of her. Many dressed in more formal attire when travelling to and from work so they were not easily recognizable as manual workers.[113]

But other women found ways to challenge the notion that their labour was of low value and status. One was to de-emphasize the personal service aspects of housecleaning work and stress instead that, as Joana Soares put it, it was "a job like any other."[114] Other house cleaners, including Mariana Batista, stressed the heavy responsibilities attached to the occupation, in being entrusted with a key to someone's home and being given alarm access codes. Certainly, employers wanted "dependable" employees.[115] A worker in the Queen's Park office complex took pride in the fact that government ministers knew her name and asked about her well-being.[116] Another similarly noted the important people who occupied the offices she cleaned. "There were many *senhores*, many *senhoras*," she noted, "who liked to see everything clean, and I liked it too, and I also liked that they valued the work that I did."[117] Still others inverted the view that cleaning was immigrant women's work and instead stressed how their ethnicity made them valuable workers. Celia Filipe proudly declared that Portuguese cleaning women enjoyed a reputation as "hard-working and honest people."[118] In making this claim, some invoked the Portuguese cleaning lady stereotype, noting, as Gomes did, that employers recommended them to their friends because "Portuguese ladies" are "hard workers, good cleaners."[119]

Portuguese immigrant cleaners' sense of dignity drew as well on the values of a gendered upbringing that associated clean homes with feminine respectability. Transferred to Canadian workplaces, these values could blur the line between their private homes and the spaces in which they laboured for wages. "We [had] to leave our house every day to do this job," noted Gomes, but "it was like we were in our home . . . cleaning our own home, washing our own clothes, taking care of people's things like they were our own things."[120] A building cleaner whose wage earning was cut short by illness said she "felt bad" about leaving work: "I always had *my* desks, *my* ashtrays, everything in order."[121] Conceptualizing the workplace as an extension of one's private home informed collective agreement negotiations where cleaners fought for the right to keep their floor assignments in office towers even after a leave of absence from work.

Nor did the increasingly contractual nature of housecleaning work eliminate entirely the personal service aspect of domestic work. Gender and class identities fit uncomfortably. Women worked longer hours without pay in order to clean a particularly dirty home because, as Gomes explained, they approached the job as though they "were cleaning [their] own home." Or, like Filipe, they performed tasks outside the realm of the contract. Faced with the disarray of her employer's makeup, Filipe bought trays and organized it. Performing this more intimate and unpaid work reflected and reinforced her self-identity as a good wife and mother—an extension of her own home and familial role—as well as a good worker.[122]

Like other low-paid immigrant workers, Portuguese cleaners also diffused the low status in their work identities by stressing family identities. Every woman interviewed expressed pride in the contribution she made to her family's financial success in Canada, even when her own husband did not acknowledge it.[123] Paid labour also allowed some women to gain some independence from their husbands. By hiding the full amount of their "cash money" from them, they could exercise more discretion over how they spent it. Usually it went "to the kids," and husbands, too, sometimes gave children gifts. But as Carolina Soares put it, "He didn't need to know everything."[124] Conversely, their jobs could also increase a reliance on husbands for social benefits, including in old age,

78   Cleaning Up

even compelling some of them to remain in unhappy or even abusive marriages.

Then, too, the cleaning workplace itself served as a site of women's integration in the wider Canadian society. Portuguese house cleaners did learn English faster than those who worked on the factory or janitorial floor alongside Portuguese-speaking co-workers. Needing to communicate with employers and occasionally follow written instructions pushed house cleaners to quickly learn English. Those employed by well-educated people developed a more sophisticated vocabulary. A good command of English combined with a knowledge of the city's various neighbourhoods and transit routes allowed them to act more independently than non-English-speaking immigrant women who had to rely on husbands, children, or kin to negotiate their lives in Toronto.

Working in an increasingly wide variety of Canadian homes led to the adoption of technologies such as vacuums and even modest attempts to incorporate new cultural trends in furnishings and interior decoration. As Gomes explained, "We didn't have money like these people . . . but on a small scale we modified our homes, like having a prettier bathroom, nicer bedcovers, or nicer curtains like we'd see in their homes."[125] Notwithstanding their preference for their own foods, these domestics, like so many others, introduced their families to foods encountered in their employers' homes: meatballs, grilled cheese sandwiches, and macaroni and cheese. Finally, working for a growing number of same-sex couples and gay men—an experience that would not have been common in 1970s and 1980s Portugal—encouraged tolerance for gay families among women who hailed from a conservative Roman Catholic society. One area of bottom-up integration that domestic workers did not experience, but janitorial cleaners certainly did, was involvement in unions, strikes, and other types of formal working-class action (the subject of chapters 5 and 6).

"Sweep and Say Union." A Cleaners' Action ESL class taught by literacy activist Mary Ellen Nettle wrote this song in the mid/late 1970s in collaboration with songwriter and trade unionist Susan Howlett. The instruction for a Calypso beat may reflect the influence of the Caribbean music scene in Toronto at this time. Courtesy of Deborah Brandt.

Chapter 4

Forging Alliances with Radical Community Workers in 1970s Toronto

A song in praise of Portuguese women cleaners' activism, called "Sweep and Say Union," emerged in the 1970s. Its story sheds light on the alliance that Portuguese female building cleaners in Toronto forged with female social justice activists and radical community workers at that time. The initial idea came from Mary Ellen Nettle, a Christian socialist and Freire-inspired educator who was teaching an ESL class for the cleaners employed in government buildings. The class was sponsored by Cleaners' Action, a St. Christopher House program founded in 1975 by the indefatigable Sidney Pratt, another Christian socialist and Freirean literacy activist. Pratt and the other Cleaners' Action staff were committed to working together with the immigrant cleaners to address their workplace challenges. Inspired by a songwriting workshop she had attended, but not herself musical, Nettle asked Susan Howlett, a songwriter and strong trade unionist, to help her get the class to participate in a collective exercise to write a song about their work. Little encouragement, it turns out, was needed. And even before Nettle had begun the class, a nighttime office cleaner who came to class after finishing her night shift supplied the title and the central theme when she noted, "All night, I swept and said union."

Sung to a calypso beat, the song's lyrics encapsulate the simple and unadorned way the women, who had at best rudimentary English, articulated their interest in organizing a union. Images central to the iconography of janitorial cleaners' activism, from the ubiquitous ashtrays and floors to clean to "dragging heavy bags of garbage," appear. As does the oft-repeated image of the women themselves as hardworking, skilled, and efficient cleaners who work while other people sleep. The simple lyrics relate to unions and a class consciousness—"We know that it's only by fighting, We can win rights, large and small"—and powerfully express the politicization of these immigrant women. Many had arrived in Canada not only without a labour or radical background, but also still reeling from the effects of the repression imposed by an authoritarian regime that outlawed labour activism and imprisoned radicals. Finally, the story of how the class produced their song—specifically, that a cleaner supplied the title and theme, and that the women's simple but effective lyrics shaped it—sheds light on both the role of community activists in the women's politicization as well as the fact that cleaners actively shaped the nature of the alliance.[1]

A variety of factors account for the rise of a class and gender consciousness among these women, including the women's dense networks of information and support and their involvement in the union campaigns and janitorial strikes detailed in later chapters. The women's growing politicization was nurtured as well by their interactions and relationships with progressive community workers who earned their trust. Significantly, the women themselves initiated the alliance by seeking out local community activists and left-leaning grassroots agencies to equip them with the tools they needed to improve their working and personal lives.

Conventionally trained social workers who dispense services to immigrants rarely seek to challenge the status quo, and this was generally true of the staff of the mainstream social agencies in early postwar Toronto. The 1970s, however, saw the rise of a new generation of community workers, many of whom had come of age during the 1960s, who were social justice activists keen to empower immigrants and effect meaningful social change. These mostly young people were inspired by the social movements of the 1960s, including Freirean radical pedagogy, liberation theology, feminism, the New Left, the civil rights movement, and the radical community organizing associated with Saul Alinsky. The women activists whose voices and stories appear here included Portuguese-speaking immigrants like Sidney Pratt, a US-born teacher and leftist who came to Toronto following several years of carrying out anti-poverty and literacy work in Brazil. Saskatchewan-born Michelle Swenarchuk, a lawyer with links to Services for Working People, an agency that handled cases involving human rights and workplace violations, and the left-led Confederation of Canadian Unions (CCU), figured among the Canadian feminists involved. These networks, made up mainly of female Portuguese immigrants, also included João Medeiros, a male literacy activist, community worker, and co-founder of the left-wing Portuguese newspaper *Comunidade*. The programs launched during the 1970s and 1980s helped to improve the everyday lives of thousands of working immigrant women. They also influenced how the building-sector unions interacted with their immigrant membership (see chapter 5). By mentoring a new generation of immigrant activists such as Marcie Ponte and Lina Costa, the pioneering activists contributed significantly towards the rise of an immigrant women's movement in Toronto.

Social Movements and Community Organizing

As their awareness of the exploitation they faced at work and at home grew, Portuguese women reached out to the community agencies in their west-end neighbourhood. They could do so because approaches to community work were undergoing tremendous change. During the 1950s and 1960s, the agencies and government departments promoting immigrant adaptation to "Canadian ways" operated with notions of family, morality, and democratic citizenship largely shaped by Anglo-Canadian liberal bourgeois ideals as well as Cold War priorities.[2] By the 1970s, however, community organizing in Toronto, particularly among the more recent Portuguese immigrants, was infused with the growing commitment of front-line activists to the ideals of social justice (both secular and Christian), feminism, working-class radicalism, and emancipatory politics.

This consciousness-raising community work grew out of the social and political ferment of the long 1960s. In Canada, the impact of international social movements was evident in the resurgence of the women's movement and the rise of the civil rights, human rights, and ethnic minority rights movements. Sixties radicalism shaped key aspects of Quebec's Quiet Revolution and the Red Power movement, as well as the anti-nuclear and anti–Vietnam War protests and the support provided to US war resisters in Canada. In the Canadian labour movement, immigrant and women workers stuck in low-wage, precarious, and dangerous jobs were among those who engaged in democratic dissent and challenged the postwar industrial regime.[3] Opposed to class, gender, race, and state oppression, the activists who developed grassroots approaches in their work with Portuguese and other immigrants in 1970s Toronto formed a current within the New Left in Canada.

Community workers in Toronto were influenced as well by the work of Alinsky, the Chicago-born activist who developed a radical model of community organizing. A left-leaning sociologist and criminologist who was radicalized by the Depression and embraced full-time activism, Alinksy began organizing workers, immigrants, and the poor, particularly African Americans, in major US cities. His approach involved uniting ordinary citizens in "people's organizations" around immediate grievances in their neighbourhoods and protesting outside of the "established" ways of expressing dissent, particularly through colourful confrontational tactics. In practice, the community organizer was usually someone from the "outside," but local organizers were quickly recruited and trained to take a lead in their communities. Community organizing among Toronto's Portuguese reflected such methods.[4]

Many of the Toronto activists emerged out of the Christian left, and they adopted a Christian model of democratic community organizing. One example of the impact of the era's social movements on Christian churches was the liberalization of the Roman Catholic Church under the Second Vatican Council, or Vatican II, from 1962 to 1965. The clergy and lay people taking up social justice causes internationally were acting on the belief that one had to practise Christ's call to "feed the hungry and clothe the naked" in a more direct and relevant way. In Britain, France, and elsewhere, activist clergy and other church-based militants worked at the grassroots level, organizing rent strikes, pickets, and boycotts against gouging landlords and discriminatory employers. They promoted neighbourhood improvement schemes and denounced segregated housing and factory closures. Much like the social gospel movement in early-twentieth-century Canada, these activists were enacting a religion based on practical social action and a populist application of Christianity. In that regard, they belong to a historical tradition in which Christian churches seek to remain relevant in the context of massive changes in Canadian society. In this iteration, closer ties were forged between Protestant and Catholic churches. An ecumenism rooted in shared social action characterized the Catholic and Protestant community workers who joined forces to improve the lives of Portuguese immigrants.

A number of these Christian community workers were particularly influenced by the ideas and methods of the Brazilian educator and philosopher Paulo Freire. A secondary-school teacher of the Portuguese language, Freire began to develop literacy programs for the poor and to embrace liberation theology by the 1960s. In the years after Vatican II moved to de-emphasize hierarchical approaches to the Church and focus instead on the laity (including the poor and illiterate), liberation theology

Cleaning Up

took shape. Its advocates stressed the Christian mission to bring justice to the poor and oppressed, particularly through political activism, and they drew primarily on Marxist political theory to develop strategies for change. Often called a form of Christian socialism, the movement enjoyed widespread influence in Latin America.[5]

In Brazil, Freire moved beyond simply teaching people how to read and write to develop a critical pedagogy of literacy education that would promote justice and equality, and raise the political consciousness of the working classes. Rejecting traditional religion on the grounds that it maintained the status quo of the powerful and denied ordinary people agency, he promoted liberation theology as a struggle for social justice for the poor and oppressed. Like Alinsky, Freire operated at the level of local communities. Teachers had roles as counsellors, not authority figures, and the voices and needs of the oppressed were privileged. A Christian socialist under the right-wing military dictatorship that emerged in Brazil in 1964 (and lasted until 1985), Freire was imprisoned and then went into exile until 1979. In *Pedagogy of the Oppressed* (1968), he laid out the principles that became the basis for a new international ESL/literacy curriculum, including in downtown Toronto. Radical projects with Portuguese immigrants were thus influenced by international currents within left-wing Christianity, particularly from South America.[6]

Much of the community organizing in 1970s Toronto was centred on women's issues; this activism contributed to the making of an immigrant women's movement that sometimes overlapped with and other times diverged from the wider women's movement of the late 1960s. Meg Luxton and other scholars show that since the late 1960s and early 1970s, a union-based, working-class feminism became a key force in the women's movement, the labour movement, and the left in Canada. Working-class and socialist feminist activists developed a strong feminist presence in the male-dominated labour movement and a significant working-class orientation in the larger women's movement, thereby ensuring that working-class and poor women's issues would receive attention in both movements.[7] The working-class feminist movement made more inroads in the public sector and in traditionally male-dominated workplaces, like the auto industry, than it did in those service sector jobs, such as cleaning, where immigrant women were concentrated. Intent on mobilizing women marginalized in both union and feminist spheres, the community and union activists who sought to improve Portuguese female cleaners' lives offered a trenchant critique of how immigrant status as well as language, ethnicity, national origin, and race circumscribed women's lives. Together, the activists and politicized immigrants formed another current in the broader women's movement.

Ideas into Practice

Many of the left-leaning organizations that sought to put progressive ideas into practice through community work with Portuguese immigrants in 1970s Toronto bore innocuous-sounding names. An early example, Services for Working People, which opened on Augusta Avenue in Kensington Market in 1969, was actually a government agency, but its staff pushed its direction leftward. A joint undertaking of the Ontario Human Rights Commission (OHRC)—which was created to administer the Ontario Human Rights Code, established in 1962—and the Manpower Services division of the Ontario Department of Labour, SFWP helped its west-end residents, particularly immigrants and unemployed youth, to better access existing services such as unemployment insurance and workers' compensation.[8] Its founding partially reflected a concern that language problems and inadequate knowledge of government resources, as well as discrimination in employment and training programs, led immigrants to turn for help to a local priest or compatriot instead of an expert, thereby stalling their full integration.[9] The OHRC was involved because of reports of growing racial tensions between southern European immigrants and Blacks (both Canadians and Caribbean immigrants) living in certain west-end neighbourhoods, including Kensington Market. After investigating a few incidents, including one involving a Portuguese pool hall that threw out some young Black men (the hall claimed the boys were underage), the OHRC attributed the tensions not to overt racism but rather to a mutual experience of alienation caused by "the traumas of transition and acculturation." SFWP was created in response to the OHRC's claim that dispensing services to immigrants in a more culturally sensitive manner would make newcomers feel more secure and integrated and thus help diminish the racial tensions.[10]

Emulating a community agency, SFWP had a "storefront" look with casual furnishings. The staff and interpreters advised on matters of employment and racial and age discrimination. They referred a rapidly growing number of clients to the appropriate office and, when required, maintained a liaison role between the client and the government office.[11] The agency's predominantly immigrant clientele included many non-English-speaking newcomers (66 percent in 1970), but the single largest group was the Portuguese.[12] Their presence owed much to the hiring of a Portuguese-speaking staffer, Fernanda Gaspar, as well as to the location. (There were no Italian-, Polish-, or Spanish-speaking counsellors in part because of their fewer numbers in the neighbourhood.) Encouraged by an extensive network of family, kinfolk, and friends, Portuguese immigrants turned to the SFWP in such large numbers that some insiders expressed concern about it being "defined" as "a Portuguese office," though little appears to have been done to attract other immigrant groups.[13]

The involvement of the Women's Bureau of the Ontario Department of Labour in SFWP is revealing, albeit in a negative sense. The provincial Progressive Conservative government of John Robarts created the Women's Bureau in 1963 in response to pressure from women's groups and unions to address women's increasing participation in the labour force, but the government's main concern was ensuring an "efficient" use of female labour in the economy. Another was to use the bureau to gauge public views on policy issues and to publicize its political initiatives in employment policy. The Women's Bureau worked with the SFWP in order "to gain insight into the attitudes and problems" particularly of low-income immigrant women.[14]

Professionals serving immigrants in the postwar years often pathologized immigrant women as victims of more deeply patriarchal cultures, but some of them understood the critical economic role of working-class immigrant women in their families. The interest of the Women's Bureau in gathering information on SFWP's immigrant female clients reflected its larger mandate to ensure that women's labour was used so as to maximize their contribution to the national economy.[15] It showed little understanding of the constraints faced by the Portuguese women they targeted. When the women resisted the bureau's goal of convincing them to learn English in order to upgrade their skills and find better employment, the counsellors blamed them for lacking "any aspirations to improve their work qualifications."[16] One frustrated counsellor put it thus: "Their low level of education does not help them to realize the value of speaking English and how it will help them with their own children let alone helping to stabilize their work situation."[17] In fact, the women's reaction was reasonable given their circumstances. They held only a grade four education but were being told to earn the grade ten requirement for learning a "skilled" trade.[18] Already balancing one, two, or even three paid jobs with their household and child-rearing duties, they did not have the time to attend English classes, except intermittently. Instead of understanding the women's situation, one counsellor influenced by the Women's Bureau dismissed them as "passive."[19]

Nevertheless, SFWP staffers like Gaspar were keen to develop a community-based approach to immigrant services that might better address the realities of immigrant exploitation. Bypassing the middle-class and male-run Portuguese community organizations, which showed little interest in the plight of their working-class compatriots, SFWP staff sought collaboration with Portuguese workers at St. Christopher House and other social agencies as well as the parishes.[20] Facing pushback from labour bureaucrats and social workers from the University of Toronto's School of Social Work who had been following the project, these efforts floundered, and SFWP generally stuck to a traditional individual services approach to immigrant work.

With one major exception. The 1970s witnessed growing grassroots involvement with Portuguese female building cleaners. SFWP staffer Gaspar, in particular, helped to mediate the workplace concerns of Portuguese cleaners working at the office-building complex of the Ontario Legislature at Queen's Park. In 1975, with Gaspar's help, the cleaners challenged the sexual discrimination in wages. In January of that year, seven women, five of them Portuguese, were asked to buff floors, a task normally performed by men. The women were being paid higher wages than a light-duty cleaner ($2.50 compared to $2.25), but not as high as heavy-duty cleaners (who started at $2.75; most were earning $3.00). In April, Modern Building Cleaning, the company contracted to clean the buildings, transferred the women out of these jobs, arguing that tenants were complaining about their work. The workers countered that the company's actions were prompted instead by the realization that the union now organizing the employees, the SEIU, would, upon winning a union contract, demand higher wages for the women. Carmina Pereira, one of the seven cleaners, declared that the women's transfers from the buffing jobs to general cleaning "have nothing to do with the quality of our work," but everything to do with the fact that, if employers "have to pay higher wages, they prefer to pay them to men."[21]

The SFWP brought the case to the Employment Standards Branch of the (renamed) Ministry of Labour under an equal pay for equal work complaint, and to the OHRC on a sex discrimination complaint. Gaspar interviewed and translated for the cleaners, and Michelle Swenarchuk, a recent law-school graduate who belonged to the Law

Union of progressive young lawyers, represented them. She had been recommended to Gaspar by the prominent labour and feminist activist Madeleine Parent. With partner Kent Rowley, Parent had co-founded the Confederation of Canadian Unions, whose goal was the establishment of an independent Canadian labour movement free of the influence of US-based international unions.[22]

Both cases failed, but there were a few bright spots. The Employment Standards officer determined that there was enough difference in the nature of the two jobs to justify the difference in salary between light- and heavy-duty cleaners, and that the women were not performing work that required the same amount of effort as the men. The women were, however, granted back pay for wages lost as a result of their transfers. Swenarchuk initiated an appeal but quickly dropped it because the laws on equal pay were still too loose: one could launch complaints about unfair wages with commissions and tribunals, but there was no legislation to proactively deal with unequal pay in the industry. The OHRC dismissed the sex discrimination complaint. The women had countered Modern's claim that they were not performing their jobs adequately by noting that they were never given the same tools as men. Equipped with a bigger mop than the women, as well as a bottled spray mixture of wax and detergent to use with the buffing machine, the men produced better results than the women, who mopped with detergent and then machine-buffed the floors. But the OHRC concluded that there was no evidence that the company was purposely discriminating against women in the higher-duty positions.[23] A representative for the Ministry of Labour did urge the government to avoid being "embarrassed by this kind of litigation" by monitoring the employment practices of its cleaning contractors, but there is no evidence that it did so.[24]

The state thus upheld the gendered divisions of labour and wages in the industry—even in its own buildings—but the campaigns revealed the women's willingness to work with community allies to fight discrimination at work. Those allies included Swenarchuk, who spent her early career working primarily with the CCU and fighting for the rights of immigrant garment workers and building cleaners.

Female Activists and Grassroots Organizing

One of the mainstream social agencies to undergo a political transformation in 1970s Toronto was St. Christopher House. Located in the city's heavily Portuguese west end, St. Christopher's conversion from mainstream settlement house to grassroots community agency was largely the work of women, both some 1970s-era progressive Portuguese newcomers and non-Portuguese activists inspired by the era's social movements. Often also immigrants, the latter group included women who already had some experience with social justice activism. They sought, in their work with Portuguese immigrant women, to put into practice the principles of Freirean pedagogy, Christian socialism, and other social movements.

This activism again originated within programs bearing apolitical names. Take, for example, the Free Interpreter Service (est. 1971), which provided translation and counselling services for immigrants in their own language. A joint venture of St. Christopher House, the International Institute of Metropolitan Toronto, West End YMCA, and University Settlement House, the Free Interpreter Service was funded by a federal Local Initiatives Program grant. Conservatives criticized the Local Initiatives Program—a Liberal government initiative to provide support for community and cultural projects that aligned with Prime Minister Pierre Trudeau's vision of "a just society"—as a special fund for radical causes, but the Free Interpreter Service and its sponsors never intended to promote a radical agenda. The personnel hired, however, pushed the service, and other St. Christopher programs, decidedly leftward.[25]

The Free Interpreter Service immediately attracted a heavily Portuguese clientele and, by July 1974, staff members were handling 700 to 900 requests for assistance a month, in some cases from longer-term immigrants who still required assistance. One of the first women staffers to respond proactively to the particular needs of the female clients was Isabel de Almeida. A college graduate who with her husband and son had left the "heavy political climate" of authoritarian Portugal for Toronto, the bilingual de Almeida (she also spoke English) landed a job with St. Christopher in 1970. Shortly after the Free Interpreter Service began operating, de Almeida became a contact for Portuguese women seeking to have abortions or leave their husbands—which drew the ire of one particular Portuguese priest.[26] Judith Ramirez, an Italian-American immigrant who became actively involved in feminist and immigrant women's organizing in Toronto, was doing the same among the Italian women who came to the Immigrant Women's Centre that she founded in the early 1970s. As she recently recounted, a number of priests, and one in particular, quietly supported her work, suggesting that immigrant Catholics like Italian and Portuguese women were not automatic recruits for the anti-abortion movement. When immigrant women's groups protested the position adopted by the May 28th Coalition for Abortion Rights in the late 1970s, their objection was to framing abortion solely as the right to choose, as this position did not acknowledge the experiences of immigrant women, both white and racialized, who could not afford to feed or raise another child, or who had been subjected to forced sterilization programs in their homelands.[27]

At St. Christopher House, the hiring of Pratt—the Christian socialist, community organizer, and Freire-inspired educator—to the staff of the Free Interpreter Service in 1972 was especially significant. Her political outlook would strongly shape the direction of work with Portuguese immigrants, particularly women. The US-born Pratt had grown up in a family that had been socially active "around the questions of slavery [and] temperance." As a high-school student, she had participated in the Model United Nations conferences, intended to encourage civic involvement among North American youth, and attended the Girls State, a program sponsored "for girls . . . interested in learning about politics and being in politics." While teaching high-school history in Indianapolis during the early 1960s, Pratt also ran a bistro and folk music club for youth, and the experience, she recalled, gave her some early insight into the "inequalities among people."

By the mid-1960s, Pratt had become a missionary for the American Episcopal Church in Brazil, where she worked in a church-sponsored girls' school and learned Portuguese. Living in Brazil during the military dictatorship, she developed her social and political perspectives on inequality and oppression. As a (Protestant) trainee in southern Brazil, her classmates were mostly Catholic priests and nuns "just coming out of Vatican II," and the "hotbed of the Catholic Left" into which she unknowingly fell exposed her to the social injustice of the regime. After moving to Recife, in the more impoverished northeast, Pratt worked with the progressive liberationist Catholic leader Dom Hélder Câmara and his team. Together with some Catholic nuns, she established an intentional community called the House of Reconciliation. There, they worked with struggling students, young factory workers, and artisans, and provided a refuge for runaway girls and battered women. Some of these efforts were also funded by the Canadian Anglican Church, an example of ecumenical relationships between Catholic and Protestant groups.[28]

Pratt's future work was influenced by contact with various people committed to social and economic justice. One of the nuns she met in

Recife was Belgian-born Cecilia Walhrave, who belonged to a European religious movement that advocated living and working with the people being ministered to. Upon returning home, Walhrave, who now spoke Portuguese, began to work with Portuguese immigrant office-cleaning women, influencing Pratt's choices when she immigrated to Canada.[29] During a 1971 trip to Geneva to study at the University of Geneva Graduate School of Ecumenical Relations, Pratt met Freire and completed a program specialization under his supervision.[30] It was particularly through her interactions with him that her work began to acquire a firm theoretical base. Further travel shaped Pratt's politics. In England during the early 1970s to participate in a literacy-teaching program, Pratt heard of May Hobbs's efforts to organize building cleaners in London. A cleaner herself, Hobbs understood that the spread of short-term contract hiring within the industry further undermined these workers. With the help of liberationist and socialist women's groups who joined the cause, Hobbs played a role in the early cleaners' efforts to join the trade union movement.[31]

Pratt had returned to the United States when she accepted an invitation from Dan Heap, an NDP city councillor, to speak at Holy Trinity Church in Toronto in 1972. Disheartened by the political situation in the United States, she decided to remain in Canada. Quickly landing a job as a Portuguese-speaking worker at St. Christopher House, Pratt brought to St. Christopher a political vision shaped by her Christian international social justice work and experience in organizing.[32]

A few years into their work with the Free Interpreter Service, Pratt and de Almeida envisioned a more grassroots approach to serving Portuguese immigrants. Created in 1974, the new Portuguese West of Bathurst Project (PISEM) targeted an area west of Bathurst Street and south of Bloor that included many Portuguese and few social services. It reflected the premise that the local residents would first help determine the needs and priorities and then "begin learning skills themselves in service delivery" until they developed sufficient expertise to assume many of the tasks initially performed by more professionally trained personnel.[33] The goal of empowering immigrants to liberate themselves from super-exploitation reflected the influence of Alinksy's radical ideas of community organizing as well as those of Freire and of liberation theology.[34]

The PISEM staff soon hired a third community worker, Claire Richard. Like Pratt, Richard was a university-educated and progressive

Christian—she was a Catholic who had taught elementary school in Nigeria through the CUSO (Canadian University Service Overseas) program—with international experience in social justice work. Richard belonged to The Grail, an international Catholic women's spiritual group committed to working through women to create a more just society. In 1972, she went to Portugal to teach English and literacy in Portuguese, in the Freire method, before it was being used in Toronto. Under Portugal's right-wing regime, the focus on consciousness-raising through literacy had to be downplayed: she and her co-workers claimed to be "just teaching people how to read." In Toronto, she met Pratt and was hired.[35]

The acronym used by the project staff better reflected their social justice goals. In Portuguese, PISEM means "to stomp on," and it stood for Projeto para Investigação de Exploração de Mulher (Project for the Investigation of the Exploitation of Women). Convinced that dispensing direct services would only perpetuate the women's situation, the PISEM staff believed that teaching women English and some basic coping skills would lessen their dependence on social services.[36] Through de Almeida and Pratt, PISEM arguably had a feminist agenda—to empower exploited immigrant women workers and challenge the status quo—though only Pratt used the term at the time. (Richard herself assumed the identity in the late 1970s). For Richard, as for Pratt, a belief that poor women were among the most exploited groups in society informed a women-centred social justice activism that sought to challenge capitalist and patriarchal power. Their activism also reflected developments in Canada, where new protest movements merged to combat racism, poverty, and sexism.[37]

There was little direct contact initially between such grassroots immigrant-women-centred community work and the more formal women's movement, but some links would be forged over the 1970s. PISEM itself had no formal links to any Christian churches, including Roman Catholic ones in the Portuguese community. Church leaders in Portugal overwhelmingly rejected Vatican II and liberation theology, and the Portuguese parishes in Toronto were mainly run by priests trained before Vatican II. The parishes provided passive support for PISEM and other efforts to mediate the negative realities of immigrant life, but they were not sites of progressive social action. Through Pratt (who began campaigning for the party shortly after arriving in Toronto) and others, PISEM did have some links with the NDP.[38]

It bears stressing that PISEM's mandate represented a marked departure from past work with Portuguese immigrants, and with immigrants

Forging Alliances with Radical Community Workers   93 in general. The shift to developing the clients' autonomy rather than simply providing aid opened the possibility of shifting agency and power from the community worker to the working-class immigrant. PISEM's founders well understood that traditional social workers might feel threatened by "the concept of developing the individual's ability to be self-determining" because "the client's dependence may be reduced or they may ask more of the workers than she/he is willing or able to give."[39] The physical distance of PISEM from St. Christopher House—the project ran out of a house located at 794 Dovercourt Road that also served as Pratt's home for a time—signalled the distancing of its staff from conventional community work. For these activists, eliminating the social workers altogether was a necessary part of the social transformation they sought. In the meantime, however, the process of encouraging poor people's autonomy and organizing community-wide development required the "total dedication and conviction" of the community workers. Staffers like Pratt worked very long hours and often at night, and willingly engaged in public and political fights.[40]

The PISEM staff's early success at mediating between the staff of the local Roman Catholic elementary school St. Veronica's, whose student population was 90 percent Portuguese, and the Portuguese parents earned them the trust of the mothers in particular. Things began in the usual way: the school principal invited St. Christopher House to help address the troubling cultural gap between the school and the parents, and the staff agreed to conduct home visits. But there the similarities with mainstream social workers diverged. PISEM staff spoke fluent Portuguese, and one staff member was herself Portuguese. Viewing this as an opportunity to establish trust with the wider community, and to "peel down" the "layers of problems" in order to identify their "core wants and needs," they spoke with hundreds of families and met with the teachers to discuss the parents' concerns. They helped to demystify the Canadian school system by sharing the photographs they had taken and the videos they had made of the children with groups of mothers. Two specific examples illustrate their efficacy as mediators. Pratt and her colleagues assuaged the teachers' anxieties over the children eating "only soup" for lunch by identifying the vegetables and other healthy ingredients that went into the hearty soups. Upon viewing the videotape that they filmed of children in physical education class, the mothers, many of them wage-earning cleaners, understood why the teachers wanted them to buy their children uniforms and sneakers, and spent their precious earnings to do so.[41]

Following their involvement with St. Veronica's, PISEM counsellors focused their attention on two arenas: reforming ESL classes in downtown Toronto, and investigating cleaners' workplace issues. In the first instance, PISEM workers understood that it would be a challenge to convince the Portuguese immigrants whom they visited, and whose English skills they assessed, to come to ESL class. They also understood that it would take creativity to enrol the women, who tended to avoid ESL classes because of the demands of the double day. One initiative involved teaching basic English to small groups of two or three neighbours in one of the women's homes, and accompanying them to the post office or a grocery store so they could practise their English. Within about sixteen months, the staff gathered all the groups in a church hall and encouraged the women, whose children were being supervised, to talk about the realities of their lives and discuss possible solutions to their problems. The classes proved to be an important site of female sociability for women with little leisure time. The greater insight staff gained into the women's lives allowed them to broaden the scope of their work with them.[42]

Indeed, reforming the existing literacy programs quickly became a main focus of an expanded network of community workers. The ESL Core Group, created in 1973 to develop new curriculum for the city's immigrant agencies, included, besides Pratt (St. Christopher House), João Medeiros (West End YMCA) and Brenda Duncombe (St. Stephen's Community House). Well regarded by his female co-activists, Medeiros joined the West End YMCA in 1972 as a community worker responsible for outreach development in the Portuguese community. Born into a large Azorean family from São Miguel, he had immigrated to Canada to avoid military service in the African wars. In Portugal, he first cultivated his left politics in a seminary run by a liberal Dutch religious order that recruited future priests from among the poor rural population. That education allowed him to complete a university degree in Lisbon, where he became acquainted with the Freire literacy movement. In Canada, Medeiros completed an additional year of studies at St. Augustine's Seminary in Scarborough, Ontario, but, like many Portuguese men of humble origins who as children had entered the seminary, in part to secure an education, he eventually left religious life to pursue a secular one.[43]

Forging Alliances with Radical Community Workers

At the YMCA, Medeiros and a group of volunteers that included another ex-seminarian student and leftist, Domingos Marques,[44] developed priorities, including ESL classes. Through the Portuguese Development Committee, a creation of the YMCA volunteers, Medeiros also helped to found *Informações*, the first paper in the community to provide workers with information about labour and citizen rights, and to communicate with them about their everyday experiences and needs. Each month, volunteers distributed some two thousand copies of the free newsletter, with its simple prose, through the local parishes. An important grassroots-organizing tool, *Informações* would evolve into *Comunidade*.[45]

Duncombe, who joined the ESL Core Group in 1974, also came out of the international Christian left. An English Roman Catholic nun with the order of the Daughters of Mary and Joseph, she went to Brazil in the late 1960s to teach English. Her politicization was fuelled by the injustice of Brazil's class system. "I was shocked," she recalled, that the many Catholics who attended church on Sunday "didn't see that the marginalization that they were responsible for was absolutely wrong and anti-Christian."[46] In Recife, Duncombe met Pratt, and a lifelong friendship began. Forced to leave Brazil because of spreading violence under the military dictatorship, she accepted Pratt's invitation to join her in Canada. Pratt found her a job in the St. Stephen's Community House daycare, where she remained for a decade. A long-time activist in the Toronto and Canadian literacy movement, Duncombe played a critical role in getting ESL classes for immigrants recognized by different levels of government and funding agencies.[47] As part of Toronto's Downtown Churchworkers' Association, she participated in the agency's shift from a charitable approach towards the "deserving" and "undeserving" poor families and workers of the downtown core to progressive community organizing, social advocacy, and ecumenism.[48]

Duncombe's co-worker was yet another Christian female activist, Mary Ellen Nettle. A United Church deaconess, Nettle first taught ESL classes to immigrant garment workers out of a van, and as noted at the outset of this chapter, led an ESL class for cleaners. In 1978, she joined the ESL-in-the-Workplace Task Force (est. 1978) that oversaw the ESL classes held in garment factories. (Besides English teachers, the task force also included union officials, community workers, Unemployment Help Centre staff, and members of Organized Working Women, an autonomous feminist labour organization of unionized women.) Later still,

Metro Toronto Labour Council ran the program in a spirit, notes historian Craig Heron, of fostering more open, democratic structures that welcomed all wage earners.[49] The new literacy activists of the 1970s also included Gabriela Castro, who joined PISEM in 1977 following a stint with the Free Interpreter Service. With Richard and de Almeida moving on, St. Christopher also hired Naldi Nomez, Patricio Urzua, Nancy Serio, and Jean Connon Unda in 1977 to work in literacy development. Unda played an important role in teaching ESL courses in the workplace.

Following Freire, the activists working among Toronto's Portuguese immigrant women workers saw literacy work as fostering a critical consciousness as well as skills building. It meant assisting the poor and oppressed to understand that the vested interests that upheld the status quo were the source of their exploitation, and equipping them with the tools to problem-solve in the short term and to develop collective strategies for their greater liberation.[50] A 1977 pamphlet that became a foundational text for revamped literacy programs for immigrants in Toronto, Ontario, and across Canada, Pratt and Chileans Nomez and Urzua of the renamed Literacy Working Group states unequivocally that, in an "conflictive and oppressive" society, literacy is a political, not a neutral, act and a fundamental human right. Conversely, "illiteracy" is a social as opposed to a personal failure. Rejecting literacy training as charitable missionary work among passive beneficiaries, the authors of *Literacy: Charitable Enterprise or Political Right?* insist upon the right of poor and marginalized people to demand literacy and to play an active role in the process of learning. The pamphlet insists that, taught in a manner that acknowledges their experiences and desires, and that seeks to assist them in becoming "masters of their own history," literacy work can contribute to the liberation and development of all people. The authors conclude by declaring that since literacy is an inalienable social right, literacy programs ought to be a matter of public policy rather than a private enterprise.[51]

The Literacy Working Group's call in 1977 for "a total revision" of Canada's literacy policies reflected a decade of front-line efforts to teach literacy, while also challenging the available texts. That work included exposing the class and gender biases in ESL content, whose stories, phrases, and character illustrations expressed the view of the more powerful and obscured the realities of the marginalized. In meetings with educators as well as in their own ESL classes, teachers critiqued commercially produced textbooks—featuring contented office workers and charitable government officials and employers, all of them white—for ignoring the realities of working-class life, be it the workplaces in which people toiled, the conflicts between bosses, managers, and workers, or the existence of unions. As for wives, they were homemakers and mothers, rarely workers juggling the double day. The textbooks' focus on white and middle-class characters, the activists noted, helped to convey the impression that success is equated with self-sufficiency, such as owning one's own business or being a professional rather than working in a factory. And that competition and individualism promoted happy middle-class individuals and families. As most of the texts were published by US companies, they also noted the need to Canadianize the content, as well as to take it out of the hands of private enterprise and into the hands of trained civil servants who would have no profit agenda. When Pratt herself entered the Ontario government in 1980, she wrote the curriculum for citizenship and, later, the curriculum on AIDS, while continuing to work tirelessly with immigrant women and unions.[52]

A basic premise of the Freire method was to begin with the students' own experiences and to introduce new vocabulary within a context that addressed their day-to-day lives. It also involved a progression, from encouraging the learners to describe their own situation in relation to a theme, then to discuss possibilities and contradictions inherent within the theme, then to address alternatives to particular situations, and finally, to generalize in a problem-solving fashion. A question like "Should Portuguese solve problems as a Portuguese community or with other ethnic and Canadian groups?" was meant to encourage students to think beyond their own situation and to mobilize around issues that they themselves have designated a problem.[53]

A 1978 documentary on these community activists offers snapshots of the Freire method in operation. (Freire himself appears in the film, whose title is *Starting from Nina*, and is listed as a co-producer.) In his mixed-gender classes at the West End YMCA, Medeiros taught English to Portuguese adults in a bilingual context that respected the learners' fluency in their mother tongue. In one scene, he holds up a photograph of a group of Portuguese men who came to Canada in 1954 to work on the railroads, and asks the adult students whether they, as immigrants working in Canada, "have the feeling that they are building up this country." A young woman replies, "Yeah, sure," but also that she is learning English so she can have a better (office) job than her non-English-speaking cleaner mother. Asked if the Portuguese newspapers provide information about Canada and their rights, another female student says no. In the voiceover accompanying these scenes, Medeiros explains the importance of "build[ing] up in this English class some kind of discussion and orientation so that they learn English and at the same time start to know their rights, and this society, and how to cope with it." He adds, "In terms of collective action," the adult learners have to address the problem that "some are unionized, others are not, some are well-paid, others are not, some are men, others are women, and they have different problems." It is all part of a longer process.

Another scene from *Starting from Nina* sheds lights on how female ESL teachers like the PISEM staff and volunteers both used and challenged the curricular materials, and also created alternative ones. The teacher is helping three Portuguese women, all working mothers meeting in a private home, to read aloud the captions of the illustrations depicting a Canadian homemaker's typical weekly routine, from washing laundry on Monday to grocery shopping on Friday. After the group reads the caption for Saturday, when "Mrs. Baker goes to the movies," the teacher asks whether they go to the cinema on the weekend. Either surprised or bemused by the question, the women say no, "I don't have the time." The teacher responds: "It seems to me that you all do different things than this. We need to make a new book, eh, a new lesson." The scene then cuts to a young Portuguese ESL teacher who explains how her class responded to the need for relevant stories by creating their own stories of a fictional Portuguese couple called Tony and Maria Medeiros. By 1983, the volunteer tutors were helping ESL adult groups produce their own newsletter, called *Writers Ink*.[54]

PISEM staff also taught English in the workplace of female cleaners employed at the Queen's Park office complex. According to the arrangement, the workers were allowed to have one paid hour off work, and they stayed one hour after work for ESL training. In contrast to classes in the garment industry, however, these workplace classes did not really take off in the building-cleaning industry, where increasing workloads and shorter work hours left workers unable to complete their nightly cleaning duties in time (see chapter 3).[55]

Cleaners' Action

In regard to labour activism, a key development was the establishment in 1975 of Cleaners' Action (sometimes spelled Cleaner's Action), the women's labour network (and PISEM offshoot) described at the start of this chapter that worked with Portuguese women cleaners to address their workplace challenges. The cleaners themselves initiated the founding of Cleaners' Action amid a contracting-out crisis they faced at the Queen's Park complex after winning a union contact in April 1975. The union drive had succeeded despite employer intimidation. The contractor had fired organizers like Leopoldina Pimentel and tried to scare others from collecting signatures door to door with work speed-ups, transfers, night-time visits to the women's homes, and threats on the job. Then, against the advice of their union, SEIU, a group of fired workers enlisted the help of lawyer Swenarchuk, who convinced the Ontario Labour Relations Board (OLRB) to order their reinstatement with full back wages.

Some months later, however, the cleaners received layoff notices from the new employer to whom a cost-cutting Ontario government services ministry had offered the cleaning contract. In response, the women turned to the PISEM staff for help because of the staff's recent success at addressing issues involving their children at St. Veronica's school. To hold on to their jobs at Queen's Park, the women were in fact forced to accept the new employer's lower wages (see chapter 5). Still, Cleaners' Action—a local initiative that was connected to cleaners' activism internationally, particularly through May Hobbs's work in London—worked for years with Portuguese women cleaners to confront both exploitative employers and complacent unions.[56]

In a recent interview, Sidney Pratt, who borrowed the name Cleaners' Action from Hobbs's night cleaners' campaign, and Marcie Ponte, an immigrant women's activist who first joined Cleaners' Action as a student placement, recalled the thinking that guided their actions: a mix of the principled (empowering the poor and oppressed) and the pragmatic ("hearing what women have to say" and letting the "dynamic" on the ground shape the "political action").[57] They taught ESL classes on the job at Queen's Park that, as Ponte recalled, "wasn't teaching the ABCs" or "the hellos, how are yous," but instead "talking about issues" and "empowering women around those issues." That might be understanding what a "boss" wanted of them or speaking up at union meetings. Cleaners' Action staff met with the women in their homes and in the office to examine union contracts and prepare them to negotiate within unions. They held workshops on health and safety issues, surreptitiously gathered evidence in support of the women's complaints, and supported direct workplace action. At one point, Ponte, the self-described political daughter of activists like Pratt, posed as a worker's daughter during a union meeting at the Toronto-Dominion Centre to observe how the union handled the cleaners' complaints. Another time, Pratt snuck into the same tower with a stopwatch to check how long it took to clean the many stairs so the women could prove that their employer was underestimating the time needed to complete the tiring task. On yet another occasion, the women, again with Pratt, convinced their male co-workers, who were paid more to use the industrial cleaners on the (familiar sexist) grounds that it was more difficult to manage heavy equipment, to let them try the machines. They were "easy" to operate, recalled Pratt, because they were "automated," but the work assignments did not change.[58]

Cleaners' Action maintained contact with cleaners through workshops, a newsletter, and social events. Workshops covered such topics as occupational health and safety, employment standards, educational opportunities, and family relationships. Through the newsletter, St. Christopher House staff were able to reach a wider population of cleaners than just those who attended formal workshops or meetings. Modelling their approach after Hobbs's major leaflet campaign in London, St. Christopher staff advertised their free services in the first newsletter to cleaners in downtown office buildings. The first issue was published in English, Portuguese, and Italian and featured their new logo, which, like the early issues of the newsletter, bore the singular name, *Cleaner's Action*.

In the initial issue, the authors explained that the newsletter was created "as an initiative to bring together all the [building cleaners] so that they know what is happening with other workers, including those working in different buildings, so we have more knowledge on our class position and the strength that we have."[59] The issue urged cleaners to telephone St. Christopher House with their individual problems, but most importantly to work collectively on long-term solutions to workplace problems. It contained an interview with Leopoldina Pimentel, the cleaner at the Queen's Park complex who spearheaded the

The Cleaner's Action logo (using singular spelling) identified activism around cleaners' issues in Toronto from the mid-1970s to the 1980s. Susana Miranda collection.

Forging Alliances with Radical Community Workers   101

Cartoon from Cleaners' Action Newsletter, year 1 (Summer 1978). A cleaner tells her supervisor, "I am afraid of the elevators," and then, "These bags smell bad."
A supervisor then informs Juliana, "You had a bad report" (a complaint about her work). Juliana is seen leaving the building, stating, "They can all go to hell!"
Susana Miranda collection; newsletter given to Miranda by Michelle Swenarchuk.

unionization drive there in 1975 (see chapter 5), speaking on the benefits of the unionization. These benefits included twelve instead of three days of holidays and some protection against the "bossa who picks on someone and wants to fire them."[60] The issue also included an explanation of the Ontario Labour Relations Act, and an account of a number of job actions taken by building cleaners in Toronto. It contained a cartoon that exemplified some of the workplace conditions that cleaners faced such as conflict with managers, heavy loads, and foul-smelling garbage—the salty language of the punchline offering an earthy response in keeping with the women's physically difficult lives.

Following Alinsky, Cleaners' Action staff focused as well on teaching the women leadership and organizational skills. By the early 1980s, some five hundred issues of *Cleaners' Action Newsletter* were being distributed each month, the work of about forty veterans of the workshops, meetings, and training sessions. They churned it out on a mimeograph machine donated by the Women's Press (est. 1971). The knowledge gained by this core group of empowered immigrant labour activists was passed on to thousands of Portuguese working women through their workplace, household, neighbourhood, and extensive kin networks.[61]

While pro-union, Cleaners' Action staff also criticized business unionism practices. In 1979, for instance, they supported the decision of the cleaners at the TD Centre to expel SEIU Local 204 in favour of the Canadian Union of Public Employees (CUPE). By then, Pratt had so antagonized SEIU organizers that they banished her from the office towers where their members worked. Not easily dismissed, Pratt would meet the women outside and, during a workplace action, she occasionally hid

102   Cleaning Up

in a women's washroom. This support for Canadian unions also aligned with the era's left-leaning Canadian economic nationalism, "a counter-movement for the protection of Canadian society and sovereignty" which strongly opposed US domination of Canadian politics and culture as well as the economy. [62]

All of this left-oriented work did not go unchallenged. Cleaners' Action staff couched their funding applications to government in neutral terms, but their direct-confrontation tactics with unions and employers attracted media coverage. One *Toronto Star* article reported on SEIU representatives, blaming the Queen's Park cleaners' claims that it had negotiated an inferior contract on "a bunch of storefront lawyers" and "student rebels," code words for Cleaners' Action staff. [63] In response, the Board of Directors at St. Christopher House—who were particularly concerned to not jeopardize their access to United Way funds—struck a committee to determine whether the group's political activities were putting funding in peril. The Review Committee, which included Swenarchuk, exonerated Cleaners' Action staff, saying they were "merely" acting to bring workers and unions into dialogue, but it also called for improved communications and guidelines. [64] The Cleaners' Action program continued, though its work with cleaners declined. Still, the decline in activity spoke to the staff's success in prodding the unions into paying more attention to their immigrant workers, including cleaners. Growing union interest in immigrant workers during the late 1970s and early 1980s was particularly associated with the rise in Canadian unions in the industry (see chapters 5 and 6).

Portuguese-Based Activism and the Immigrant Women's Movement

In addition to the support they provided Portuguese immigrant working women, grassroots programs such as PISEM and Cleaners' Action contributed to the growth by the mid-1970s of a wider immigrant women's movement in Toronto. Its leaders were linked to a constituency of community workers and helped to radicalize others. Focused on southern European women and immigrant women from countries in Latin America, the Caribbean, and Asia, the wider network of grassroots agencies included the Centre for Spanish Speaking Peoples (1973), COSTI's Centro Femminile (1975), and the YWCA's West Indian Women's Program (1976). Three of the activists who founded Women Working with Immigrant Women (WWIW) in 1974 as an umbrella organization for agencies and women that worked with immigrant women in Metropolitan Toronto were Pratt, Nettle, and Duncombe. Its main goals were consciousness-raising and public education, as well as lobbying for funds to develop appropriate resources for immigrant women. The Centre for Spanish Speaking Peoples, which was analogous to the Free Interpreter Service, sent its cleaner clients to Cleaners' Action, whose staff sent clients with specific legal problems to the centre's legal aid clinic. Pratt was a continuing member of WWIW and took part in its ESL/Literacy committee. In fact, WWIW, which held monthly meetings with the female representatives of its thirty different ethnic service agencies, shared office space with PISEM in 1975–76. Such cross-agency communication contributed to a collective sense that community workers were part of a movement for immigrant women, rather than simply involved in isolated efforts to help specific ethnic groups.

Portuguese women's initial reason for turning to community agencies founded by immigrant women such as Taman McCallum (then Judith McCallum), a Caribbean left-wing feminist activist who came to Toronto via London in 1970, as well as Pratt (American) and Duncombe (English), was employment, but their participation in these grassroots organizations encouraged them to address other issues. Take, for example, the Working Women Community Centre (founded as the Women's Community Employment Centre in 1974 before becoming the WWCC a year later). The WWCC, which catered to Spanish-speaking newcomers such as Chileans who had fled their authoritarian homeland as well as Portuguese women, not only provided vocational counselling and other labour-related services. The staff also offered advice and support to women dealing with abusive husbands and divorce and/or with physical and mental health challenges.[65]

Mentors and Portuguese Immigrant Activists

The legacy of the pioneering community workers at St. Christopher House is evident in the emergence of a new generation of Portuguese Canadian activists. Involved with the Working Women Community Centre since its early beginnings in the mid-1970s, the San Miguel–born Ponte served on WWCC's board of directors across a period of twenty-five years. Getting hired as its executive director in 1999, she said, "was like coming home."[66] As "the proud daughter of the era of Sidney Pratt, Brenda Duncombe, and Mary Ellen Nettle," Ponte remains indebted to the mentors who showed her how to do community development "from the ground up and not the other way around."[67] They also influenced Ponte's private life by helping her move out of her mother's home at a young age to pursue an independent life at a time when it was unusual for young single women to leave their immigrant parental homes. The personal relationships between community workers, as we have already seen, were as important as the working ones.

One of the significant Portuguese programs developed at WWCC was Modistas Unidas (1979–83), the first immigrant women's co-operative. Made up of independent skilled garment workers, these women resisted factory and piecework exploitation through collective organizing.[68] Another was the Portuguese Women's Group, which brought in speakers to discuss issues such as patient rights, stress, and sexuality, and offered women an outlet to talk about their problems and concerns. The women also shared their traditional craft skills with each other, and developed their confidence and leadership skills by organizing group activities. Other immigrant women's agencies emerged from WWCC, which, overall, holds an important place in the historical development of the immigrant women's movement in Toronto, and it emerged partly from early work being done with Portuguese women at St. Christopher House. Under Ponte's directorship since 1999, in October 2022, WWCC provides services for a diverse range of newcomers in about twenty-five languages.[69]

Another Portuguese activist "daughter" of the St. Christopher generation was Lina Costa, whose activism focused on assisting victims of domestic violence. A young twenty-four-year-old teacher who left Portugal in 1973, Costa pursued a social services program at Ryerson Polytechnic Institute (now Toronto Metropolitan University). After a stint working in the computer field, Costa got a job at St. Christopher House and worked in the Cleaners' Action program. The domestic abuse programs that emerged for immigrant women in the 1970s reflected a marked shift in how community agencies dealt with this form of gender oppression. Whereas 1950s and 1960s era social workers often counselled immigrant women to remain with their abusive husbands unless the situation proved exceedingly hopeless, their 1970s counterparts advised immigrant wives to leave abusive relationships if they so desired. The larger women's movement had taken up the issue of domestic violence by this time, and in that regard, the wider women's and immigrant women's movements intersected. But the former was also criticized for failing to meet the needs of immigrant women, who felt restigmatized by agency staff that did not speak their language or show a sensitivity towards their culture.[70]

Costa's involvement with counselling abuse victims began at St. Christopher House. During Cleaners' Action meetings, staff noticed that some women cleaners always wore long-sleeved shirts in the middle of summer. Others, however, could not hide the bruises on their faces. It is a sign of the trust forged between the two groups that, once Cleaners' Action workers asked the women about their bruises, they disclosed instances of physical violence by their husbands.[71] The absence of Portuguese community programs limited women's options to telling a priest, or in extreme situations, the police, neither of which offered permanent solutions.[72] In response, Cleaners' Action launched the Domestic Violence Group Project in 1982, targeted initially at Portuguese women.[73]

Whether due to patriarchal indifference or the concern that exposing such dirty linen in public would increase hostility towards a minority group, Portuguese community leaders either denied there was a problem or said the women would never talk about it publicly.[74] Undeterred, St. Christopher House workers reached out to the women through the Cleaners' Action and ESL programs. That the women responded is suggested by an article on wife assault that appeared in the *Cleaners' Action Newsletter*. It featured the following declaration:

> We Portuguese women tend to suffer in silence and to put up with even intolerable situations because we believe that as wives and mothers we have to accept things. This is not true and it is not right. A husband never has the right to abuse his wife for any reason and no woman ever had to put up with abuse as if it were normal. Such violent treatment is against the law.[75]

Costa and colleagues secured the support of parish priests in the Portuguese community, who announced the program in church, allowed flyers to be passed out, and explained in their sermons that the Church did not condone domestic violence. Up to fifty women attended the workshops held in the parishes after mass. Attendance was not usually immediate; most women held on to a flyer for a long while so that husbands would not be suspicious. But for most of the meetings held at St. Christopher House, women could attend them without arousing much suspicion because husbands were accustomed to wives using the many services offered there.[76] The group meetings actually dealt with a wide range of issues, from obtaining a driver's licence and birth control to dealing with lawyers. Of course, not everyone left their abusive husbands. One of the women who did had joined the first domestic violence class in 1982. A thirty-three-year-old mother of three children (aged 13, 11, and 8) who endured ongoing physical and verbal violence at home, she felt empowered enough by the support she received from the four other women in the group to leave her husband and move into an apartment with her children. When her husband refused to acknowledge that she had any rights, she took him to court and won legal custody and child support. Only then did he promise never to beat her again and beg for her return. She agreed, but continued to attend group meetings and made it clear that she would never again tolerate his violence.[77]

As news of the program spread, hospitals, legal clinics, women's shelters, and the police alerted St. Christopher staff about women like Ana, whose husband's vicious beating put her in hospital. The lawyer to whom she was referred contacted the Portuguese-speaking counsellor at St. Christopher House, who invited Ana to join the women's group. The women, Ana recalled, helped someone who "felt that it was [her] duty to suffer patiently for the sake of the children, hoping and praying for things to change" to see that "in fact, nothing would change and that [she] was not born to suffer."[78] Ana divorced her husband.

Instead of the stereotype of the passive, isolated, and victimized Portuguese woman, these women showed what one community worker aptly described as "great courage and tenacity." [79] From 1982 to 1990, more than 750 Portuguese women sought counselling in this program.[80] Their response also underscores the importance of culturally appropriate support services—and, moreover, that feminist and ethnocultural sensibilities are not mutually exclusive. In 1990, a new independent centre called Abrigo (shelter) began providing counselling to battered Portuguese-speaking women (not only those from Portugal). Costa became a counsellor there. Community work around abused Portuguese women contributed to a larger immigrant women's movement in Toronto.

Conclusion

In reflecting on her activity as a literacy worker and social justice activist among Toronto's Portuguese immigrants, Pratt noted that she and her mostly female co-activists openly criticized Canada's rhetoric of multiculturalism. They did so, she explained, because they wanted "to call attention" to "the contradictions of saying that Canada was a multicultural, open, literate society, when, in the experience of our [working-class and poor immigrant] clients, this was just not true."[81] At the same time, PISEM and Cleaners' Action activists like Pratt were actively involved in laying down a foundation for the Canadianization of immigrants. So, too, were activists like Nettle, who taught ESL classes out of a van, and Medeiros, a left-wing immigrant who ran the West End YMCA classes.

The difference, however, is that, unlike the mainstream social workers and agencies who proceeded them, these front-line community organizers were offering a different, indeed more progressive, way of being Canadian—even as they themselves were adjusting to life in Canada. Through the PISEM programs, the English classes, the direct workplace actions, the ESL curriculum, the domestic violence classes, and so much more, Portuguese immigrants were becoming Canadianized from the bottom up, rather than the top down. In the process of forging alliances with radical community workers, Portuguese immigrant women were not simply being acted upon by outsiders, or socially controlled by experts or elites, but instead were learning about the ways to be "Canadian" in a progressive, multicultural, working-class environment.[82]

The activists, recalled Duncombe, wanted their students to "understand" that they were not just individuals with specific problems but "a whole group of people" who had "political problems." They "suffered the same thing, a kind of injustice" and "if they got together they could do something about it." "We were," Duncombe added, "very politically active." Through that activism, they helped to revise and revamp the tools and goals of community organizing among poor and working-class immigrants.[83] Portuguese women's growing politicization had much to do with the harsh material realities of their lives, but it was nurtured by their interactions and relationships with progressive community workers who worked tirelessly on their behalf. Equally important was the emergence of the workplace solidarities that are detailed in the next chapters.

Chapter 5

Battling Corporate Giants:
Union Activism in the 1970s

In an early expression of the workplace militancy of Portuguese immigrant women in Toronto, a large group of night cleaners employed by Modern Building Cleaning, which held the contract to clean the Toronto-Dominion Centre, launched a wildcat (illegal) strike in June 1974. Located in the downtown core, the skyscraper's three towers and pavilion were clad in bronze-tinted glass and black-painted steel. The project was funded through a joint partnership between TD Bank and the Bronfman-family-owned Fairview Corporation (later Cadillac Fairview). In addition to housing the bank headquarters, the building provided rental office and retail space for many other businesses. Designed by elite architect Ludwig Mies van der Rohe, the TD Centre was hailed as a fitting symbol of Toronto's emergence as Canada's financial capital and its growing importance as an international city.[1]

The towers may have glistened, but the mostly female Portuguese cleaners who walked off the job at the TD Centre's tallest tower, the Toronto-Dominion Bank Tower—or, as the women called it, the "building *preto*" (black building)—did so because of the garbage. Stinking used garbage bags, to be exact. The foul smell of the organic-waste-tainted bags was making the women, particularly the pregnant women, gag and experience the dry heaves. On the grounds of human dignity and workers' right to a healthy workplace, they rejected their employer's cost-cutting directive to reuse plastic bags emptied of the refuse of the building's many wealthy tenants.

In dealing with the imperious company manager, W. S. McFarlane, the workers exhibited an earthy female militancy in keeping with their physically demanding labouring lives and their transplanted cultural displays of informal protest. When union steward Idalina Azevedo was summoned to the manager's office for defying orders, she thrust a smelly bag under his nose and that of the police officers he had called in. By the time Dan Heap, an NDP city councillor from a Portuguese-dominated ward, arrived on the scene, he found McFarlane "flanked by security Guards and two Metro police, trying through interpreters to force a hundred angry women (mostly speaking only Portuguese) to use re-cycled garbage bags."[2] When the company later violated a promise to rescind the order, the women walked out. The strike was illegal because it occurred during the life of a legally binding collective agreement signed between Local 204 of the Service Employees International Union and Modern. The women scored a victory when the Ontario Labour Relations Board ordered a ban on the use of dirty bags.[3]

The history of this cleaners' strike challenges many of the stereotypes of Portuguese women workers. Research on immigrant women has held an important place in Canadian labour and left history; here, immigrant women feature prominently, indeed centrally, in our historical analysis of unionization.[4] The cleaners' 1974 wildcat strike and other union activism featured here (and in chapter 6) challenge older portraits of politically apathetic Portuguese immigrants, and in the case of women, housebound, docile, and submissive. It illuminates the experiences of non-English-speaking immigrant women in Canada's expanding service sector after the Second World War and their willingness to fight for their rights in the workplace.[5]

Often married with children, Portuguese female cleaners contributed to the dramatic increase of married women in the postwar Canadian workforce and to the growing rates of unionization among women workers. The many newly unionized women included teachers, nurses, and civil servants as well as auto, electrical, and other workers.[6] Here, we highlight the "foreign-speaking" immigrant women who, like Azevedo, toiled on the lowest-paid janitorial workforces of Toronto's private and public buildings. We explore how these precariously employed nighttime women cleaners initiated, and arguably helped to shape, female service workers' activism within the lower ranks of the service industry.[7] In reflecting on the 1974 wildcat strike more than thirty years later, Azevedo noted that, although afraid of losing their much-needed income, the women's deepening resentment towards an exploitative company that also used the police to intimidate them had emboldened them to defy their employer and the law. So, too, had the Carnation Revolution, the left-led military coup that overthrew the Estado Novo regime on 25 April 1974 in Lisbon.[8] The decision to contact Heap to help them settle the dispute captures the women's resourcefulness in using sympathetic allies to address their workplace concerns.

Feminist specialists of immigrant and ethnic women workers have noted the limitations of labour histories whose concepts of working-class femininity, female respectability, and militancy largely derive from research on dominant-majority (such as Anglo-Canadian) women. As Julie Guard notes, a good deal of Canadian feminist labour history has been concerned with the apparent contradiction between prevailing bourgeois norms of feminine propriety and working women's participation in "unruly" behaviour, street politics, and picket lines. The contradiction has certainly applied to many working women, most particularly, perhaps, to dominant-majority women such as white Anglo-Canadian Protestant women in Ontario towns and cities.[9] However, as Guard adds, and a growing literature well documents, "the presumption of a single and undifferentiated standard of respectable femininity obscures the complexities of class, ethnicity, and race that shaped women's varied experiences of gender."[10]

When Heap arrived at the TD Centre during the Portuguese cleaners' altercation with the Modern manager, he not only heard the women's loud and angry "foreign" voices. He also witnessed the assertive finger-pointing and thrusting hands and arms that offered a dramatic example of the "rhetoric" of the labouring female body.[11] Our analysis of Portuguese female cleaners' militancy sheds light on the rough-and-tumble proletarian culture of southern European women who, as scholars of Italian women workers observe, drew simultaneously on their capacity and pride in performing demanding physical labour, their "sharp tongues," and the close link between their protest strategies and their commitments to family obligations.[12]

Like other supposedly "unorganizable" im/migrant women— whether Italian garment workers in early-twentieth-century New York, or the Central American and Mexican workers involved in the Justice for Janitors struggles in late 1980s and 1990s Los Angeles—Toronto's Portuguese female cleaners have important union stories to tell. In taking on big capital in late-twentieth-century Toronto, their actions reveal a feisty womanhood rooted in family and community life that is consistent with their identities as respectable, hardworking—and indeed breadwinning—wives and mothers.[13]

Unlike LA's Latino/a janitorial workers, some of whom arrived in the US already radicalized, these women had no prior experience with unions in Portugal, where the Estado Novo dictatorship had outlawed unions and imprisoned militants and radicals. This is not to say that they did not bring with them rural expressions of informal protest towards exploitative commercial farmers and other employers. But it makes their campaigns for unionization all the more impressive. Still more noteworthy is the critical role played by Azorean women in these labour struggles, for they have long been caricatured as the most backward, passive, and submissive of all Portuguese. Motivated by material need and family duties, and demanding respect as essential service workers, these women led union drives, went on strike, and worked with community allies to critique, even oust, complacent union leaders.

Postwar Labour Movement

What did the Canadian labour movement look like as Portuguese immigration to Canada took off in the late 1960s and early 1970s? The union movement had been based mainly in the resource industries, in mass production, in parts of the construction industry, and in small pockets of the service sector. A small number of women were unionized compared to men, but their numbers were increasing with the growth of white-collar unionism, particularly in the public sector. By 1975, about a third of the country's workers were covered by collective agreements. Unionized male workers in these years generally prospered, gaining higher wages and better job protections. The proportion of immigrant women in unions remained small, though their presence increased within public sector unions that represented, for example, teachers, government employees, and some nurses.[14]

Building cleaners, however, were decidedly marginal to the union movement. Organizing efforts among Toronto's Portuguese cleaners took place within the context of the Ontario Labour Relations Act, which provides procedures for the certification of a union. To be certified, a union needed the support of a simple majority of the workers at a given workplace, who registered their support by signing union cards. As the officially recognized bargaining agent, the union then negotiated with the employer to secure a collective agreement that established wage rates, benefits, and workplace measures for the life of that agreement.

A successful union drive opened the door to but did not necessarily result in a collective agreement. The fact that the labour market was segmented along gender and racial-ethnic lines—as it still is—made it difficult to organize "low-skilled" immigrant workers like the nighttime female building cleaners hired on contract. In addition, the so-called postwar compromise that saw unions trade off a new industrial regime of state-sanctioned collective bargaining for managerial control of the labour process led to a certain complacency among the established unions, making them less interested in organizing blue-collar, immigrant, and women workers.[15]

One established union that did organize building cleaners was the Service Employees International Union. A member of the older, once craft-based American Federation of Labor (AFL), the SEIU had been actively organizing service workers in the United States since the early twentieth century. In 1955, when the AFL and its long-time rival, the Congress of Industrial Unions (CIO) merged, the SEIU became an AFL-CIO affiliate. Nevertheless, business unionism still ruled in the SEIU during the late 1960s and the 1970s, and minorities and women had a weak voice in the union.

The rise of Canadian unions in this era would challenge the SEIU's dominance in the service sector. The Canadian Union of Public Employees came to play a significant role in organizing cleaners, particularly in the public sector. By the 1970s, more overtly nationalist unions that belonged to the left-led Confederation of Canadian Unions sought to organize immigrant workers like building cleaners. Still, except for some larger workplaces, the janitorial staff in the building services sector were not organized in large numbers.[16] Most small workplaces never experienced the benefits of unionization. The building owners' increasingly common practice of contracting out the cleaning to out-of-house companies that competed for the contracts drove down the price of labour and made organizing cleaners both difficult and unattractive. These workers had little bargaining power in this highly competitive system, and the industry's low wages meant correspondingly minimal union dues. For some unions, the cost of organizing these workplaces was not worth the benefits accrued.

SEIU Organizes the Toronto-Dominion Centre

Founded in Chicago in 1921 as the Business Service Employees International Union (BSEIU), the SEIU was the first union to organize cleaners in Canada. Following some initial success among office custodians and window cleaners in Vancouver in 1943, the union turned to Toronto. In 1944, a charter was issued to BSEIU Local 204 for elevator operators, and a year later, for hospital service workers at Toronto

General Hospital. Locals in Quebec and the prairie provinces followed. By 1960, Canadian membership numbered over twelve thousand. To more accurately reflect its varied membership, "Building" was dropped from the union's name in 1968.[17]

The Canadian (B)SEIU generally focused on the hospital sector, but Toronto's Local 204 came to organize building cleaners in Toronto. By the 1960s, the local included janitorial cleaners at the Metropolitan Toronto School Board and the University of Toronto, both of which hired their own cleaners. It also covered those hired by cleaning contractors supplying janitorial workers for a variety of office buildings in the downtown business district. By 1968, Local 204 held Canada's largest cleaning contract, at 275 workers, who had unionized the year before, with Modern Building Cleaning at the new Toronto-Dominion Centre, which then consisted of the one office tower called the Toronto-Dominion Bank Tower.[18] Surmising that they might be facing "a potential membership of 8 to 10 thousand people," Local 204 president Albert Hearn admitted in a 1971 memo that his local had "neither the manpower or the money" to organize on this scale.[19]

The SEIU's business unionism justified forming close working relationships with building managers and cleaning contractors on the grounds that employers and workers in the sector shared "a communion of interests." In a 1964 article in *Building Management* magazine, Hearn spoke in terms of a building's public image being linked to an employer's fair treatment of its cleaning staff, who in turn would provide "good, reliable service."[20] However, as more contractors entered the industry, increasing the competition for tenders, the union tried but failed to organize them in an effort to set minimum wages in the industry. But having forged a relationship with Modern, a Canadian company that provided janitorial services for public and private buildings, SEIU negotiated agreements with the company that allowed the union to represent Modern workers at many offices and hospitals in Canada.

The unionization of the TD Centre occurred without conflict. Indeed, SEIU organized the cleaning workforce even before the building opened, partly, it appears, because of the relationship it was cultivating with Modern, which got the nod from building owners TD Bank and Fairview Corporation. According to the first agreement signed in March 1967, and effective for the period 1 January 1967 to 31 December 1968, the first fifteen employees and all new employees (up to three hundred) were now covered by the collective agreement.[21]

From the start, the cleaning workforce at the TD Centre was overwhelmingly Portuguese. With 90 percent of its 275 members Portuguese immigrants, the collective agreement was printed in Portuguese.[22] For Hearn, the ability to communicate with these workers also meant "introducing New Canadians to our way of trade union life" and "showing them what kind of protection they are getting from their trade union contract."[23] The acculturation process, as James Barrett has argued in the US context, could occur from the bottom up as well as the top down.[24] While the SEIU in the late 1960s and the 1970s hardly emulated the early-twentieth-century socialist unions Barrett studied, even mainstream unions offered an arena of alternative values in contrast to those of employers and the state in which immigrants might learn to become "Canadian." For Portuguese immigrants with no prior experience with unions, participation in the SEIU, and other unions, played an important part in their Canadianization. By 1972, Local 204's membership numbered about seven hundred workers.[25] And while Portuguese cleaners did not initiate the unionization of the TD Centre, they would urge the union to meet their needs.

Portuguese immigrants in Canada—as elsewhere, including in 1970s England[26]—exhibited workplace militancy already in their early years of arrival. In Toronto, the women were decidedly militant. One of the earliest actions in Toronto was a short-lived sit-down strike in April 1973 at Ryerson Polytechnic Institute. Maintenance workers angry over the administration's decision to deal with budget cuts by firing them occupied the fourteenth floor of Jorgenson Hall, the institute's main building. The wives and children who joined them attracted media attention, likely because reporters considered their presence unusual, but they were there as critical participants in a working-class family economy (see chapter 6).

A week into the strike, the photographs accompanying the Toronto *Globe* coverage of the "occupation" featured Emiliana Pedro, Maria Couto, and Martha Ribeiro in a kitchen preparing the hearty lunchtime soups for which Portuguese women became known. The reporter's identification of them as the wives of the striking janitorial workers was bolstered by the accompanying images of young children skipping rope in the corridor and arm-wrestling with female students from the institute's social service program. But these women may well have been nighttime cleaners doing double duty as the family's main cook and child minder.

A year later, the media coverage of the 1974 wildcat strike at the

TD Centre's tallest office tower over dirty garbage bags featured the women as workers and militants, though the strike did not resolve the problem. At the time of the strike, Modern employed about two hundred women on nighttime contracts to clean the TD offices from 5:30 p.m. to 10:30 p.m., Monday to Friday. As the women began reacting to the smelly recycled bags, Azevedo, as union steward, and others contacted the Local 204 representative Joe Jordan, who called the city's department of public health. The chief public health officer met with company representatives, and an agreement was reached that only bags containing no organic waste could be reused. But as company pressure to reuse the dirty bags continued, the women turned to Heap, the city councillor who represented their ward (Ward 6) and had already shown them support, to help settle the dispute. In possession of a letter of support from the chief public health officer, the women, Heap recorded, "were insisting on their rights" to a healthy workplace. By the time he showed up to pressure McFarlane into respecting the promise not to reuse organic-tainted bags, the women had taken matters in their own hands.[27]

Acting assertively is not necessarily the same as being fearless. The women who swarmed the company manager and later walked out on their jobs were afraid. Azevedo, who had become a union steward after learning to speak some English, assumed a leadership role during these events. In recalling the confrontation with the Modern manager, she emphasized just how frightened she and the others were when he ordered the police to remove her from the building. For many immigrants, the police are a visible marker of the state, prompting fears of jail and deportation. When the police officers asked her why she would not use the recycled bags, she lacked the English vocabulary to answer it. But using her female labouring body, she mimed the motions of a woman gagging and gestured with outstretched hands to indicate the figure of a pregnant woman. And then she thrust the smelly bag in the men's faces. The police reacted as she no doubt hoped they would, twitching their noses and turning away from the smell. Then, when they asked to meet separately with manager McFarlane, the union representative, and Heap, Azevedo's heart, she recounted, "filled with happiness" because it looked like they might actually be heard. It took four hours to get McFarlane to agree to provide the staff with new bags until a Board of Arbitration ruled on the matter.[28]

During a recent interview with CHIN radio conducted in connection with the unveiling of the mural to Portuguese women's labour activism in October 2021, Azevedo recounted a related story that was both personal and political, and spoke as well to transnational connections. After winning the battle of the dirty garbage bags, with police support, a group of women headed to a nearby parking lot to eat their snack. There, they picked up Azevedo in celebration and thanked her for what she had done for them. To which she, now every bit a militant, recalled replying: "It was not me, it was all of us. The people united will never be defeated, which was 25 April, was very alive at this time."[29] Politicized in response to her mistreatment in Canada, Azevedo also drew inspiration from the toppling of a dictatorship that had ruled her homeland with disregard for the struggling people of the far-flung Azorean islands.

Women Cleaners Organize Queen's Park

Portuguese female cleaners not only joined unionized workplaces, but they also led organizing drives in the face of stiff employer opposition. The campaign to organize the Queen's Park office-building complex in 1975 offers some insight into why and how these "neophytes" did it.

Located east of the provincial legislature, the vast compound of older and newer buildings houses many government ministries, and thousands of civil servants and other staff work in the offices. Four large towers that were built between the mid-1960s and 1971 were surrounded by gardens designed by Japanese American architect Hideo Sasaki. The women who cleaned the offices at night did not, however, get to enjoy or contemplate the serene garden landscape.[30]

The contract cleaners hired by Modern Building Cleaning, which also held the contract tendered by the Ministry of Government Services to clean its buildings, were particularly vulnerable workers. They earned lower wages than the cleaners hired directly by the Ontario government to clean other provincial buildings in Toronto ($2.40 versus $3.74 an hour for women).[31] The women resented the fact that the better-paid "heavy cleaning" jobs (which involved operating a simple machine) went only to men. There were also complaints about management switching their jobs without notice and firing workers without just cause.[32] The situation worsened with the hiring of a female Portuguese supervisor who callously docked the workers' pay for being only a few minutes late for work. (She had evidently left another building when the cleaners there unionized.[33]) In response, the janitorial staff came to agree that the only route to better wages and working conditions was a union, though none of them had had any experience with forming one.

But various factors worked in their favour. Especially important were the strong ties of mutual aid and community forged among Portuguese immigrants in Toronto. The dense networks of kin, friends, and neighbours provided critical information. News of the concrete gains made at other workplaces softened the women's views towards activists as so many dangerous radicals. From relatives and neighbours who had benefited from their interactions with the community workers at St. Christopher House and elsewhere, these cleaners learned the value of alliance building and empowering themselves through collective organization. The value of unionization was transmitted as well through family members who worked in unionized workplaces, whether in buildings or on construction sites. When asked why she had joined the union drive at Queen's Park, Elena Afonso replied that she had learned from her husband and other male relatives who belonged to construction unions "that unions were good for workers."[34]

The family and ethnocultural ties among the workers, combined with the shared class experience of exploitation and collective sense of grievance, favoured union activity and likely allowed for a greater degree of militancy. In other words, ethnic solidarity fostered activism. There are parallels here with what Ruth Milkman and others later found among militant Latino/a janitors in Los Angeles. Being deeply enmeshed in ethnic social networks that were embedded in certain occupational settings, such as building services, facilitated union mobilization. Unlike some Latino/a workers in the United States, Portuguese immigrants to Canada could not draw on a radical past, but rather were radicalized by the experience of migration.[35] No strangers to anti-immigrant prejudice, their position as precarious contract workers heightened their awareness of class exploitation. The gender discrimination faced by the women served to further anger and embolden them. Acutely aware that they stood at the lowest ranks of low-paid workers in the building-cleaning sector, Portuguese women came to view unions as a source of hope for a better life. This ethnic and gender unity fostered collective action, particularly in workplaces where they made up the bulk of the workforce. As in other female strikes, the activists would organize at kitchen tables in their neighbourhoods.[36]

Still, choosing to unionize the Queen's Park complex on their own was an audacious plan for women with little to no union organizing experience—or English. Predictably, they faced stiff employer opposition. When a Modern official got a whiff of union talk, he summoned one of the leaders, Azorean Leopoldina Pimentel, to his office and fired her. On the next day, two male Portuguese-speaking company representatives showed up at her door, demanding that she turn over the list of names of those interested in forming a union. Having already destroyed it, Pimentel insisted that she alone face repercussions for union activity.

The company staff then urged the women to sign a form indicating their refusal to join a union. Knowing their jobs were on the line, almost all of them did so. The two who refused were fired. Worried but undeterred by the company's tactics, the campaign leaders turned to their own neighbourhoods. The organizers went door to door, explaining the benefits of unionization to their co-workers (and the workers' families), and collecting signatures for those who joined the certification drive.[37] In response, Modern unleashed a campaign of intimidation. In an obvious attempt to scare them off, it dispatched company men to make nighttime visits to the organizers' homes. It imposed speed-ups that made it impossible for the women to complete their assigned workload. It transferred various pro-union workers to other workplaces, and fired yet more women suspected of joining the certification drive. The women remained resolute in the face of such tactics and, on 29 April 1975, SEIU Local 204 was certified as the bargaining agent for 106 workers who cleaned at the Queen's Park building complex.[38]

Also resolute were the eight Portuguese cleaners who had been fired for union activity. In keeping with conservative business unionism, the SEIU and its lawyers had urged the women to take a settlement and give up their jobs. Rejecting that advice, the women turned to the outside community agencies and the activists who would become important allies and work with them to found the Cleaners' Action labour network (see chapter 4). Fernanda Gaspar, a progressive Portuguese-speaking staffer with the Services for Working People, an OHRC agency, convinced the first woman to contact her about the firing to encourage the others to follow suit. To the chagrin of SEIU Local 204 leaders, SWFP promised to bypass the union and help the women "seek protection under the relevant labour laws." The lawyer who filed the application with the OLRB for full compensation for lost wages and the return of their jobs was Michelle Swenarchuk, the young left feminist lawyer recommended to Gaspar by Madeleine Parent, a prominent feminist and co-founder of the left-led CCU (see chapter 4). At the OLRB hearing, which Gaspar attended along with the applicants, Swenarchuk convincingly argued that since it was illegal to fire workers for union activity

Battling Corporate Giants

when a union was certified, the women were legally entitled to their back wages and jobs. The board reinstated their jobs and they were paid 100 percent of the back wages.[39]

When asked why vulnerable immigrant women with little knowledge of unions or labour law had fought so hard to form a union, Afonso said the answer was easy. She and her co-workers had come to understand that the union could provide workers with some security and prevent employers from "getting away with doing whatever they wanted."[40] As others recalled, these women knew, too, that unlike the Portugal they'd left, Canada allowed them some space to fight for their rights as workers. Leveraging the opportunity, they successfully negotiated some power for themselves in the workplace. In that regard, this immigrant women's strike arguably reflected the women's transformation from exploited greenhorns to class-conscious workers, as well as better-informed new Canadians. (Male cleaners were not absent from this and later union drives, but their comparatively more privileged position made for muted involvement.) This episode also points to an early tension between the SEIU and the female activists who provided the cleaners with linguistic, legal, and other forms of support.

Before barely savouring the victory, however, the newly organized cleaners faced a major challenge. During the bargaining process that began in July, Modern refused to agree to a wage increase on the grounds that they were restricted by the terms of their contract with the Ministry of Government Services. They could raise wages, they argued, only if they received a more favourable contract. The Ontario government, however, refused to recognize itself as an "employer" that ultimately had the power to retain the cleaners' jobs by renewing its contract with Modern. Instead, like many corporate owners of buildings, it cast itself as a neutral player in the negotiations. Modern issued its employees notices of termination. In response, the Ministry of Government Services opened up bidding for the cleaning contract.[41]

The cleaners knew they would probably lose their jobs at Queen's Park if they continued to push for higher wages, but insisted that was preferable to once again settling for minimum wage levels. The economic context is significant. By the early 1970s, workers' wages were not keeping up with the escalating cost of living, and minimum wage earners would have scarcely been able to make ends meet as their "real wages" were eroded by inflation.[42] When the union called a vote on Modern's proposed new wage rates—the $2.85 quoted for light-duty cleaners and

$3.74 for heavy-duty cleaners equalled those paid to SEIU Local 204 members who cleaned the TD Centre—the Queen's Park cleaners voted 45 to 29 against accepting them.[43] According to Swenarchuk, that meeting was "particularly important in the process of politicization of the cleaners, most of whom had never voted before on any question." "There was a sense of power," she added, "in saying, through the symbol of the ballot, to the company and to the SEIU, whose role in the entire process came under increasing criticism, that the workers were determined to continue the fight."[44] Viewed from the perspective of a bottom-up Canadianization, the experience spoke to the workers' increasing adaptation to Canadian society.

Azorean immigrant office cleaners become labour heroines. Idalina Azevedo (right) led a wildcat strike, over dirty garbage bags, against Toronto-Dominion Centre in June 1974. Leopoldina Pimentel (left, her physical gesture emphasizing a point being made) spearheaded the union drive at the Queen's Park office complex in April 1975. York University Libraries, Clara Thomas Archives & Special Collections, Domingos Marques fonds, ASC61142.

The women's insistence on higher wages reflected their status as critical wage earners. Far from supplementary income earners, many of them were family breadwinners. This was true of Maria Pacheco, who was pregnant with an unemployed husband. "If I didn't work," she bluntly told reporters, "I don't know what we'd do for money." Like many others, she was already supplementing her income by working as a hotel chambermaid to make ends meet. These women's willingness to risk their jobs for a bigger wage increase reflected their determination to improve the family's standard of living. As Ana Pacheco put it, the small wage increase was "just not enough" to support their families. The injustice of their low wages was amplified by Modern's healthy profits (over $1 million in the previous year).[45] These contract workers knew, too, that cleaners hired directly by the government made significantly higher wages. In interviews with reporters, cleaners like Piedade Silva exposed the company's scare tactics, which included threatening workers with dismissal unless they accepted the offer. Supervisory personnel were harassing the workers on the job to do the same.[46]

Cleaners' Action founder and activist Sidney Pratt discusses a workplace strategy with Queen's Park office cleaners in 1975. St. Christopher House (now West Neighbourhood House) collection.

These women gambled and lost. Exploiting the fierce competition among the growing number of contractors offering bids, the ministry awarded the cleaning contract to a different company, Consolidated Maintenance Services. And in the end, the cleaners were forced to accept low wages in order to keep their jobs. The contracting-out crisis of 1975 was a bitter pill to swallow, though the women's resourcefulness in turning for help to community activists led to the birth of Cleaners' Action (see chapter 4). Their tenacity also impressed their allies. An SFWP counsellor observed that "contrary to a much-spread belief that immigrants are apathetic and little inclined to organizing, these women . . . have acted courageously and intelligently in the face of many difficulties." Also giving the community allies their due, she added that the availability of the community workers' services and the women's trust in them "provided the stimulus necessary for them to voice and act on their own aspirations."[47]

Rejecting Business Unionism, Joining Canadian Unions

In a dramatic example of workers' bottom-up unionism, the mostly female Portuguese cleaners employed at the TD Centre expressed their increasing contempt for an unresponsive union by successfully voting to decertify it in 1979. SEIU Local 204 may have printed its collective agreements in Portuguese, but it proved wholly inadequate in representing particularly its female immigrant members. As Mercedes Steedman observed in her study of the early-twentieth-century garment industry, business unionism in female-dominated workplaces impedes women's participation. The union bureaucracy tends to be male, and decisions are made with little to no input from female members. Most workers in the building-cleaning sector were women, as is still the case, and they, too, found themselves peripheral in union decision-making.[48]

More specifically, the origins of the cleaners' defiant action against SEIU Local 204—which metaphorically amounted to raising a collective middle finger to the union—lie within SEIU's history in Toronto. Already by 1976, the complaints were piling up. SEIU members at the University of Toronto noted that the absence of interpreters at the ethnically mixed membership meetings left immigrant workers in the dark. An excessive focus on the hospitals, they added, meant little discussion about their "problems at UofT."[49] Similarly, TD Centre members reported that, with no Portuguese-speaking staff in the union office, workers found it very difficult to communicate workplace grievances, including firings and harassment.

By 1978, the growing frustration over SEIU's evident disinterest or slowness in responding to their complaints led a group of cleaners from Ward 6 to turn to Heap. Once again intervening on behalf of his constituents, Heap asked Neil Wood, president of Cadillac Fairview Corporation, to at least address the underhanded tactics of Modern's new assistant manager. The man was assigning older workers the heaviest jobs so they would quit. He was playing favourites when assigning overtime hours or layoffs, and even pressuring male employees to join his soccer club. Both SEIU Local 204 president Hearn and the manager of the cleaning contractor rebuffed the charges, saying no such complaints had been received. To the workers, the denial confirmed SEIU's too-cozy relationship with Modern.[50]

The women cleaners' increasing willingness to consider ousting the SEIU in favour of a more democratic and militant union also owes much to the alliance they forged with the Cleaners' Action activists of St. Christopher House. Since spring 1975, Sidney Pratt, Swenarchuk, and others had been listening to the women's complaints, informing them of their labour rights, discussing strategies for addressing their workplace grievances, and engaging in direct workplace actions that enraged SEIU leaders (see chapter 4). As a campaign worker for Heap and the NDP, the Portuguese-speaking Pratt continued to solidify her relationship with the cleaners and their families during her door-to-door visits to what she said was "millions" of Portuguese homes. (She also rode the bus and subway at night to hear the women's stories.) Pratt may have "hated" the banana liqueur she was repeatedly served during her home visits, but she drank it out of respect and solidarity with the Portuguese workers who offered it. "By the end of the day," she later recalled, she would be "royally drunk but warm."[51]

Cleaners' Action staff had become critical allies in part because the cleaners' union stewards, who were mostly daytime male workers, were out of reach. As were the union meetings, which were held in the evening, when the women worked. That the better-paid heavy-duty cleaning jobs that involved simple-to-operate machinery went only to the men continued to rankle. As did the union's lacklustre efforts to convince TD Centre management to allow ESL in the Workplace classes to be held. So, too, did the sexism and condescension of SEIU representatives. One example of it appeared in a report that referred to the 1974 wildcat strikers, most of whom were married with children, as "housekeeping girls." All of this made the women interested in accessing a new union that would be accountable to them.[52]

That the Cleaners' Action activists openly criticized SEIU Local 204 for poorly representing their members and counselled representation by a Canadian union also mattered. Their advice was in keeping with the larger movement in Canada at this time to have workers represented by Canadian unions rather than US-headed international ones. Pratt (though US-born) and Swenarchuk belonged to a loose coalition of nationalists whose opposition to American unions was part of a larger political agenda for full economic, social, and cultural independence for Canada. But like many left-wing activists, they also viewed the campaign for independence as part of a struggle to bring about a more egalitarian or socialist society. As Local 204's contract with Modern was expiring in spring 1979, the cleaners, already schooled in the relevant procedures, were ready to act.[53]

The Cleaners' Action staff had organized a meeting to decide on what the workers wanted in a new contract. The women, however, arrived upset and agitated over the employer's latest antics, and the meeting quickly morphed into a barrage of complaints about SEIU's latest blunders. Women voiced their anger over the union's failure to help a dozen older workers (in their sixties) who had lost their jobs; Local 204 had neither filed any grievances nor counselled anyone on making a complaint of age discrimination to the OHRC. They criticized SEIU for not properly training the stewards, thereby limiting their effectiveness. They accused the union of cynically replacing one bad business agent (Jordan) with another one (a Mr. Hamuluk). The union dues, they noted, kept increasing, but wages rarely did. In response to what a reporter with the left-wing *Comunidade* newspaper described as the workers' increasing consciousness of their union's "profound disinterest" in them, about forty TD Centre cleaners held more meetings and elected a special committee to draw up a list of workplace complaints.[54]

Labour-management tensions at the TD Centre climaxed with the firing of a young Portuguese male cleaner who spoke English well and had joined the cleaners' special committee. Again, Local 204 did nothing about the unjust firing. Then Modern accused the cleaners of theft and, despite their vehement denials, hired security guards to search them. One woman was so shaken by the experience that she ended up in hospital for acute anxiety. When, again, the union did nothing, the cleaners turned to the OLRB to get rid of the union.[55]

The workers faced the OLRB with their trusted feminist lawyer Swenarchuk, who later described the meeting of the mostly Portuguese cleaners as a "big" turning point in their radicalization. For four years, she recalled, Pratt had been working with this group, and while "these workers have always fought the company and their union," there "wasn't any indication that they wanted to change unions until now." Given the "very high" stakes, Swenarchuk was "sure the SEIU [would] use all its financial resources" to try to defeat them.[56] But almost every one of the 300 workers who attended the OLRB meeting had signed a petition to decertify the SEIU. Despite SEIU protests that only the special committee, and not the general membership, opposed the union, the OLRB held an official secret vote on decertification on 1 May 1979. All but a dozen of the 306 members who cast votes voted to get rid of the SEIU.[57]

In the meantime, a commission of TD workers began to look for another union to represent them. Predictably, given Swenarchuk's connection with the Confederation of Canadian Unions, she and Pratt favoured a CCU union. It had yet to organize a cleaning workplace, but some cleaners signed the union cards. Another faction favoured the Canadian Union of Public Employees. Formed in 1963 through the merger of the National Union of Public Employees and the National Union of Public Service Employees, CUPE represented more than 78,000 workers in some 500 locals across Canada. There were long-standing tensions between SEIU, which had a top-heavy structure, and CUPE, whose more decentralized structure and autonomous locals gave it a more democratic profile. In addition, CUPE (and its predecessors) painted the SEIU as an untrustworthy international union that collaborated with employers via sweetheart deals, kept down public sector wages, and undermined class consciousnesses by encouraging identification with employers.[58] CUPE had also enjoyed some success in challenging SEIU's status as an organizer of cleaners in Toronto, mainly in hospitals (including Sunnybrook Hospital) and school boards (Metropolitan Toronto Separate School Board).[59] And it got the nod. As members of CUPE Local 2295, the TD Centre cleaners joined the country's largest union.[60]

Still, on certain issues, like wages, CUPE was as ineffective as SEIU. On a number of occasions, for example, it was forced to accept wage freezes in order to retain the cleaning contract. Overall, CUPE never made serious inroads in the contract cleaning industry. Nor did its decentralized structure—wherein locals ran their daily affairs and CUPE National became involved only in the event of arbitration or during negotiations—necessarily work well for new immigrants still learning the ropes. When CUPE representatives did attend meetings, they could not understand the workers. CUPE did incorporate more women into the local's executive, but tensions around ethnicity and language continued with CUPE, much as with the SEIU.[61]

Ultimately, however, the Canadian union that made substantial inroads into the building cleaners' industry was a CCU affiliate. In 1979, the Canadian Food and Associated Services Union (CFASU) organized the mostly Portuguese cleaners at First Canadian Place. Built in 1975 by the Reichmann-owned Olympia & York Developments, First Canadian Place was the tallest of the glitzy skyscrapers that were transforming Toronto's skyline. Together, the tower and associated buildings occupy almost an entire block (see chapter 6).[62] The CFASU, which began as a private restaurant-based union in British Columbia, enjoyed its first success outside BC in 1977, when the Windsor Arms Hotel in Toronto was certified. Two years later, First Canadian Place was organized. In 1981, the union changed its name to the Food and Service Workers of Canada in an effort to represent the variety of membership in the union.

The affiliation of CFASU/FASWOC with the CCU was significant. Founded in 1969 as the Council of Canadian Unions at a convention hosted by the left-led Mine-Mill union in Sudbury, the CCU (which was renamed the Confederation of Canadian Unions in 1973) was composed of left-leaning unions that were expelled or that withdrew from the mainstream labour movement, in response to conflicts that Canadian members had with their US-based unions.[63] It was established as an alternative to the Canadian Labour Congress, which at the time was dominated by US-based international unions. A nationalist as well as left-wing union, the CCU encouraged rank-and-file democracy. CCU unionists also appeared more willing than the internationals to fight tough economic battles in sectors where marginalized immigrant workers predominated.[64]

The link between FASWOC and the First Canadian Place cleaners was another one that came through St. Christopher House. A year earlier, Pratt and her colleagues had supported CFASU's efforts to organize the cleaners at Commerce Court, one more glitzy office-building complex. The workers with links to Cleaners' Action led the pro-union lobby. However, the contractor, Federated Building Maintenance, had defeated the campaign by resorting to a common employer tactic. It offered the workers a higher hourly wage (in this case, 5 cents more) than that paid to union members (SEIU members at the TD Centre). Other CCU-affiliated unions were enjoying some success with immigrant women in other industries, however. For example, the Canadian Textile and Chemical Union organized the McGregor Hosiery Mills factory (commonly called McGregor Socks) on Spadina Avenue, where many Portuguese women also worked. Despite the setback, Cleaners' Action staff and cleaners got the word out about the value of unions and, specifically, the idea that international unions should be rejected in favour of Canadian ones.[65]

As at Queen's Park a few years previously, it was Portuguese immigrant women (the overwhelming majority at this workplace) who spearheaded the 1979 campaign to unionize the cleaners at First Canadian Place. According to Wendy Iler, a hotel chef who became a CFASU/ FASWOC organizer, she responded to the request from a Portuguese cleaner to visit her workplace by quietly bringing union cards. The women had gathered outside of the building just before their shift was to start, and Iler signed almost everyone that night. It was "like a riot," she said of the women's boisterous behaviour, with the women repeatedly calling "*Senhora, senhora*, more cards" until she ran out of them. The security guards and company supervisors watching from inside the building did not initially understand what was going on, but once they did, they threatened to fire the lot. One of the women to sign a union card that night was Emilia Silva, an immigrant from central Portugal. Years later, she vividly recalled the transformation in the women's physical demeanour after they signed that piece of paper; each of them held their head up high and marched triumphantly into the building. Silva herself was elected president of the local without running for the position. In recalling why she had become a committed unionist, Silva noted that, for her, a union was not only about "wanting higher wages and benefits," but also having a safe base where one was "free from being belittled."[66]

Much as at Queen's Park, the tensions with management had prompted the women to unionize. An unfair supervisor named Lina generated much resentment. If cleaners finished their work slightly early, she would dock their pay. And it was infantilizing to try to hide from her until they could punch the clock. As Lucia Ferreira recalled, the workers also believed that Lina, whom they clearly considered a sell-out who'd betrayed her community for personal gain, had gotten rid of several women just out of spite. The injustice of firing women who were trying to support their struggling families, she added, led her to support a union that would defend their rights.[67] The comments issued by Silva (and others) about a union meaning that managers "couldn't get away with belittling the workers" underscored the women's identity as hard-working immigrant women who deserved—indeed, demanded—to be treated with respect and dignity in the workplace.[68] Economic goals also mattered; in addition to higher wages, the women wanted basic benefits such as holidays, sick pay, or overtime pay.

The SEIU had been trying to organize First Canadian Place, but as a FASWOC representative noted, the cleaners "didn't want to join the American Union."[69] Once again, the cleaners' ties with St. Christopher House community activists influenced developments. In this case, Goretti Cabral, a Portuguese staffer and the cousin of First Canadian Place worker Fernanda Pimentel, played an active role in supporting the women's certification campaign.[70] As a CCU union, FASWOC had valuable experience with "ethnic" organizing. It also had strong links to the Canadian women's movement through activists such as CCU co-founder Parent and colleague Laurell Ritchie, then a CCU organizer. As socialists and feminists active in the National Action Committee on the Status of Women (NAC) and its provincial counterparts, and pay-equity and other lobbies, Parent and Ritchie (and others) helped to ensure that class and union issues, and immigrant working-class women's demands, remained on the agenda. FASWOC Local 51 was made up of female organizers and staff members, and also hired Portuguese-speaking female staff. Compared to the SEIU, and even CUPE, this union was more gender and ethnic inclusive, and is an example of some major shifts in the labour movement's response to women and minoritized workers.[71]

As at Queen's Park and Commerce Court, the cleaners met with employer resistance. Federated (which also held the Commerce Court contract) argued that First Canadian Place employees enjoyed better wages and benefits than "any other" cleaners in "downtown Toronto bank buildings," including the unionized workers at TD Centre, who had to pay union dues. "You do not need a Union to achieve good wages and benefits," declared one memo, because "these have been achieved without an outside union."[72]

The anti-union strategy of raising wages in line with unionized buildings was common enough among cleaning contractors.[73] But Federated went one step further by trying to formally block the union's certification on the cynical grounds that most workers' inability to understand the Ontario Labour Relations Board notices posted in English made them ineligible to petition for a union.[74] (As per normal practice, copies

Cleaners from First Canadian Place and their children attend a union meeting in 1979 with representatives of Canadian Food and Associated Services Union (CFASU), later Food and Service Workers of Canada (FASWOC).
York University Libraries, Clara Thomas Archives & Special Collections, Canadian Auto Workers Union Local 40 fonds, ASC07682.

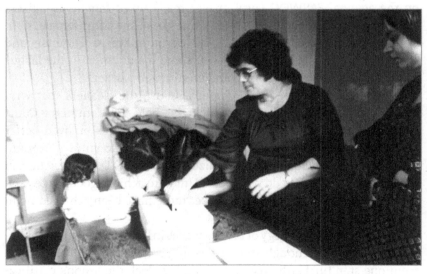

A recently unionized cleaner who had probably never voted in authoritarian Portugal casts her ballot in 1980 on the first contract with CFASU.
York University Libraries, Clara Thomas Archives & Special Collections, Canadian Auto Workers Union Local 40 fonds, ASC07681.

Cleaners vote to ratify the two-year collective agreement that their union, CFASU, negotiated with Federated Building Maintenance at First Canadian Place, 1980. York University Libraries, Clara Thomas Archives & Special Collections, Canadian Auto Workers Union Local 40 fonds, ASC07680.

of the OLRB's Notice to Employees of Application for Certification and of Hearing had been posted in various locations in the workplace.)[75]

Once again, Swenarchuk represented the cleaners at the OLRB hearing. To support their case that the women could not understand what they were doing, Federated humiliated a cleaner who stood silently as their lawyer peppered her with questions in English that she could not comprehend.[76] But this obvious attempt to diminish the women's intellectual and political capabilities failed. The women clearly understood the collective action they were undertaking. All employees were in attendance on the board's premises during the hearing, having been subpoenaed by the employer, in English. And not one of them came forward to support the employer's protest. Instead, 96 of the 120 eligible cleaners had signed union cards, well above the 55 percent required for automatic union certification. The chair of the OLRB ruled that language had no bearing on the validity of the union's application, and in October 1979, FASWOC was certified to represent the employees of Federated at First Canadian Place.[77]

Battling Corporate Giants

Conclusion

In contrast to SEIU's unionization of the TD Centre in 1967, the cleaners' union activism in the 1970s very much represented a bottom-up form of labour mobilization. The union drives, the wildcat strike, and the ousting of a complacent, even neglectful, international union in favour of a more militant and democratic Canadian one reflected the growing politicization of mainly female immigrant workers to the exploitative conditions of the job. The dense family and social networks that prevailed at the immigrant Portuguese dominated cleaning workplaces facilitated labour mobilization as the bonds of class, gender, and ethnicity overlapped those of family, kin, and neighbour.

The impressive degree of bottom-up mobilization also owed much to the work of the grassroots community workers and social movement activists who worked closely and respectfully with, but also counselled and influenced, the women's choices and strategies. Foreign, female, and fighting for their workplace rights, the Portuguese cleaners often initiated the relationships they forged with left-wing community workers and feminist activists, but the bonds of trust and continuity in communication across several years arguably served to make those cleaners more militant or at least union savvy than they might have otherwise been. The various unions involved differed in terms of ideology, organization, and openness to the rank and file, but generally speaking, offers and instances of support occurred largely in reaction to the requests and actions of the women workers and their community allies. At which point, they brought in unions cards, provided some financial support, and tried to solicit positive media coverage and sympathetic public support for the workers' cause.

Nevertheless, labour victories within a highly competitive industry like the building services cleaning sector, where fierce competition between contractors bidding on cleaning contracts imposed a downward pressure on wages, are never secure. Five years after First Canadian Place was organized, the mostly Azorean women who still dominated the cleaning workforce at this complex would rise again to fight exploitation and other employer abuses. Indeed, it was the women whom everyone, including mainland Portuguese immigrants and elites as well as the labour movement and wider Canadian public, considered the most passive, submissive, and in the shadows—immigrant women from the impoverished Azores—who would spearhead the most explosive cleaners' strikes of the period. As we shall see, the lengthy 1984 strike marked the high point of Portuguese immigrant women's labour militancy. It also offers an especially revealing case study of these immigrant women's earthy militancy.

Chapter 6

"We are women and immigrants but we can fight": First Canadian Place Strike, 1984

On 27 June 1984, a group of striking Portuguese female office cleaners crowded into the lobby of First Canadian Place in Toronto's financial district. Given the role particularly of Azorean women in the union drives of Toronto janitorial workers during the 1970s, certain community and union activists may not have been entirely surprised to find the women occupying the marble-and-glass skyscraper. But to the thousands of other people who walked past them—bankers, lawyers, secretaries, store clerks, and shoppers—these women would have looked out of place. They usually cleaned at night, after businesspeople had gone home. It was unusual to see these ordinarily invisible and silent women emerge en masse during the day in the building's public space, wearing everyday clothes rather than uniforms, holding strike placards, chanting political slogans, dancing, and denouncing scabs. For six weeks between 4 June and 13 July, these immigrant women spoke truth to power in the heart of corporate Canada.

Located near the corner of King and Bay Streets, First Canadian Place is Canada's tallest skyscraper (298 metres). Built in 1975 by Olympia & York Developments and designed by Canadian-owned B+H Architects, the tower and associated buildings house the headquarters of the Bank of Montreal as well as other businesses. The Exchange Tower, a skyscraper added to the complex in 1981, houses several tenants, the most permanent being the Toronto Stock Exchange. With millions of dollars' worth of transactions taking place there every business day, First Canadian Place offered yet another towering symbol of corporate capitalism.

Although inflation was devouring their inadequate paycheques, the striking cleaners wanted a wage increase of just 50 cents an hour. Federated Building Maintenance, the company contracted to clean First Canadian Place, refused any increase. As for the building owners, the

Reichmann brothers of Olympia & York, they denied any role in the labour dispute. But with the strike now in its third week, an Olympia & York representative confronted the women in the lobby. He scolded them for embarrassing the building's well-to-do tenants and insisted they move outside. When they refused, the police were called in. Some women shouted in Portuguese and others cried as they saw those arrested being led to the police van. Surrounded by police, a striker shouted in imperfect but emphatic English, "I'm stayed. I'm stayed," as she defiantly threw down her megaphone. Also arrested was Lucia Ferreira, a union representative with the Food and Service Workers of Canada, which belonged to the Confederation of Canadian Unions. It took six uniformed officers to get a screaming Ferreira into the police van.[1]

This and other developments during the 1984 strike attracted plenty of media attention, particularly from English-language reporters who thought it remarkable that a group of marginalized foreign-speaking women had taken to the streets to demand better treatment. For the workers involved, the lengthy strike marked the high point in cleaners' activism and in the women's transformation into radical political subjects. In defiance of big capital, cost-cutting employers, surly supervisors, and pathologizing stereotypes, it was largely women from the Azores—namely, the sisters, cousins, co-villagers, neighbours, and friends of the female islanders who from the start had driven much of the labour militancy in Toronto's postwar building-cleaning sector—that waged the most militant episode of Portuguese female resistance in Canada.

An analysis of the 1984 strike both underscores key themes related to the politicization of immigrant women who became militant labour unionists and illuminates the social and cultural features that informed their public displays of militancy. The strike again reveals the family breadwinner status of immigrant women, who were often dismissed as dependants or worse, and reveals a good deal more about the role of children and husbands in the women's activism. An assessment of the women's picket-line behaviour and the iconography (images, songs, slogans) of the strike contributes to our understanding of the role of im/migrant and minoritized women in service workers' activism in late-twentieth-century Canada and North America. The 1984 Toronto strike predated the Justice for Janitors campaigns in the United States, and still later, in Canada. In regard to the strikers' actions, however, this strike arguably foreshadowed the "in-your-face" politics particularly of the US-based J4J movement (see below and chapter 7).[2]

Whereas the activism of earlier certification drives occurred mainly behind the scenes, the 1984 strike was a very public event, with many observing and recording the women's words and actions. Together with the union records and retrospective interviews, the newspaper coverage of the strike allows for a more in-depth analysis than did the materials on the certification drives of the earthy militant women from southern Europe. The female militants not only protested with their sharp tongues and aggressive body gestures, but they also animated the picket line with popular dances and ethnocultural and religious rituals, as well as labour songs and chants of international solidarity. And, like Azorean-born Leopoldina Pimentel, who led the Portuguese cleaners' 1975 union drive at the Queen's Park office complex (see chapter 5)—or Michelina Mior, the Italian "Norma Rae" of the 1979 Lancia-Bravo strike by immigrant food workers in Toronto (see below), or Fatima Rocchia, the Portuguese immigrant garment worker who became a leader of the dramatic Montreal garment strike of 1983[3]—the 1984 Portuguese cleaners' strike in Toronto produced labour heroines worth remembering.

In addition, the strike reveals some apparent paradoxes. On the one hand, the strikers openly identified themselves as non-citizen immigrants (as opposed to new Canadians or citizens) who nevertheless had a right to decent wages, basic security, and respect in a country that had long defined itself as an enlightened, liberal, immigrant nation. A decade after Canada adopted multiculturalism as official policy, the women's protests exposed the limits of liberal pluralism even as their picket-line activities revealed a rich hybrid culture that fused together various cultural forms and political ideals. On the other hand, the relationships the women forged with union organizers, community activists, and other allies once again indicate a pattern of acculturation little addressed in studies of immigrant adaptation, namely that grassroots organizations and progressive unions can provide an alternative, more bottom-up, and even more radical path to Canadianization than that offered by middle-class gatekeepers promoting bourgeois models. Ultimately, the women's practice of saying one thing, that they were non-citizens, occurred at the same time as they were being "Canadianized" through their labour activism. More broadly, these relationships speak volumes on the power of alliances and bottom-up organizing in class struggle, something that the union movement and the left repeatedly ignored or denied, preferring instead a "we know best" top-down approach.[4]

"We are women and immigrants but we can fight"

On Strike

In early spring 1984, FASWOC Local 51 was bargaining for the third time with Federated Building Maintenance. Several months after being certified in October 1979 to represent Federated employees at First Canadian Place, the union negotiated a two-year collective agreement covering the period 13 April 1980 to 12 April 1982. A second collective agreement executed in 1982 again covered a two-year term, to 12 April 1984. During the 1984 negotiations, female cleaners were earning an hourly wage of $5.83 (minimum wage was $3.85) and the men, $6.97. Local 51 members wanted an hourly increase of 50 cents each year for two years beginning with the expiry date of the contract. On 3 June, they voted to reject the two-year contract offer from Federated, which included an hourly wage increase of 30 cents effective in January 1985. The next day, 250 cleaners, 90 percent of whom were Azorean women in their thirties and forties with children, went on strike.[5]

The cleaners' actions reflected the fact that, in a period of heavy inflation, Federated's proposed wage increase would have no practical impact on their lives. As elsewhere, many nighttime cleaners were already holding day jobs as factory workers or private cleaning ladies to help make ends meet. During the years 1981–84, Canadians experienced the worst recession since the Great Depression. The construction industry, where most Portuguese men worked, was hit particularly hard, and unemployment levels soared.[6] The pressure on female cleaners at First Canadian Place to sustain their families through an economic crisis increased exponentially. Male janitors like Jose Belchior were also struggling: he and his wife, a cleaner at the Toronto-Dominion Centre, were raising seven children.[7] Predictably, Federated countered with the argument that, with Olympia & York refusing to increase the amount of the cleaning contract, agreeing to a wage increase would mean losing a profit and possibly the contract.[8] An Olympia & York official bluntly told reporters that "the hard fact of life is we have a contract [with Federated] and any wage increases will come out of [the Federated owner's] hide unless we change that contract. If he goes down the tubes, everybody goes down with him."[9]

Significantly, given the degree of female militancy exhibited, most of the striking women were on strike for the first time. They knew that any job action could result in the loss of the cleaning contract and their union, but they were determined to act. Indeed, their decision to strike was made independently of the male janitors, who voted not to go out.

The union leadership did not explicitly recommend striking, on the grounds that the workers might not have jobs to come back to. Instead, voting 96 percent in favour of a strike, the cleaners actively pursued their own agenda.[10]

Various factors explain the strikers' courage and resolve. First, the unwavering demand for higher wages had much to do with the still little known fact that many of these women were the family's main income earner, or in other words, family breadwinners. Many Portuguese immigrant men in Toronto toiled in the construction industry, where even in good economic times jobs were seasonal and risky. While pregnancy or childbirth might interrupt a wife's income earning, most Portuguese women cleaners were lifelong workers whose wage earning continued during a husband's winter slack period. The reality of workplace injuries for husbands in construction made women's income earning all the more necessary. Although not listed as such on the census or other official records, these women were often the family's main or sole income earner.

Many more Torontonians learned such eye-opening details about the women during the 1984 strike, because many strikers (whose average age was forty-four) were profiled in the newspapers across a lengthy six-week period. Reporters like the *Globe and Mail*'s Suzanne Goldenberg were clearly taken with the stories of women such as Margarida Correia. She explained that she would not quit the strike because, with an injured husband who had not worked for nearly four years, she was the sole support to their three small children. Equally compelling was Maria Estrela's story. She was a mother of four young children whose husband had been unable to work for seven years. These women's narratives, which also underscored the precarious position of low-income families, typified the experiences of the female strikers, most of whom were married with children.[11]

These women's activism was rooted in their everyday material realities and familial responsibilities. As migrants, though, those familial obligations extended to families back home (see chapter 3). In their interviews with reporters, some strikers cited their inability to buy and send clothes to struggling families in Portugal as an impetus to fight for higher wages. A second factor informing their activism, then, was their status as transnational subjects helping to sustain family economies stretched across the Atlantic Ocean.[12]

Third, while most of these women were participating in their first strike, many if not all of them already knew a fair bit about job contracts, unions, strikes, and employer intimidation. Since the 1960s, Portuguese building cleaners were being politicized in response to the workplace exploitation and anti-immigrant prejudice they faced. In the 1970s (as chapter 5 detailed), women led successful union drives among janitorial cleaners. Buoyed by the support of radical community workers and feminist activists, they traded the business unionism of an international union for left-leaning Canadian unions. The presence of radical allies is key to understanding immigrant militancy, when the immigrants themselves did not arrive in the host society already radicalized. Like Italians, Portuguese immigrant workers were not consistently militant (or conservative) in locales across the diaspora. But in certain places and at specific historical moments—whether Italians in turn-of-the-twentieth-century Ybor City in Tampa, Florida, with its multiracial but heavily Latino/a and leftist cigar-making workforce; or the Portuguese in late-twentieth-century Toronto—activists influenced by transnational social movements could nudge aggrieved and minoritized workers into embracing labour militancy.[13]

All this suggests that, despite being novices, the Portuguese female cleaners who went on strike at First Canadian Place in 1984 had a good understanding of what that decision entailed. The dense kin networks of information and support among the heavily Azorean janitorial workforces, and their alliances with progressive community workers like the Cleaners' Action activists, had taught them about contracts, workers' rights, and even defying their union leaders.[14] Of course, the overwhelmingly Azorean profile of the strikers makes a mockery of the discriminatory attitudes within mainland Portuguese and Portuguese Canadian society as well as in Canadian society that positioned these women as especially insular and "primitive."[15]

More Than Wages: Critiquing Canadian Myths

Like other non-English-speaking women who arrived in postwar Canada from the rural villages of southern Europe through the family sponsorship system, Portuguese women garnered little attention in official discussions of immigration policy or in public debates over national identity—except as dependants and mothers in need of modernizing. Despite their high rates of employment, officials rarely spoke of the economic contribution of such women to Canada. The women on strike at First Canadian Place were well aware of their vulnerable and inferior position as immigrant women and "low-skilled" workers in the Canadian work-force. Equally strikingly, however, they were prepared to talk about it publicly and to assert their rights and dignity as workers in ways that criticized the liberal myths of the Canadian nation.

In their coverage of the strike, Toronto journalists noted the deep-seated disappointment expressed by women who, having come to Canada prepared to work hard and sacrifice much to attain their visions of a better life, found the cards stacked high against them. Maria Gouveia, forty-eight, told a *Star* reporter, "I came to Canada for a dream [that] I know I must work hard [to] find," but, ten years later, all she had to show for it was a heart attack caused by the stress of working days that stretched from 7:30 a.m. to 2:30 a.m. Another striker, Maria Cruz, articulated the problem well. "I knew I had to work hard here," she said, "but I didn't know" about those in power "trying to exploit the immigrants, especially the immigrant women [who] do not speak English [and thus] have no rights." Using the media's rare interest in them, workers like Gouveia and Cruz were challenging their employer in an effort to attain the goals they had hoped for in migration, including ensuring a better life for their children.[16]

Notwithstanding their political rhetoric of no rights, the strikers knew, too, that, compared with Portugal's (now toppled) dictatorship, Canada allowed workers some space to fight for their rights. Not only did they pursue that opportunity through labour activism, but they also highlighted the importance of the 1984 strike in part by drawing links with the 1974 Carnation Revolution that initiated Portugal's turbulent transition to democracy after decades of authoritarian rule.

Through their actions, the women directly challenged Canada's self-proclaimed liberal image as a benevolent nation of immigrants that offered newcomers the opportunity to work and eventually enjoy the status and entitlements of citizenship. In their communications with the press, as well as with employers and state representatives, the striking women sometimes positioned themselves as non-citizen immigrants being exploited as cheap labour. This, despite the fact that roughly half of them were Canadian citizens (the other half were landed immigrants with certain rights). Disappointment over the fact that citizenship had not protected them from exploitation helps to explain why, but so, too, does the strategic potential of the argument. As president of FASWOC Local 51, Emilia Silva tried to help bring an end to the lengthy strike by invoking a shared immigrant status among the janitorial workers and the wealthy building owners. The Reichmanns were Hungarian Jews who had escaped the Nazi occupation of Austria and later immigrated to Canada. In her letter to Olympia & York president Albert Reichmann, Silva appealed to his newcomer status, saying: "Surely you can understand our situation. We are immigrants to this country. We take pride in our work and we work hard. We are trying to make a better life for our families."[17]

The strikers also well understood that the taunts and insults they endured at the hands of critics and passersby—antics that were also covered in the press—belied the image of Canada as a home for hardworking immigrants. On the picket line, the women faced shouts of "go back to your country" from some tenants of the building and spectators.[18] Far from encouraging a sense of collective belonging to a pluralist Canada, the experience fuelled a sense that laying claim to equal rights on the basis of an acquired citizenship would not succeed. In fighting to gain economic justice in a context where neither the wider society nor the state perceived them as citizens, regardless of their actual status, the strikers instead sometimes appealed to the public's increased awareness of human rights. In such instances, they positioned themselves as poor immigrant women unscrupulously exploited by a rich corporation. [19]

Children and Husbands

Another notable feature of the 1984 strike was the significant presence of the women's children and husbands on the picket line. Like other strikes involving married women, including immigrant and ethnic women, children became very much part of the strike.[20] The press reported on the games of tag played around the buildings. "On most evenings," one reporter noted, "children strut along the sidewalk, carrying signs, slurping popsicles, shouting through a megaphone or generally annoying their mothers."[21] The presence of children on the picket line owed much to the women's inability to pay babysitters at times when their (able-bodied) husbands were at work and could not care for them. But it also served a strategic purpose. As visible reminders that the women had families to support, the children's presence reinforced the justice of their cause. The children, many of them family interpreters, were also important allies who alerted their mothers to strikebreakers trying to sneak into the complex.[22]

More than simply fun and games, the children's actions reflected a knowledge of their parents' difficult lives. The 1978 documentary

142   Cleaning Up

made about Freire-inspired community workers and teachers working among the Portuguese and other inner-city residents of Toronto's west end underscores this point. In a scene featuring one of the elementary schoolteachers seeking to legitimize her students' working-class experiences, the children answer questions about their parents' dangerous jobs. One Portuguese girl explains that her mother's eyesight has been damaged by the constant exposure to the foil wrapped around the frozen TV dinners she gathers from the assembly line and places into delivery boxes. Another, that her father was hospitalized with broken fingers after the large sewer pipe he was installing fell on his hands. Her distraught mother, she adds, spent all night phoning relatives to find out what happened. A Portuguese boy reports that while his stevedore father had thus far escaped injury, three of his co-workers were killed while loading and unloading ships on Lake Ontario. Finally, a Portuguese girl earning $5 a week for sweeping and washing the halls of the apartment complex where she lived had first-hand experience with the labour of cleaning buildings.[23]

Many husbands responded to the union's call to join their striking wives on the picket line. Their presence offered a rebuke to stereotypes of Portuguese women being controlled by patriarchs who kept them at home. Having developed a union consciousness and a commitment to the labour movement through their experience with construction unions, these men supported their wives during their picket-line duties, even though it meant less time spent on domestic and familial responsibilities. Like many Canadian men, these husbands may well have aspired to be breadwinners supporting homemaker wives, though as former farmers, they were accustomed to wives who had worked alongside them in the fields. Moreover, their union experiences did not promote a sense of working-class masculinity that excluded women from unionism, but instead led them to support their wives' activism.[24]

The critical factors at work here were a couple's shared goal of attaining the financial security hoped for in migration and a desire for respect as hardworking immigrants. As Ferreira told a *Star* reporter, "My husband supports me. For sure, he would like me at home, but he knows why I am here and sometimes he comes to walk on the line."[25] Indeed, this husband played a key support role in the strike, shuttling women to and from the picket line. And Maria Cruz reported that her husband, Antonio, was unwavering in his support, telling her to stay strong.[26]

"We are women and immigrants but we can fight"

Picket-Line Bodies and Culture

As with other immigrant strikes, the ethnic identity of the strikers helped shape the character of the picket line at First Canadian Place. The cultural displays of picket-line behaviour and dissent reflected a fascinating blend of Portuguese rituals (including festive rituals and dances), workers' international solidarity, and Catholicism. At times, the picket line was reinforced with the sort of Portuguese band that liberal pluralists would have welcomed as a publicly orchestrated display of multiculturalism. Other times, portable stereos—commonly called "ghetto blasters" because of their popularity among racialized inner-city youth—blared music as women danced, sometimes quite flamboyantly, directly across from an upscale restaurant favoured by politicians and corporate leaders.[27] Many if not most of the women were afraid of getting arrested or assaulted, but they did not adopt the polite manners associated with a bourgeois womanhood. Nor were they constrained by notions of working-class femininity and respectability rooted in an ideology of domesticity. Rather, they acted in strikes as they did in daily life—with an earthy, assertive, and mouthy femininity rooted in the harsh realities and struggles of rural and urban working-class life.[28]

A booklet of songs sung on the picket line illustrates how transplanted homeland cultures influence working-class culture in host societies, while the women's performances put their negotiated hybrid identities as immigrant women, workers, and labour militants on display. The booklet includes English-language songs, but the women sang only those in Portuguese, including a Portuguese translation of "We Shall Not Be Moved," the African American slave spiritual that became a popular union and protest song during the civil rights movement. Predominantly Roman Catholic, the women's equally frequent singing of a Portuguese song to St. John the Baptist, who is celebrated each year on 23 June, attested to the importance of their religious faith to their union activism. So, too, did the declaration of the union activist who informed a reporter, "Jesus gives me strength to continue fighting."[29]

Things could turn decidedly upbeat when the women (and their children) sang and danced extravagantly to a wedding and party favourite, "*Passarinhos a Bailar*" (the Bird Dance). Created by a Swiss accordion player in the late 1950s, the Bird (or Chicken or Duck) Dance was a popular novelty tune in North America from the 1980s onward. The decidedly unfeminine movements to this oompahpah tune involved mimicking a bird or a chicken with five easy steps: moving one's hands to simulate

Cleaning Up

a beak quacking; flapping one's arms; wiggling one's hips or shoulders in a downward motion, as though flapping one's feathers; clapping; and then locking arms with a partner to twirl polka-style. Ferreira recalled the dancing drawing a delighted audience. The building's female tenants, who were generally more sympathetic than the male tenants towards the strikers, would come down to watch the picketers dance. And the strikers enjoyed making the tenants laugh. In Silva's memories of the strike, the *festa* atmosphere of the picket line looms large. The women, she recalled, were "always singing" and most everyone who walked by stopped to watch them sing and dance. Silva's memories, like the wistful tone with which Ferreira remembered the dance interludes being "a lot of fun," suggest that the shared laughter among picketers and tenants offered a welcome relief from the tensions.[30]

The picketers also engaged in acts of mischief. In symbolic reference to the garbage they cleaned up, the women shredded newspapers and scattered the pieces about. They threw raw eggs at the main building and watched as the yolk splattered down the wall. Mothers even brought Magic Markers so their children could write and draw on the building's marble floors and walls. Making First Canadian Place look dirty was an act of defiance intended to covey the sullied public image of the owners and employers who put profits before people. The stunts also called attention to the vital role these women played in keeping the premises clean.[31]

Just as quickly, the picketers could turn overtly political, expressing their commitment to a people's politics from below by embracing the slogans of the era's international solidarity movements. With raised fists and thrusting arms, the women frequently chanted the Latin American rallying cry: "*O povo, unido, jamais será vencido*" ("The people, united, will never be defeated").[32] Shouting a slogan that originally emerged out of the Chilean resistance against the Pinochet dictatorship was neither merely coincidental nor gratuitous, for it had also become the central rallying call of the Portuguese Revolution in 1974. In repeatedly chanting it, the women and their families were drawing a symbolic link between the struggle for democracy in their homeland and the cleaners' struggle for justice in their hostland. Chanting the slogan arguably offered, as well, a nod to international solidarity.[33]

More than simply performative acts intended to gain public attention, these ethnocultural expressions of militancy and solidarity offered a way of claiming a political identity. In this context, the women's "expressive acts" (to use historian Ian Radforth's term for popular demonstrations and celebrations in the streets) served to distinguish the Portuguese strikers from Anglo-Canadian society, even as the strike confirmed that the cleaners had much in common with other working-class women.[34] The overlapping bonds of ethnic, class, and gender solidarity reinforced the cohesiveness of the mainly Portuguese strikers, the women's multiple identities fuelling a particular form of radicalism.

Overall, though, the strikers' militancy marked the strike as exceptional for this group of immigrant women, who, like other southern European women, were assumed to be submissive before husbands and employers alike. Portuguese women, as earlier chapters document, did engage in everyday acts of resistance at home (such as daytime house cleaners not disclosing the full amount of their payment for cleaning private homes) and at work (as when private cleaners exerted control over the labour process). The 1974 wildcat strike of Portuguese office cleaners at the TD Centre publicly exposed the women's growing militancy, however briefly. The ten-week strike by 260 members of Local 530 of the Canadian Food and Allied Workers Union against the Lancia-Bravo factory in Toronto's west end did the same for the (mostly) Italian and (fewer) Portuguese women who, with their immigrant union brothers, won wage increases, improved benefits, and the compulsory dues checkoff. (The checkoff offered a form of union security by requiring all workers, even non-union members, who benefited from a collective agreement to pay union dues.) Much like Idalina Azevedo, Azorean leader of the 1974 wildcat strike, Michelina Mior, the Italian immigrant woman who became "chief whip of the picket lines" at the Lancia-Bravo pasta-and-sauce-making plant, had gone from a greenhorn worker who knew nothing about unions to defiant organizer and strike leader.[35]

Still, the pronounced public militancy and violence on display during this overwhelmingly Portuguese immigrant women's strike more dramatically challenged Canadian perceptions of how Portuguese women, and Azorean women in particular, would act. The union itself had doubted the women's ability to remain steadfast in the face of a lengthy strike. A non-Portuguese FASWOC representative, Isabel Saez, publicly admitted that "these women are stronger than any of us thought they would be."[36] In defying the stereotype of the passive Portuguese cleaner, the women enlarged the definition of who could belong to an active and militant working class. In that regard, they redefined the political and made themselves public, militant, female subjects.

146 Cleaning Up

Some journalists likened the strike to a David-and-Goliath struggle, where normally "docile women, keepers of home and hearth" were transformed into "a bitter, vociferous group intent on fighting their employers." One headline declared: "Picketing Cleaners Tackle Bay St. Giant." Another, "Cleaning Ladies Fight Goliath," and still another, "Cleaning Women Battle Corporate Giant." Although steeped in problematic portraits of housebound wives emerging from the shadows, such media coverage helped to elicit public sympathy for the strikers by focusing on the gross disparities of wealth in Canadian society.[37] In positioning the strike as a battle between "good" (hardworking women) and "bad" (rich capitalists and profit-hungry employers), the biblical analogy endowed the strike with a social justice mandate.

Fury Unfurled

The picket line, of course, can be a site of tensions as well as solidarity. A key source of conflict was related to the strikers' biggest challenge: blocking the dozen street-level entrances and additional underground entrances to First Canadian Place. From the start, tensions flared between strikers and those wanting to cross the picket line. On the second day, a striker trying to prevent the entry of a delivery truck was arrested. When two husbands intervened, they, too, were arrested and charged with assaulting a police officer.[38]

Tensions mounted further when the police began to help scabs (replacement workers) cross the picket line. Many of them were students referred by the Canada Employment Centre for Students, a federally run agency. Their fury unfurled, the picketers shouted at the youths, with some using swear words such as *filho da puta* (son of a bitch) to express their anger. According to FASWOC representative Wendy Iler, the union representatives ignored the swearing mainly because they figured that most of the onlookers would not have understood the women's words. Even so, the fierce tone, high-pitched voices, and coarse language used to scold, taunt, and occasionally threaten the strikebreakers reflected the women's membership in the rough plebian culture of *o povo*, the struggling lower classes.[39] Speaking in blunt English, an angry Maria Serafin was "neither ladylike nor deferential" when she bluntly instructed the reporters covering the students' arrival, "Tell them not to take my job because I have a family to feed."[40]

On 3 June, a few days after the arrival of the first batch of student strikebreakers, three female strikers stationed at the tunnels were assaulted by a private security guard escorting more strikebreakers past their picket line. Suffering from bruises and scratches and one sprained hand, the women received medical attention at Toronto General Hospital. In response to the incident, the union suspended the pickets and called a meeting in order to calm down the furious women. But as a taxi containing scabs pulled up, the women rushed the car, pounding on it with their hands and shouting loudly. Later, the police arrested striker Maria Medeiros for hitting a male supervisor from Federated Building Maintenance with her umbrella. Such incidents not only scared and angered the strikers, but also alerted them to the ugly truth that they were fighting the government as well as Olympia & York and Federated. Incensed over the state collusion, through the recruitment and police protection of the strikebreakers, the women viewed their aggressive actions as fully justified. In short, state-sanctioned actions that aided corporate owners and employers at their expense deepened the women's militancy.[41]

The striking women's anger was again on full display when, on 13 June, a group of about ten co-workers were escorted across the picket line to return to work. Some of the women had brought older children to protect them from the shouting and shoving by cleaners committed to the strike. One shoving match ended with an arrest and four strikers being sent to hospital with injuries. In a tone that conveyed the strikers' resentment over this challenge to their solidarity as well as a sense of rough-and-tough justice, striker Maria Feitor declared, "We pushed those ladies to the outside, we don't want them working here."[42]

A male union representative tried to downplay the divisions in the ranks by telling reporters that the women who had crossed the line did so "under pressure from husbands to give up the strike and return to the kitchen in the Portuguese tradition." But he missed an obvious point. The women were returning not to their kitchens but to their jobs. Women's paid work was not the problem. Some husbands may have objected to a wife being associated with a highly publicized and occasionally violent picket line. Other husbands might have considered it an embarrassment to the Portuguese community, though the elites were utterly indifferent to working-class or Azorean immigrants. Even so, a woman's decision to quit the strike had far less to do with a husband's notion of an obedient wife or respectable community member than with an immediate need for money. Acutely aware that the loss of their regular paycheque was causing their family hardship, these women were also acting on the fear that losing the strike would mean being fired.[43]

148   Cleaning Up

Such fears were in fact widespread, and yet most of the Portuguese strikers stood firm. The women's defiance, and the physicality of how they expressed it—by shouting and swearing, raising their fists, thrusting their arms, pushing and shoving, and even kicking or slapping the strikebreakers—underscores a critical point raised in chapter 5. In contrast to what some scholars have found with respect to Anglo-Canadian women workers' discomfort over the evident contradiction between prevailing norms of feminine propriety and their participation in "unruly" street politics and picket lines, hegemonic gender norms of the polite, demure, and accommodating woman did not dampen the militancy of this group of immigrant female strikers.[44] A deep-seated sense of female honour framed the Portuguese female strikers' desire for respect and dignity in the workplace, but as in other strikes involving non-Anglo immigrant and ethnic women, they were not constrained by dominant notions of bourgeois femininity or by working-class ideals of female domesticity. Rather, an "in-your-face" defiance, physicality, salty language, and activism were an integral part of these working women's immigrant experience in Canada.[45]

Solidarity and Victory

With hard-fought gains often undermined by the contracting-out system and other practices, the Portuguese cleaning woman became a symbol of the new era of assaults by big business and the state on the working class (see chapter 7). This helps to explain the support the strikers received from the labour and feminist movements and the NDP; indeed, the groups themselves reflected overlapping networks among labour, feminist, and socialist or social democratic activists.

Although the strikers belonged to a smaller CCU union, members of large international unions affiliated with the Canadian Labour Congress, such as the United Auto Workers, joined their picket line. So, too, did the Canadian Union of Postal Workers, including its president Jean-Claude Parrot. Other CCU members as well as CUPE locals supported the strike as well. The presence on the picket line of many Portuguese cleaners from the TD Centre, and who were now CUPE members, helped forge a wider solidarity among Toronto's downtown cleaners.

Feminist support came from leftist groups like the International Women's Day Committee, which decried the women's "poverty wages" as well as the employer's "dirty tricks" and the misuse of students "desperate for work" as scabs during the strike.[46] Also there in solidarity was

Organized Working Women, an independent organization of unionized women that supported women's struggles for equality within their workplaces and unions as well as in the wider labour movement and broader society. An issue of their newspaper, *Union Woman*, featured a group of the strikers wearing their FASWOC on Strike posters as they walked the line. The Red Berets, a socialist feminist group that sang at feminist and labour demonstrations, as well as singer Arlene Mantle, supported the tenacious strikers.[47] Susan Howlett, a Red Beret and one-time factory worker who had been involved in the successful campaign by the Canadian Textile and Chemical Union (a CCU union) to organize McGregor Socks, wrote a song about the cleaners. Having first learned about the strike through CTCU organizer Laurell Ritchie, Howlett sang her song at a rally in support of the strike:[48]

If you come to King & Bay
At the end of the day,
You'll see the cleaners striking,
Demanding better pay

Five-eighty-three an hour
Doesn't go too far these days
Fifty cents an hour,
We're asking for a raise

We'll fight, fight, fight,
Take a stand, take a stand,
We'll strike, strike, strike,
'til we win

Policemen on horses
Came down to help the scabs
To "serve and protect" the rich
The poor don't have a chance

Sixteen doors and tunnels
To First Canadian Place
Picket signs spread all around
We've got to cover ground

We clean the floors of Stock Exchange
Where money's just a game
For us it's such a struggle
Just to earn a living wage

This is not a summer job .
It's all that we have
Students won't you listen
Don't go working as a scab[49]

Prominent politicians, particularly those with ties to the NDP, also supported the cleaners. High-profile NDP members of the Ontario Legislature such as Bob Rae and Dan Heap, a long-time supporter of Portuguese cleaners (see chapter 5), joined the women on the picket line.[50]

By contrast, the leaders and journalists of the mainstream Portuguese community were absent from and silent about the strike, though the Portuguese Canadian Democratic Association and the Portuguese Pastoral Council offered their support.[51] The scant evidence indicating a gendered response to the strike among the building's tenants includes a *Toronto Star* reporter's interview with some of them. Two women, a secretary and an insurance claims consultant, sympathized with the strikers. Perhaps reflecting on their own experience, one of them argued that the cleaners "should get more" money because "women shouldn't be underpaid." Conversely, a male lawyer thought the current wage rate "reasonable" for cleaners. Calling scab labour a "fabulous" thing, the far better paid head of Price Waterhouse complimented the strikebreakers as people who actually want to do the work. Corporate leaders and elite law firms were hardly going to support the strikers. But as women who experienced discrimination in the workplace, some of the female tenants and staff expressed some sympathy for the strikers.[52]

Bolstered by the support it did receive from various circles, FASWOC sought to pressure Olympia & York into settling the strike by getting it to acknowledge its role as an employer that effectively controlled Federated's bargaining position. A letter from the Portuguese priests may have tested the conscience of Albert Reichmann, a devout man, by asking him "to contribute to resolution through open dialogue, according to the principles of justice and good faith."[53] The NDP caucus at City Hall also wrote Olympia & York, citing the "ridiculous" offer of a 30-cent

"We are women and immigrants but we can fight"

A woman on the picket line of the First Canadian Place strike in 1984 looks straight ahead into the camera. Her image is captured in the mural unveiled by Lisbon artist Vhils in Toronto's Little Portugal, October 2021.
York University Libraries, Clara Thomas Archives & Special Collections, Canadian Auto Workers Union Local 40 fonds, ASC07886.

raise, and admonishing the company for risking its reputation "to save a little bit of money on the backs of its hardworking cleaning staff."[54] Aware that any acknowledgement of its role in the dispute would be bad for business, the corporation denied any responsibility.[55] The union tried to force the issue by issuing a claim before the OLRB that Olympia & York Developments qualified as a related employer under the Ontario Labour Relations Act on the grounds that its policies determined wages and that it exercised some control over Federated staff.[56] As it turned out, Olympia & York did finally come to the bargaining table at the last minute, which helped to settle the strike.

Labour Heroines

After six weeks on strike, the cleaners accepted Federated's new offer of a 35-cent hourly increase retroactive to when the old contract expired (13 April), and a further 25-cent increase in the second year of the agreement. In total, a 60-cent increase. In addition, the sick leave concessions that the employer had demanded in mid-strike bargaining were dropped,

The picket line during the First Canadian Place strike in June–July 1984 was often boisterous, but this image captures a quiet moment as a boy holding what appears to be a juice box guards a pile of strikers' belongings in front of the building's marbled lobby. His T-shirt reads: "Inside this T-shirt is one terrific kid."
York University Libraries, Clara Thomas Archives & Special Collections, Canadian Auto Workers Union Local 40 fonds, ASC61151.

and the five strikers who had been fired over strike incidents returned to work.

Having accepted the contract, the victorious cleaners chanted "*O povo, unido, jamais será vencido.*" Shouting into her megaphone, Local 51 president Silva told the jubilant crowd: "We have proven to everyone that

The children who accompanied their mothers on various picket lines were often seen shouting into a megaphone, defacing a building with (washable) markers, dancing, or shouting at strikebreakers. But like the striker captured here in mid-stride on the First Canadian Place picket line in 1984, mothers also had to deal with children who got tired, upset, or angry. York University Libraries, Clara Thomas Archives & Special Collections, Canadian Auto Workers Union Local 40 fonds, ASC61145.

NDP MP Dan Heap joins the overwhelmingly female picket line during the strike by FASWOC (Food and Service Workers of Canada) at First Canadian Place in 1984. York University Libraries, Clara Thomas Archives & Special Collections, Canadian Auto Workers Union Local 40 fonds, ASC61144.

FASWOC striker Lucia Ferreira takes time from her kitchen duties to address the crowd during the party to celebrate the victory at First Canadian Place in July 1984. Children, mostly girls, are gathered around the stage, just as they joined their mothers on the picket line during the strike.
York University Libraries, Clara Thomas Archives & Special Collections, Canadian Auto Workers Union Local 40 fonds, ASC61149.

we have courage. We proved to Canada and to Olympia & York that we are women and we are immigrants but we can fight." And then, noted FASWOC representative Iler, "the workers pushed back the chairs [in the room] and danced in front of the TV cameras."[57]

More than four hundred people attended the victory party held in Casa do Benfica, a Portuguese hall named after a popular Portuguese soccer team. In line with Portuguese as well as Canadian gender patterns, the women cooked the five-course meal and did the clean-up. Dressed in their nicest dresses with aprons overtop, they ran back and forth between the kitchen where they prepared the food, the stage where they gave speeches, and the dance floor. As on the picket line, the children participated in the celebrations. Dressed in their best Sunday outfits, a group of them told the crowd: "Us children have helped our mothers during the strike. We have stopped cars, even ladies, from going into the office building." Some cleaners defied the law and brought their homemade wine to the victory *festa*. A large cake was decorated with the familiar ode to the power of the people. And people danced until three in the morning to the music of Nazaré Praia Disc Jockey, named after Nazareth Beach, in Portugal.

The Portuguese immigrant female cleaners accomplished an immense feat by winning a strike against a major corporation, thus belying the notion that immigrant women were simply passive victims of an exploitative industrial-capitalist economy. In recalling the strike years later, feminist union leader Laurell Ritchie was eloquent in her appraisal of the strikers. "These were feisty, hard-headed women," she noted, "and quite sophisticated in their political strategies." Ritchie added, "They had to be—given the rough and tumble of the industry they worked in. Many people foolishly underestimated them."[58]

The portrait of feisty, wilful and politically sharp immigrant women cleaners certainly applies to leaders such as Silva, FASWOC Local 51 president, and Ferreira, a union representative. However ambiguous the legacy of their service sector activism, they, and others, deserve recognition as labour heroines. The women's pride in having won hard-fought-for rights lingers with the cleaners to the present day. A quarter of a century later, Ferreira proudly noted that the women still talk about the strike.[59] At the unveiling of the mural celebrating Cleaners' Action in Toronto's Little Portugal in October 2021, the mainstream community leaders—who had earlier ignored the women's impact on the cleaning industry and its unions—heaped praise on the militant women being honoured. But the event also triggered an outpouring of memories among the striking women and other cleaners who, thirty-seven years after that strike, are still with us (see epilogue).

The enormous and enduring impact of the strike in the lives of the women is also evident in the permanent casting out of the women who returned to work. In the eyes of those who endured a six-week strike, the women who crossed the picket line are forever marked as traitors. At the victory party, Silva identified the "enemies" by name. An unsigned poem in the union records dubs them *desgraçadas* (disgraces) and Judases. A quarter century after the strike, Ferreira grew visibly upset as she recalled what she considered these women's deep betrayal of their campaign for respect, dignity, and a better life.[60]

And Yet

For all of its importance, the 1984 strike did not secure long-term rights and security for immigrant cleaners. Short-term gains were outstripped by long-term losses. As part of the strike settlement, Federated Building

Maintenance agreed to reinstate the five fired workers. The courts' relatively lenient position towards the strikers and the one husband facing criminal charges for picket-line violence reflected a certain sympathy towards non-English-speaking workers who were confused about what constituted legal activity during a strike and who did not understand the police who approached them. But the workers facing charges were also admonished to learn the laws of their new home.[61]

Moreover, Olympia & York exacted its revenge on the workers two years later. By February 1986, the 250 cleaners at First Canadian Place were in danger of losing their jobs because Olympia & York was putting the cleaning contract up for tender just when the collective agreement was set to expire. A delegation from FASWOC met with Liberal Ontario premier David Peterson and labour minister Bill Wrye to introduce successor rights legislation, but were unsuccessful. The point of such labour code provisions was to ensure that a union's collective agreement with one employer (such as a cleaning contractor) would carry over to another employer. In such a scenario, the successor employer would be responsible for meeting the terms of the collective agreement their predecessor signed with the union until its term expired.[62] In 1992, under the NDP provincial government, successor rights for contract cleaners were incorporated into changes to the labour law through Bill 40. A few years later, Bill 7, the first major piece of legislation introduced under the "open-for-business" Progressive Conservative Mike Harris government, eliminated successor rights. Since then, successor rights in the building services sector in Ontario have contracted and expanded (see chapter 7).

As for the First Canadian Place cleaners who had spearheaded the six-week strike, they accepted Federated's 1986 offer of a 35-cent pay raise, an increased workload, and fewer working hours on the grounds that, by allowing their employer to remain competitive for the Olympia & York contract, they could keep their jobs and the collective agreement.[63] The contract was renewed on the backs of female cleaners forced to accept lower wages and give up other gains made during the strike. The language barrier would keep all but a few Portuguese women from assuming high-level leadership posts in their unions. Outside the big downtown buildings, many Portuguese women continued to toil in smaller workplaces untouched by unions.

In addition, the 1990s saw new unions and cleaning companies enter the industry. The Labourers' International Union of North America (LiUNA) Local 183, which represented many cleaners' husbands in construction unions, successfully raided First Canadian Place in 1990. Like the SEIU before them, LiUNA would attract heavy criticism for "sweetheart" deals with cleaning contractors. In the meantime, SEIU revitalized itself through the Justice for Janitors campaign, which included large numbers of women. As sociologist Ruth Milkman notes, the US-based campaign arrived in Los Angeles in 1988 following some modest successes in smaller American cities, most notably Denver, and then later spread to other parts of the United States.[64] Arguably, the campaign did not really take off in Canada until 2007 in Toronto (and Ontario).[65]

There are some key differences between the Portuguese cleaners' union drives and strikes in 1970s and early 1980s Toronto and the later J4J campaigns, the first dramatic victory of which was led by the SEIU Local 399 in Los Angeles in 1990. For one thing, the 1984 Toronto strike, like the earlier union drives, emerged initially out of the bottom-up activism of rank-and-file immigrant workers without a union or radical background, whereas the SEIU's J4J campaign initially reflected the union's top-down organizing strategies, though already radicalized Latino/a immigrant workers later played a key role in mobilizing rank-and-file activism. For another, the SEIU's J4J strategy of unleashing a wave of strikes across the building-cleaning industry in LA differed from the pre-2007 Toronto pattern of focusing on one specific workplace.

But there were also certain similarities, including the use of "in-your-face" tactics that attracted media and public attention. In some respects, the physicality and boisterousness of what Ritchie called the "feisty," "hard-headed," and quite politically sophisticated Portuguese women cleaners during the 1984 strike at First Canadian Place—like the mix of festive, political, ethnocultural, familial, and theatrical elements that shaped the picket line—paralleled, even foreshadowed, the J4J campaigns in the United States. By this we mean their use of guerilla street theatre, such as targeting and embarrassing employers and politicians dining in their favourite restaurant or country club, and large street demonstrations that included families in order to attract attention and support. As in 1970s and early 1980s Toronto, the later J4J campaigns involved an active outreach to sympathetic political allies and progressive community organizations. Again, though, the initial outreach in Toronto was from the bottom up (the women who turned to St. Christopher House workers to support them in their labour struggles) rather than the top down (the union leadership.)[66]

158   Cleaning Up

Conclusion

The cleaners' strike at First Canadian Place in 1984 reveals much about the position of immigrant women within the Canadian postwar economy, labour movement, and neoliberal state. Portuguese women were crucial to the expansion of the service sector in these years, even transforming its workforce. Yet, despite rhetoric to the contrary, these formally uneducated immigrant women became militant participants in the labour movement at a time when labour faced increasing limits on workers' power. Class, gender, and ethnic realities as well as identities converged to drive this group of workers to assert their commonalities with other workers, as well as their distinct concerns as ethnic workers. By taking protest to the street in the heart of Toronto's financial district, and by attracting plenty of sympathetic press attention, the women successfully brought their usually "invisible" labour and lives into the public realm. Or put another way, they became political, even radical, subjects. At the same time, their presence reinforced a gender and ethnically stratified workforce that was low paid and toiled under inferior conditions. These conditions were supported by state laws that limited the women's ability to unionize and to retain their unions through the contracting-out process. One of the biggest challenges they faced—and bravely took on—was fighting the contracting-out process and lobbying for successor rights.

Chapter 7

Fighting Contracting Out
in the Workplace and Political Arena

My name is Lino Medeiros, I am 10 years old. Please let my mom have her job. My dad had an accident and he cannot work so please let her keep her job, if you don't know who I am talking about, is Maria J. Medeiros. Please let her keep her job, you know that I love my mom and she loves me so don't let her lose her job now. When we are big we are going to take care of her but now she takes care of us. Don't let her lose her job. Your friend, Lino.[1]

Lino's letter offers yet another poignant example of how aware the children of Toronto's Portuguese immigrant cleaners were of their mothers' critical wage earning but difficult labouring lives. It was included in a 1985 petition addressed to powerful men: Prime Minister Brian Mulroney and Ontario premier Frank Miller, as well as Bernard Ghert, president and CEO of the Bronfman-owned Cadillac Fairview Corporation, and Richard Thomson, chair and CEO of Toronto-Dominion Bank. The signatories were the mostly Portuguese female cleaners in danger of losing their jobs at Toronto-Dominion Centre, as building owner Cadillac Fairview put the cleaning contract up for tender for the first time since the complex opened in 1967. Like Lino, they wanted Cadillac Fairview to renew its contract with Modern Building Cleaning, which employed 260 cleaners, because not doing so would surely mean widespread layoffs.

Unmoved by such appeals, Ghert curtly replied that his "responsibility" and "obligation" was "to ensure that the cleaning costs borne by the tenants of the TD Centre were in fact competitive."[2] His decision to tender the contract sparked a crisis in hundreds of families who feared losing crucial incomes. The women shouldered the heaviest burden, however, because, like Lino's mother, many of them were the family breadwinner.

In the end, the TD complex was divided between two contracts, one with Modern and the other with Empire Building Maintenance. The former retained some of their cleaners; the latter hired some of the others, but at lower wages and with loss of benefits.

Between 1975 and 1995, the Portuguese immigrants who dominated the janitorial staff of Toronto's major office buildings confronted and protested the nefarious neoliberal practice of contracting out cleaning services in the building services sector. They lobbied in favour of reforms to the labour law that would provide better protection for their jobs, their unions, and other hard-fought gains. Together with a loose coalition of allies, some better resourced than others, these workers sought to raise public awareness and sympathy about the adverse effects of this cost-cutting practice on them and their families. They pressured the provincial government to limit the odious practice and to ensure successor rights—the carryover of collective agreement provisions from one employer to another—in labour law.

Building cleaners protested the contracting-out practice in both public spaces (such as provincial and municipal government buildings) and private business spaces. While men also participated, women cleaners were at the forefront of the anti-contracting-out movement largely because they were the most vulnerable to its effects. Fighting the practice through petitions and other means constituted an important aspect of their labour activism, and progressive community workers and feminist activists again provided critical support. Perhaps to a greater degree than union drives and strikes, however, anti-contracting-out activism took these women beyond the workplace and into the formal political realm. Particularly noteworthy was their success in enlisting the active support of concerned NDP politicians, whose interest, in turn, in gaining the support of the Portuguese community also explains their involvement. An exploration of cleaners' activism against contracting out sheds light not only on how a state increasingly committed to a pro-business neoliberal approach "acted upon" these immigrant women, but also how the women "acted back" in an attempt to shape state policy. In doing so, they carved out a public and political place for themselves in Canada's wealthiest city.[3]

Contracting Out

By 1975, contracting out had clearly emerged as one of the strategies by which big capital and the state would restructure economic relations and undermine workers' collective power in the emerging neoliberal era. The practice was not new, especially with respect to tendering contracts for the cleaning and maintenance of public buildings, but in the mid-1970s, the process accelerated, spreading quickly to sectors such as health care and the civil service. It was also an uneven process: governments at every level looked to downsize and reduce budgets, while the lucrative contracts offered to the private sector were considered a stimulus to the larger economy.[4]

Profit-driven companies contracted out the cleaning of their private buildings for various reasons. For example, building owners could take some workers out of the coverage of existing collective agreements by turning to non-unionized cleaning contractors that paid much lower wages and so cost less. Employers could escape state policies designed to promote equity and fairness (such as pay equity) and abdicate work-related responsibilities. Contract workers, for example, did not qualify for coverage under employer-based benefits, and even under some government-mandated social insurance programs (such as unemployment insurance, if their hours and wages were too low).[5] Notwithstanding their public status, budget-conscious government departments were equally enamoured with the practice. Contracting out services and other non-standard forms of work increased sharply in the 1980s and 1990s, as both private and public employers increasingly adopted "flexibility-enhancing" strategies.

In the late 1970s, some of the unions, alarmed by the transformation of more secure jobs into insecure contracts, particularly in the public sector, tried to fight back. Large public sector unions such as the Canadian Union of Public Employees urged their thousands of members across Canada to introduce clauses in collective agreements to restrict employers from contracting out jobs. A 1978 CUPE publication noted that "hardly a week passes without one of our locals"—whether in food preparation, laundries, hospital cleaning, garbage collection, data processing, or some other sector—"being forced to prepare a brief, organize a demonstration, launch a PR campaign, or conduct a strike to stop contracting out."[6] As hospital and long-term care facility cleaning jobs were contracted out, unions like the Hospital Employees' Union faced the same challenge.[7] Also an important player in the health care industry, the Service Employees International Union grew more vocal in its opposition to the privatization of health care services, which adversely affected nurses' aides and home-based nursing jobs. SEIU did not overtly protest

Fighting Contracting Out in the Workplace 163

the practice of contracting out in the building-cleaning sector, where it had a much longer history, although it did step up its efforts to protect its most important membership base, namely janitorial workers, as they became increasingly targeted for such cost-cutting strategies.[8]

Certainly, the anti-contracting-out stance of unions and other labour bodies was mainly about protecting their members' jobs and unions and maintaining favourable working conditions. There are also other arguments to be made against the now ubiquitous practice, including that it adversely affects taxpayers and the larger community. In the long run, profit-driven private contractors drive up the costs of these services, especially as some of those contractors become more powerful. And since contract employees tend to be low paid and transitory, the quality of their services invariably declines. Furthermore, the practice breeds corruption in the form of overruns, overcharges, and kickbacks to public officials with power to determine which business gets a contract.

In addition, because contracting out reduces workers' standard of living through lower wages and limited or no benefits, there are costs to the welfare state and thus on taxpayers: injured workers effectively "increase costs" for health care or workers' compensation (see chapter 3), and children who forgo education and training in order to start earning an income may be trapped in low-wage work, creating a vicious cycle. On social justice grounds, labour leaders stressed that those most adversely affected by the practice were the already most disadvantaged groups— women and minoritized workers. In practice, though, unions could do little to stop the spread of contracting out across public and private buildings in Canada.[9]

Building Cleaning

In both the public and private sectors of the building services industry, major building owners and developers could effectively cut costs and increase profits by unloading the cleaning service onto private contractors. The low profit margins fuelled the fierce competition between contractors, whose chances of winning or losing a bid hinged on that most costly item—wages. Since contract cleaners had no successor rights, any gains the workers made from collective bargaining were easily lost with the tendering of new contracts. Certain workers in the primary labour market were protected by strong collective bargaining legislation. By contrast, secondary-tier workers like building cleaners fell under the minimum standards legislation, and the decline in such standards resulted in "sweatshop conditions" for cleaners. Further, when the cleaners at a building were effectively re-employed by a successful bidder on a contract, they were considered "new" employees under the Employment Standards Act for the purposes of wages and benefits and entitlements such as payments for vacation, termination, severance, public holidays, and pregnancy leave.[10]

The collective bargaining model in Ontario is premised on an individual workplace rather than a sectoral or regional level, and so it favours the large workforce concentrated in one place. The model has proven far less useful in creating bargaining units strong enough to survive in small workplaces. Or in facilitating union efforts to organize workers who move frequently among employers (or whose employers frequently change in one workplace) within a sector, such as the building-cleaning industry. Unlike a factory owner, the service contractor is not attached to a particular site of operation, making it difficult to identify the employer and bargaining unit. But only the contractor is defined as the "employer," and not the building owners, even though they largely determine the cleaners' wages and working conditions by defining the price and terms of the contract. Freed of employer obligations under the Labour Relations Act, building owners are keen to subcontract services to the lowest bidder.[11]

In the mid-1970s, the SEIU did try to organize cleaning contractors in Toronto at a sectoral level in order to set minimum guidelines for the industry. In keeping with its business unionism, SEIU Local 204 president Albert Hearn approached contractors reportedly receptive to the idea that "some form of unionism" could "eliminate the cutthroat bidding" by setting a standard price for their services that, in turn, would establish standard wages in the industry. Contractors could ensure labour peace in exchange for union recognition and wage concessions. When Hearn's proposal that Toronto office buildings over twenty-five floors be unionized and that a building owners' association deal with union contracts received support from various contractors and even the presidents of TD Bank and Bank of Montreal, SEIU negotiated directly with contractors with little to no input from workers. Criticism came from within the SEIU, whose international president George Hardy accused the contractors of using the union to attain an illegal outcome, "setting price levels so as to eliminate competition." A related concern, it appears, was that SEIU was complicit in setting wage levels in the industry too low. In the end, the proposal failed, and intense competition and low wages continued to prevail.[12]

The SEIU did enjoy some success in lobbying for minimum guidelines for the building-cleaning industry in the United States and Quebec. In the US, the Service Contract Act (1965) required government agencies to guarantee the prevailing level of wages and benefits as well as working conditions on federal service contracts. A 1972 amendment required new contractors to respect wage rates based on a preceding contractor's collective bargaining agreement (which might be higher than the minimum guidelines), even when not hiring the same workers. Four years later, the coverage was extended to white-collar workers.[13]

Following an earlier breakthrough, SEIU Local 298 negotiated a master contract with the Quebec government in 1975 that outlined the minimum wages, hours, and working conditions of fifteen thousand cleaners employed in public buildings in the Montreal area.[14] Like the US Service Contract Act, the agreement covered both union and non-union employees. Union members did, however, enjoy additional benefits negotiated in their collective agreements, such as a grievance procedure, maternity benefits, and more holidays.[15] This master agreement set wages higher than in Ontario, where building cleaners earned minimum wage.[16]

The Ontario Labour Relations Act was inadequate to meet the needs of a workforce made increasingly insecure as a result of new neoliberal economic policies. The restrictions on the ability of contract workers to retain their unions through the contracting-out process fit with the larger effort of the Canadian state to undermine workers' collective power. Ontario governments, both Progressive Conservative and Liberal, have historically been unresponsive to calls for amendments to the Labour Relations Act that would ensure successor rights.

Contracting-Out Crisis, Queen's Park, 1975

Just as the cleaners' successful union campaign at the Queen's Park office complex in 1975 constituted labour activism (see chapter 5), so, too, did their resistance to contracting out. Here, the main player was the Property Management Branch of the Ministry of Government Services, which arranged for janitorial services in thirty-three Ontario government buildings in Toronto. Pleased that their first foray into subcontracting the cleaning of a government building (Frost Building South in 1965) had reduced the bill by one-half, the ministry continued the practice. By 1976, twenty-eight (or close to 85 percent) of their buildings were

166   Cleaning Up

being cleaned by fourteen contractors from the private sector. Ministry people might justify their use of subcontracting on the grounds of efficiency, especially in small office locations, but the monetary savings were the chief concern. After comparing the relative costs of hiring contract cleaners (43 cents per square foot per year) and directly employing in-house staff ($1.55), a government report stated the obvious: "It is far more economical to have janitorial work carried out by contract."[17]

The contracting-out crisis experienced by the mostly female Portuguese immigrants hired to clean the offices at Queen's Park in 1975 offered an early tough lesson in capitalist exploitation in the industry (see chapter 5). In response to the newly unionized cleaners' demand for higher wages, Modern Building Cleaning cancelled its contract with the Ministry of Government Services, the workers were laid off, and the ministry awarded the contract to another cleaning company with a lower bid (based on lower wages for cleaners). The episode also signalled the beginning of a larger public awareness of the plight of building cleaners and contract workers in general. In this and later episodes, the Portuguese cleaning woman was invoked as the canary in the ever-deepening coal mine of neoliberalism. The vulnerabilities and precarity of office cleaners exposed by these episodes accurately warned of the coming of even greater assaults on the working class by big business and the state. In press reports and political debates on the contracting-out crisis at Queen's Park, Portuguese immigrant women were consistently identified as the main victims of these unfair labour practices.

These women were also the impetus behind the fight for higher wages and resisting the contracting-out policy at Queen's Park. But it was their allies—activists like feminist lawyer Michelle Swenarchuk and St. Christopher House worker Sidney Pratt—who helped to bring their struggle to a larger audience. As chapter 4 details, Cleaners' Action emerged out of the crisis. By building links to unions, women's and community groups, the press, and politicians, the workers' supporters brought larger awareness to their plight. But aware of the disinterest of the Portuguese community's male leaders, the workers did not turn to them for help in their struggle.[18]

The workers' allies made a calculated decision to involve the media in this labour struggle. They contacted journalists and held press conferences meant to embarrass and pressure the provincial Progressive Conservative government of Bill Davis, then in the midst of an election campaign that saw the NDP record some concrete gains, to act in the

Fighting Contracting Out in the Workplace 167

cleaners' interest.[19] Holding press conferences to call attention to the huge gap between the wealthy and influential property owners (including government), and the impoverished and powerlessness workers who cleaned their buildings, would become a mainstay of the campaign of Justice for Janitors in the United States in the 1980s and early 1990s. Aware that imposing direct pressure on cleaning contractors was ineffective because the contractors were so easily replaced by lower-cost, non-union ones, even if they agreed to union representation and terms, organizers sought to "shame" the more wealthy building owners into retaining jobs, recognizing unions, and increasing cleaners' wages even though they were not the workers' legal employers.[20]

At the first press conference held in 1975, the Portuguese cleaners and their allies explained how contracting out hurt the workers' wages and union. They called on the government to hire cleaners directly and to protect their livelihood by amending the bidding process so that a new contractor had to hire the previous company's workers. And to consider factors other than the size of the bid in awarding contracts.[21] Government Services Minister James Snow callously replied that the government policy of accepting the lowest bid when tenders were being called would save taxpayers money. Here, then, the state and employer were one and the same.

The Ontario government cast its decision to hire Consolidated Maintenance Services, a US-based company that underbid Modern by $70,000 on a two-year contract, as a neutral business decision. But it had effectively decided to lay off all the cleaners. The women turned to the deputy minister to ask for his help in getting their jobs back, the novelty of speaking to a high-level government official underscored by the fact that they would meet in the very offices they cleaned at night. When he refused, they marched over to Dan Heap's house because they knew he had supported the TD Centre cleaners during their wildcat strike over dirty garbage bags two years earlier. Heap agreed to rally other NDP members to the cause.[22]

On the day before the cleaners were to lose their jobs, a press conference held at the Queen's Park press gallery reflected a much larger support base. Co-sponsored by the Ontario Committee on the Status of Women (OCSW) and the Civil Service Association of Ontario, it featured representatives of the Ontario Federation of Labour and City Hall as well as the NDP. Building a community-based coalition of social justice forces to bring pressure on corporate players is another progressive strategy

168   Cleaning Up

adopted by the contemporary J4J campaign.[23] For Toronto's cleaners, this broadly based movement-building began with the 1975 episode.

The participation of the OCSW signalled the beginning of an association with the wider women's movement. The OCSW in fact focused on contracting out as a women's issue. Noting that in the cleaning industry the practice primarily affected immigrant women, OCSW member Pat Lundie argued that "if Ontario continues to sub-contract it should deal only with companies who undertake to pay competitive wages and who permit their employees to form collective bargaining units." The "present practice," she added, "is highly unjust, retrogressive and unbecoming to the government of Canada's largest province, particularly in International Women's Year."[24] The OCSW later met with ministry representatives and urged them to either reconsider the contracting out of cleaning work or to include fair employment guidelines in its contracts.[25]

This episode also brought the cleaners into contact with the National Action Committee on the Status of Women, which also issued a statement of public support.[26] Swenarchuk and Pratt, both of whom were involved in working-class and feminist organizing through the Confederation of Canadian Unions (see chapter 4), played key roles in mobilizing labour and feminist groups around the cleaners' cause. True to its conservative business unionism, the SEIU took a far less active role in supporting the cleaners; Hearn, of Local 204, even disapproved of the leftists. Writing about the 1975 crisis, he later attributed the "considerable upheaval in the Portuguese community" to "the left wing element headed by one Miss Sidney Pratt."[27]

With their children in tow, as they could not afford babysitters, the cleaners crowded into the room where the press conference was held, but the children were hardly passive props. To the surprise of journalists and others, they commanded attention. In what would become a familiar feature of their activism, the women used the platform to educate the public about their critical role as family breadwinners. Staring straight ahead, Germana Travassos said that with seven children and an underemployed husband to support, she had to work. With their husbands in the construction industry, others noted, come winter they would again be the only income earner. And when the journalists reacted by asking what their husbands thought of them acting so publicly, the cleaners brushed them off and instead focused the discussion on their work.[28]

The women also called on the state to treat immigrant workers with fairness. "It's no good for us to organize for fair wages," noted

Fighting Contracting Out in the Workplace 169

Piedade Silva, "when the government allows us to be fired so that they can save money."[29] In declaring that she "did not want to go on welfare," Travassos and others positioned themselves as hardworking citizens who deserved some rights, not supplicants. In a classic case of treating immigrant women as the source of their own problems, Minister Snow, who attended the press conference, told them to learn English and reiterated the point that tendering contracts made "good business sense."[30] In "othering" the cleaners as uneducated and unskilled immigrants from an inferior culture, Snow ignored how systemic racism and sexism serve to marginalize immigrant women.[31]

Asserting themselves in the public and political arena, the women instead defined themselves as valuable members of the Canadian community who deserved respect and an adequate standard of living.[32] The public sympathy they garnered, along with the pressure applied by their network of allies, forced Snow to do something. In a response that would become a long-standing pattern in the cleaning industry, he agreed to speak to a representative of the current contractor, Consolidated, and ask them to hire the cleaners. The pressure applied on Consolidated brought the company's vice-president to town from New York. After meeting with Snow and some of the cleaners, as well as Swenarchuk and Pratt, he agreed to hire all the workers if they would "take what he gave them."[33]

Alas, their dire circumstances led the women to accept a new contract with Consolidated at a salary less than that previously offered by Modern. And by cutting the working hours while retaining the same workload, Consolidated further reduced the value of the workers' wages. Meanwhile, Snow and Consolidated cast themselves as benevolent actors who saved jobs. Rehiring the cleaners was positioned as a compromise between saving taxpayers' money and securing the cleaners' livelihoods. But since the legal conditions of contract building cleaning did not change, similar crises would keep recurring in the industry.[34]

There were positive outcomes stemming from this crisis. First, due to public pressure, both Modern and Consolidated accepted the fact that the cleaners should earn more than the minimum wage, even though both offered only a slight improvement to salaries. Second, the Ontario government later agreed to implement regulations that required firms receiving government contracts for cleaning, maintenance, and security to pay the going industry wage rate as determined by the Ministry of Labour. That is, the government would no longer accept the lowest bid based on minimum wage. Requiring bids to reflect the existing negotiated wage rate and benefits meant that the incumbent contractor was not disadvantaged by others offering lower bids. And when new contracts were tendered, previous workers would have a right to retain their jobs under the new contractor, thus also preserving seniority. In effect, these changes amounted to informal successor rights for cleaners in Ontario government buildings. Private cleaning companies with no vested interest in how the public viewed their labour practices, however, enjoyed greater leeway in how they conducted their business and treated their workers.[35]

Having met with the Queen's Park cleaners to inform them of their new rights, Minister of Labour Robert Elgie admitted to being quite impressed by the "concerned group of women." Evidently moved by their personal stories, he wrote about the woman who "frankly told [him] that as the end of each two year contract came up, her 'stomach tightened right up' and she had great fears and concerns about her ability to get a new job and survive economically."[36] Forged largely in response to the activism of the cleaners and their allies, the new labour policy was indeed a positive development for the cleaners at Queen's Park, and it also explains why the turnover at this workplace has historically been low.[37] But the Portuguese cleaning lady would appear again in the public sphere in her fight for economic security.

Metro Police Headquarters, 1977

When the issue of contracting out in government buildings again drew public attention, it was in the municipal realm. Metro Police Headquarters, at 590 Jarvis Street, was in 1977 the only municipal building that contracted out cleaning services. It was all about saving money. When, a decade earlier, the city had purchased the premises for a new police headquarters, the building was being cleaned under contract at "substantially lower rates" than the city (Metropolitan Corporation) paid its in-house janitorial staff. So, apart from two daytime cleaners employed directly by the city, the night cleaning was contracted out. They earned minimum wage: $2.65 and $3.20 an hour for light- and heavy-duty cleaners, respectively. With no union, they had few benefits and no grievance procedure to protect them. By contrast, the two daytime cleaners hired directly by the municipality were, like their counterparts in other municipal buildings, members of CUPE Local 79, earned more than $5 per hour, and had benefits and job protection. Neither Metro Executive Committee (an advisory body to city council chaired by the mayor) nor Metro Toronto Council (the legislative body of the municipal government of Toronto) discussed what the discrepancy meant for the ten Portuguese contract janitors—seven women and three men—but the cleaners would make themselves heard.[38]

The wider context matters. The police headquarters may have been the only municipal building that contracted out its cleaning, but from the early 1970s on, Metro Toronto had been cutting costs by hiring contract workers for various services. The parks, property, and road and traffic departments, for example, contracted out laundry services, printing, painting, mechanical and electrical work, and construction and demolition work. At one point, the chair of the Board of Commissioners of Police, Judge C.O. Bick, complained about the quality of the cleaning at police headquarters but, rather than hire cleaners directly, Executive Council tendered the contract and awarded it to another contactor (Y&R Properties). In 1980, Councillor Heap raised the alarm bells, noting that contracting out was "big stuff" at City Hall and that Metro Council had recently "adopted an official policy of contracting out everything they can."[39]

The nighttime cleaners at Metro Police Headquarters spoke out about their predicament, not in response to a contracting-out crisis but to expose the injustice of their situation. It was an offensive rather than a defensive action. Once again, the cleaners themselves initiated matters. One woman in particular, Arminda de Sousa, who is the source of the following story. When Pratt knocked on her door as part of a community outreach effort to inform people of the services available in Portuguese at St. Christopher House, de Sousa explained her problem. She and her husband, a cleaner at Eaton's department store, could barely support nine children on their low wages, but her English was too poor to issue a formal complaint. In addition to helping with the complaint, Pratt contacted Heap, who became an important ally in a struggle that would last for many months. De Sousa's courage is underscored by the response she recalled giving relatives who warned her off speaking out: "If I lose my job, I'll go and find another."[40]

In January 1977, Heap appealed to Metro Council Executive to discontinue the annual contract with Y&R and hire unionized in-house staff, but they refused. The difference between hiring Y&R, and hiring in-house staff and providing supplies (at $135,000 per year), was $38,000.[41] When the Executive Committee's recommendation to hire Y&R was discussed in city council, Heap and the presidents of CUPE Local 48 and

Local 79 asked to refer the matter back to the Executive Committee with a request to hire Metro Toronto employees for a one-year period. City council agreed to not renew the contract with Y&R while various government departments looked into the matter.[42]

In the meantime, Heap shared the cleaners' pay stubs with the city's Fair Wage Officer and asked for an investigation into Y&R's practices at police headquarters. Y&R, it turned out, was paying not the rates required under Metro's fair wage policy ($3.05 and $4.16) but instead minimum wage. The Fair Wage Officer negotiated back pay for the employees (the group total was over $2,400). De Sousa recalled feeling

Arminda de Sousa speaks to the Metropolitan Executive Committee at Toronto's City Hall in 1977. St. Christopher House (now West Neighbourhood House) collection.

Fighting Contracting Out in the Workplace

emboldened enough to chide her boss, telling him, "You are robbing us. You take advantage of us because we can't speak English." Nevertheless, Metro's Management Subcommittee rejected on financial grounds the request from Heap and John Sewell, a reform-minded city councillor who would be elected mayor a year later, to cancel the contract with the untrustworthy Y&R Properties and hire the cleaners directly.[43] Again, saving money trumped the welfare of the cleaners who toiled in Metro Toronto buildings.

In response, Sidney Pratt and the cleaners at police headquarters met with the Metro Executive Committee. In a letter to the committee, Pratt had cited the "unfairness of having some buildings cleaned by workers with a secure position and others by employees of private contractors who allow their workers few means to protect themselves."[44] At the meeting, de Sousa addressed the committee through an interpreter. "Because we have no union, such as public employees have with CUPE," she said, "we have very little security." She continued:

> Some of us have been fired after being away sick. Others have been threatened with being fired if they didn't come back to work the third day after reporting that they were sick—this happened to me. We have no rights and benefits like those of other cleaners in buildings used by the municipality.[45]

When, thirty years later, de Sousa explained why she and her co-workers had spoken up—"We wanted our rights, because others had them and we didn't"[46]—she reiterated the claim they had made to membership in a city community and municipal space. Refusing to be othered, they argued instead for inclusion in a community that offered rights to those who belong to it.

If the cleaning contractor lied about its employees' paycheques, the bureaucrats manipulated the numbers to make contracting out appear more attractive to elected officials. There was a significant difference between the janitorial staff requirements drawn up by the personnel department and the reality, which involved a smaller crew, far fewer heavy-duty cleaners (who were more expensive), and fewer working hours than claimed. In practice, more women were doing the work that personnel staff claimed as higher-paid, heavy-duty, male work—but for less money.[47] Using their immigrant status against them, the government responded by arguing that cleaners without English should not be rehired by the municipality.[48] For such immigrants, the authorities appeared to be saying, minimum wage and substandard working conditions were acceptable. Pratt responded by pointing out that language had little bearing on the workers' ability to perform their jobs. After all, she added, the current boss at Y&R was Greek and could communicate with his staff only minimally in English. She also called upon the city to arrange for English classes for these workers. Certain conservative councillors, including Mel Lastman, rejected the idea of hiring the cleaners as municipal employees on the grounds that it amounted to "stealing" employees from Y&R.[49] And in the end, Metro Executive voted to recommend that council give the cleaning contract at police headquarters to Y&R Properties.

Heap and the NDP continued to support cleaners' rights through the 1980s. Heap kept in close contact with the SEIU over the issue, even delivering a speech on cleaners at the SEIU's Ontario convention in 1979. A year earlier, at Heap's urging, the NDP Provincial Council initiated research aimed at securing better legislation in Ontario for contract cleaners so as to bring standards in the industry up to those of Quebec.[50] These efforts were part of a larger NDP strategy to mobilize support within the Portuguese community, which Joe Pantalone (Ward 4 city councillor) and Ross McClellan (member of provincial parliament, or MPP, Bellwoods)—both self-defined socialists with large Portuguese constituencies—described as one of the city's newest and largest working-class immigrant communities. Bob Rae (NDP MP until May 1982, and MPP from November 1982) also became more active in the Portuguese community, and specifically became involved in the fight for successor rights legislation.[51]

Municipal governments continued to contract out services, but the ongoing pressure applied with respect to the new Metro Police Headquarters, which opened in 1988, led to the decision to make the cleaners municipal employees and members of CUPE.[52] The cleaners' determination and action made an impact at this workplace. Indeed, as their lawyer noted, "the cleaners had done much of the work themselves, only requesting assistance from Sidney [Pratt]."[53] In short, they were activists in their own right.

Toronto-Dominion Centre, 1985

In early 1985, Toronto's Portuguese cleaners faced another contracting-out crisis, this time in private corporate space. As described at the outset of this chapter, 260 cleaners at the Toronto-Dominion Centre (which now had a fourth office tower) faced layoffs in March of that year because, just as the collective agreement between Modern Building Cleaning and CUPE was to expire, Cadillac Fairview, the building owner, chose not to renew its contract with Modern but instead put it out for tender. (By contrast, the Queen's Park crisis in 1975 was triggered by the *contractor* backing out of the cleaning contract after the cleaners demanded higher wages.) The current TD Centre cleaners, some of whom had worked there for decades and may well have been involved in the 1974 wildcat strike, earned among the lowest hourly wages in the industry ($6.39 and $7.36 for light- and heavy-duty work, respectively), but had no opportunity to negotiate better wages and benefits. John Sousa, president of CUPE Local 2295, attributed Cadillac Fairview's actions to its wanting to prevent a militant strike like the First Canadian Place strike of the previous summer (see chapter 6). Aware that TD cleaners had actively supported that high-profile strike, including on the picket line, the company, Sousa charged, was trying to pre-empt any worker action. Indeed, Sousa accused Cadillac Fairview of "trying to take away [the] union's right to strike." Predictably, the corporation denied any such connection.[54]

For many of these workers, the TD Centre complex had been their sole workplace in Canada and thus was inextricably linked with their migration experience. In their petition to government officials and corporate representatives, the cleaners claimed that "for some workers" the towering complex "is a second home" and "a big part of our lives here in Canada."[55] In likening the complex to a second home as well as a means to support their families, were these mostly female janitorial workers simply being strategic? Or were these heartfelt sentiments? The following flyer they sent to the building's tenants suggests a mix of both, though the related theme that also stands out is their sense of pride.

> How do you feel about having new cleaners come in to clean your private offices? How do you feel about having strangers come in to your private offices after hours? We have been part of the TD Centre family for 17 years and have built an excellent reputation. We have always maintained a good relationship with you and enjoy keeping your offices clean. Are you willing to let Cadillac Fairview Corporation throw that all away and start anew?[56]

The women's sense of pride in their work permeates another flyer distributed to tenants, suggesting that they wanted recognition as first-class cleaners. "We are the 260 cleaners who clean your offices, clean your washrooms, wash your windows, wash your carpets and keep the TD Centre so impeccably clean," it stated. "We pride ourselves in being the cleaners who keep the TD Centre one of the cleanest office complexes in Toronto."[57]

During the 1985 episode, the cleaners were less at the forefront of the anti-contracting-out activism than in the past. Rather than a grassroots action, this episode reflected a far more organized, even institutional, movement. By this time, unions were taking more initiative on cleaners' issues, and CUPE had a leading role. Again, the cleaners and their supporters used the media and political allies to bring public attention to their cause. In addition to the petition addressed to the political and corporate leaders that opened this chapter, and the flyers sent to the building's tenants, CUPE Local 2295 turned for support to Toronto City Council, the Toronto and provincial NDP, and Labour Minister Russell Ramsay. Toronto mayor Art Eggleton came through with a letter to Cadillac Fairview that called on CEO Ghert "to do [his] utmost" to avoid terminating the jobs of long-serving workers, as it would cause "tremendous hardships" for them and their families.[58] A letter signed by fourteen Toronto aldermen urged Cadillac Fairview to appreciate that the workers are "mostly immigrant women whose income is essential to the livelihood of their families."[59] TD Bank and Cadillac Fairview were bombarded with letters from both allies and the general public that indicated growing public awareness of and sympathy for working immigrant women who ought to have the right to retain their jobs.[60]

Cadillac Fairview still refused to reverse its decision to tender the contract. Ghert even publicly chided Eggleton for getting "drawn into a union matter" from which he "cannot emerge a winner."[61] Downplaying his responsibility to the cleaners on the grounds that he was not their legal employer, Ghert praised Modern "as a responsible corporate-citizen" that, should the company win the contract, would surely "look after their long-term employees."[62] The inability of unions to fight contract tendering was underscored by the fact that the CUPE local executive recommended a one-year pay freeze to try to keep their employer competitive.[63]

Public pressure did, however, compel the minister of labour to meet with Cadillac Fairview and the cleaning contractors in the bidding, in order to ask that any new contractor hire the cleaners currently working in the building: a familiar "solution" to contracting out. As a private sector building, Cadillac Fairview was not affected by the fair wage and job security policies that applied to provincial-government-hired cleaners working in their buildings. Once again, public and political pressure appeared to be the only way for cleaners to retain their jobs, and ideally, their union. In the end, Modern was awarded the contract for only one of the towers, employing about sixty people. Empire Building Maintenance was given the contract for the remaining office buildings, which together employed about two hundred cleaners. All the public scrutiny and political persuasion led Empire to agree to hire most of those two hundred workers, to respect seniority in hiring, and to recognize the union. But the workers suffered a wage cut and most of their benefits, including a drug plan and paid sick leave, were eliminated.[64]

On the union side, CUPE Local 2295 now represented TD cleaners under two separate collective agreements. Sousa noted that the union could claim "a victory in that we saved most jobs and we didn't let them bust our union," but Cadillac Fairview had clearly weakened the bargaining unit by dividing the workplace into two. It reduced the price of the cleaning contract by forcing down wages and benefits. And there was nothing to prevent the same scenario from being repeated again and again. In response, Sousa and others emphasized the need for municipal and provincial cleaners to obtain successor rights in law. Saying, "we can't just fight this one local at a time," he called on all the affected unions "to get together and organize to make sure we have legal protection so that a new contractor must respect the terms of the previous employer."[65] One year later, another contracting-out crisis in the downtown core would see the formal coming together of unions, and others, in the struggle for successor rights legislation.

First Canadian Place, 1986

When a contracting-out crisis broke out at First Canadian Place in February 1986, it generated more public controversy than the others because of the publicity given to the dramatic strike that had taken place there in 1984 (see chapter 6). The scenario was familiar enough: 250 cleaners were in danger of losing their jobs, their union, and their hard-won rights because Olympia & York was putting the cleaning contract for First Canadian Place up for tender—for the first time ever—just as the collective agreement was set to expire.

Wendy Iler of FASWOC suggested that the tendering process was part of a scheme to force the union to water down its demands around wages and benefits during collective bargaining.[66] Another motive may have been to punish the cleaners whose publicity-grabbing picket-line antics had given Olympia & York a lot of bad press. Also, Olympia & York had been forced into paying a higher contract price to Federated Building Maintenance to reflect the higher wages for which the cleaners had fought. Not that anyone at Olympia & York said as much. Instead, company representatives spoke of occasional tendering as sensible business that protects the tenants' interests and that encourages a contractor and their staff to work together "to ensure a continued quality of service ... at an acceptable cost."[67]

But what distinguished this crisis from others is that, thanks to the 1984 strike, the mostly female cleaners in this building were now more familiar both to their supporters and to the general public. Liberal premier David Peterson faced an onslaught of public pressure from community groups, unions, and politicians, who wrote letters and made phone calls in support of the cleaners. Even tenants of the building expressed support. One such letter offered a ringing endorsement of the cleaners and also captured their strong work ethic. "My desk," it read, "is always clean in the morning with things left exactly as they were the night before." On the occasion when the writer had "forgotten things of value" in their drawers or on top of their desk overnight, the items "have never been touched by [the] present cleaning staff." Adopting a scolding tone, the tenant concluded: "The honesty, loyalty, integrity and pride in their job must be worth something to you when figures on your balance sheet are tallied."[68]

The public pressure helped Premier Peterson to persuade Olympia & York to inform the potential contractors that they would have to offer first right of job refusal to current employees. The issue was protecting jobs, not the union or wages and benefits. As Peterson quipped in the legislature, "I am more concerned about protecting jobs than I am about protecting unions."[69] To reporters, he remarked, "It's a free country" and "These contracts can go out for tender."[70] For their part, Olympia & York made no long-term commitment to cleaners in its buildings. Given the situation, the workers had little choice but to accept Federated's offer of a pay raise of just 33 cents in the first year, 27 cents in the second, and a half-hour reduction in their shift despite an unchanged workload. They did so because it allowed their employer (Federated) to remain competitive and in order to keep their jobs and their collective agreement.[71] In the

Fighting Contracting Out in the Workplace

end, the cleaning contract was renewed, but the cleaners were forced to give up many of the gains made during the 1984 strike. As in the case of Queen's Park, the provincial government refused to alter the labour law, but the government, and Olympia & York, took on "benevolent" roles by helping the cleaners keep their jobs even if it was at substandard wages and conditions.

Similar scenarios occurred repeatedly throughout the 1980s, including at the O'Keefe Centre (SEIU) in 1984. Two years later, workers faced job loss at the Ontario Science Centre (Ontario Public Service Employees Union—OPSEU), the Aetna building (LiUNA), and the Scarborough Letter Processing Plant (Canadian Union of Postal Workers—CUPW). In some cases, public pressure helped the cleaners facing layoffs to retain their jobs with a new contractor, but the precarity of the work, particularly in private corporate spaces, remained.[72]

Committee for Cleaners' Rights, 1986

A unionist well captured the contract cleaners' dilemma in a 1986 interview with the *Toronto Star*, saying that, because they had no rights under the Ontario Labour Relations Act, they had to "make every set of negotiations a public campaign and a political fight."[73] But it was the 1986 episode at First Canadian Place that gave cleaners the momentum they needed to press for changes to the labour law. With a mandate to get successor rights legislation passed in Ontario, the founding of the Committee for Cleaners' Rights in February 1986 represented the culmination of more than a decade of struggle by cleaners and their allies for workplace justice. The membership included unions, such as FASWOC, CUPE, CUPW, OPSEU, SEIU, and LiUNA, and community organizations such as St. Christopher House and the Portuguese Interagency Network, which was formed in 1978 to represent Portuguese Canadian social agencies. The NAC was also involved in this labour struggle that was to a significant degree a women's struggle. Already associated with the cause of the Portuguese cleaning lady, the NDPers on the committee included Heap, Pantalone, and Rae.

Early on, a Committee for Cleaners' Rights delegation convinced Mayor Eggleton to sponsor a resolution at city council to make changes in the provincial labour laws that would protect the jobs of building cleaners when contracts changed.[74] The proposal was twofold: introduce successor rights clauses in the Ontario Labour Relations Act, and approve an amendment to the Employment Standards Act that would see even non-unionized workers retain their wages and benefits when the contractor changed.[75] The shift in target coincided with a change in the movement. Just as the committee finally began to make some political headway, the workers who, with their Portuguese-speaking allies at St. Christopher House, had been at the forefront of the struggle receded into the background. The committee's activism extended to workplaces that were not largely Portuguese, though the majority of workers in Toronto's downtown cleaning industry still were.

The Committee for Cleaners' Rights may have shifted the direction of organization from a bottom-up (or rank and file led) to a more top-down model, but it proved effective at mobilizing the Portuguese immigrant community in support of the cause. In less than a year, the committee had gathered ten thousand signatures, mostly Portuguese, on a petition calling for the government to change the Labour Relations Act.[76] People signed petitions at work, in union meetings, and at community social and cultural events. Encouraged to do so by their priests, parishioners at St. Mary's, St. Helen's, and other churches gathered after mass to add their name to a petition. During the Festa do Senhor Santo Cristo dos Milagres (the Feast of the Lord Holy Christ of the Miracles), a major Portuguese *festa*, twenty-six pages of signatures were obtained. The unprecedented degree of community mobilization reflected the committee's more organized, institutional, and political character, but it would not have achieved success had the issue not resonated so deeply with so many working-class Portuguese.[77] The 1,300 signatures collected on International Women's Day in 1986 reflected the support of feminists, left activists, and unionists for the cleaners' cause. During the organized community canvases, high-profile local NDPers Rae, Pantalone, and Heap helped to gather signatures door to door in the west end.

Riding on a crest of public support, Rae and NDP labour critic Robert Mackenzie (Hamilton East) introduced a private member's bill (Bill 132) in the Ontario Legislature—where Peterson's Liberal government held power with the support of the NDP—that was meant to tighten the successor rights portions of the Ontario Labour Relations Act. Flanked by two female Portuguese cleaners, Rae told the reporters and others who attended the press conference that these women workers were "one of the most vulnerable and exploited groups in our society." The newspaper coverage echoed his language. To make the case for successor rights, NDP members invoked the Queen's Park 1975 episode, noting that when the provincial government required new contractors to hire previous

Fighting Contracting Out in the Workplace

employees and honour their collective agreement, the union could obtain higher wages for light-duty cleaners (women) than those prevailing in the industry in general.[78] During a lobby organized by the Committee for Cleaners' Rights at Queen's Park in November, a crowd of cleaners, union representatives, NDP members, and community activists visited the offices of Liberal and Progressive Conservatives MPPs and asked them to support the bill. Idalina Azevedo, who had been an SEIU union steward at the TD Centre during the wildcat strike in 1974, spoke in favour of the bill at the NDP press conference that day. "As immigrants," she said, "we love this country" because "we have a chance to make a better life for us and our families." Then she added, "But we deserve to be treated like human beings."[79] The Committee for Cleaners' Rights devoted considerable resources to getting Bill 132 passed, and when it went up for a vote, cleaners congregated in the halls of Queen's Park to ask members from all the parties to support it.

The debate on the bill underscored the tension between workers' rights and neoliberal ideas. The NDP MPPs framed the issue as one of workers', women's, and immigrant rights. Mackenzie called the cause "one of simple justice and fairness" for the workers who have organized for better pay and benefits. His remarks also made clear that he recognized the issue affected the Portuguese, and women, in particular. McClellan recalled that the first issue he'd handled as a newly elected MPP was the 1975 contracting-out crisis at Queen's Park. He noted that a community coalition had successfully fought for those jobs and forced the government to back down, but that such "firefighting exercises" were no longer enough. He also highlighted the particular vulnerability of the many Portuguese cleaners to these onslaughts against working people. Contracting out, he stated, "has come to symbolize the kind of struggle that has faced them in this country." Fighting it, he added, "symbolizes an opening, a breakthrough and a way of achieving a decent standard of living, through working hard and through fighting for collective rights, not excessive rights but simply rights to a decent reward for their labour and to a decent standard of living for themselves and their children."

The remarks did not go over well with everyone. Liberal MPP Rick Ferraro (Wellington South) reduced the matter to a "socialism versus free enterprise" debate. He erroneously referred to the First Canadian Place crisis as a one-time event and insisted on the right of Ontarians "to enter into contract or compete for business contract with whomsoever they wish." Claiming that forcing businesses to unionize would drive jobs out of the province, he called the bill "wrong and undemocratic." Liberal MPP William Barlow (Cambridge) expressed sympathy for the plight of the Portuguese cleaners—his riding had a large Portuguese constituency—but said he could not support the bill because it would "smother the very lifeblood of business itself."[80] Bill 132 was defeated (41 to 23) with all the Liberals voting against it, and all NDP and three Progressive Conservatives voting in favour of it. By 1989, in the wake of the failure, the Committee for Cleaners' Rights had disbanded.

Conclusion

It was not until 1993, under the first NDP provincial government in Ontario under Bob Rae, that successor rights for contract cleaners were incorporated, through Bill 40, into changes to labour law. These rights would soon be the first casualty of Mike Harris's "common sense revolution." The first major piece of legislation introduced by the Harris government in 1995 was Bill 7, which eliminated successor rights. The intention was to curtail union power while privileging the private sector.[81] Even the cleaners at Queen's Park, who had a favourable agreement with the provincial government in terms of wages and job security, lost those rights. Now, contracts would be tendered to the lowest bidder, and new contractors had no obligation to maintain existing wages and benefits or workers. As one SEIU representative noted, these workers were losing "one of the most envied contracts in the business."[82]

The Committee for Cleaners' Rights has been criticized for concentrating on successor rights when it did little to fight against the downward pressure on wages in non-union workplaces affected by the competitive nature of contract cleaning. Also, as Bill 7 demonstrated, legislation can change when new governments are formed.[83] The SEIU in the US avoided campaigns to change labour law and instead formed the Justice for Janitors campaign in 1985. Organized by geographical area rather than individual worksite, the J4J campaign sought to bring workers together into larger groupings in order to better fight the larger corporations. J4J used master contracts that were market-wide and thus allowed for standardization of the local labour market. With the founding of a Canadian Justice for Janitors campaign in Toronto in 2007, the SEIU focused on organizing contractors in Toronto (as they did in Montreal) in a system much like that proposed in the 1970s, rather than organizing site by site. While initially a top-down, or leadership-led movement, today rank-and-file immigrant workers and their communities are active players in the campaign. Through J4J, the SEIU has sought to build a contemporary social justice movement around janitors in the US and, since J4J's arrival in 2007, in Canada.

Epilogue

On the evening of 19 October 2021, a ceremony was held in a west-end parking lot in the city's Little Portugal for the unveiling of a striking mural to commemorate the labour activism of Toronto's Portuguese immigrant women office-building cleaners during the 1970s and 1980s. Engraved on the wall of an older house at 1628 Dundas Street West, the sepia-toned mural was the work of the internationally celebrated Lisbon street artist Vhils (Alexandre Farto). Known for his "highly unorthodox mediums in art," he has described his method of carving, cutting, drilling, and blasting to expose the layers in the materials as a sort of "archeological process" that makes stories emerge from walls.[1]

Plans for a mural by Vhils had been in the works since 2019, but they were disrupted by the COVID-19 pandemic. Two years later, in summer and fall 2021, a theme for the mural was chosen and work commenced. The organizers of the mural—including the Portuguese Consulate, Toronto Deputy Mayor Ana Bailão, and the Little Portugal on Dundas BIA (Business Improvement Area)—proposed the theme of cleaners' activism to Vhils, whose art often depicts social justice issues and leaders, and he accepted.[2] In partnership first with Bailão and then with the Little Portugal on Dundas BIA led by AnaBela Taborda, the cultural attaché for the Portuguese Consulate in Toronto, Rita Sousa Tavares, secured funding and organized the logistics. These included funding from the City, facilitated by Bailão, for the street art project. The wall itself was made available by Vitor and Marina Tavares, Portuguese immigrant owners of the two-storey, late-nineteenth-century house. Historians Gilberto Fernandes and Susana Miranda, co-author of this book, were interviewed and provided historical context, photographs, and other archival materials to Vhils's research team, who also used the material to produce two short videos about the cleaners and the making of the mural.[3] Support came as well from the Toronto and York Region Labour Council and from two construction unions that now represent a significant number of Portuguese men. LiUNA Local 183 and the International Union of Painters and Allied Trades District Council 46 helped with contributions of time and materials (cement, lifts) as well as the plastering.

Vhils's team flew to Toronto in advance to gather photographs, conduct research on the topic, interview people associated with cleaners' activism, and prepare the wall. The images for the mural were then chosen. Finally, Vhils arrived, and the mural, which forms part of his *Scratching the Surface* project, was created. A large gathering of people from the Portuguese Canadian community as well as the wider labour movement and a number of leftists and other progressive people attended the unveiling ceremony.

As feminist labour historians, we are, of course, keen to bring a dramatic chapter in immigrant women's resistance in Canada out of the shadows and into the classrooms, union halls, community centres, and other public spaces to be noted and debated by students, working people, immigrants, and middle-class folk. In this regard, the mural sheds light on some of the merits as well as perils of doing public history. On the positive side, this work of art is truly beautiful and gives one great aesthetic pleasure. Designed as a faded newspaper, the mural features the Portuguese cleaners who animate our book. It conveys the drama of the past events being commemorated through the juxtaposition of individual labour and community activists and a group image of workers on strike. An entire section of the mural, on the right side, is dominated by the strong and pensive face of Idalina Azevedo. The Azorean immigrant, whose story is among those featured in this book, led the wildcat strike at the Toronto-Dominion Centre's tallest bank tower in 1974. To the left of her is an image of Jean Connon Unda, a St. Christopher House community worker who was hired to work in literacy development (see chapter 4). She is holding up a copy of the *Cleaners' Action Newsletter*. Beside Unda stands a group of cleaners holding up strike placards ("FASWOC on Strike") during the 1984 First Canadian Place strike. Not only those who attended the unveiling, but also the friends, family, and colleagues we have taken to the mural have been impressed with the intensity it conveys.

Also positive is that the mural both builds on the work of committed public historians and enhances it through its wider public reach. As founders of the Portuguese Canadian History Project (est. 2008), whose website declares "Preserving the collective memory of Portuguese Canadians / Democratizing access to historical knowledge,"[4] Miranda and Fernandes had launched public history initiatives with content on the cleaners. These included a photography exhibit, a walking tour, and a podcast of a talk by Miranda at the Toronto Public Library.[5] In addition, the Department of Public Memory, a grassroots organization that commemorates community organizations, designed a memorial sign about Cleaners' Action that was unveiled at Nuit Blanche in 2017. That sign was located near the Queen's Park complex, but was taken down, presumably by the City, shortly afterwards.[6] The mural, however, represents the broadest public recognition to date of the Portuguese female cleaners' labour activism in Toronto. This is in stark contrast to the lack of support the women received from within the Portuguese community *while* they were engaged in their job actions in the 1970s and 1980s. As we recount in the book, only a small group of leftist community activists offered them support.

What changed by 2021 within the Portuguese community that allowed women's activism in the cleaning industry to be celebrated so publicly? In the 1960s and 1970s, as this book also recounts, the recently arrived Portuguese community in Canada struggled with the legacy of homeland politics transplanted to Toronto, that of an authoritarian political culture that suppressed left-wing politics and intensified class, gender, and regional divisions. The revolution that toppled the right-wing dictatorship in Portugal occurred only in 1974, so the act of supporting left politics, including that of labour unions, was still a new experience for many, if not most, Portuguese immigrants. Furthermore, the organized Portuguese community in the 1970s and 1980s was still largely composed of middle-class men from mainland Portugal, and it ignored issues that affected their working-class counterparts, including women and Azorean immigrants. Indeed, Azoreans, though in the majority numerically, were often treated as second-class citizens within the community, whose leaders showed little interest in giving public voice to their needs or struggles.[7] In a pattern common among new immigrant groups, community-building among the Portuguese in the 1970s and 1980s was about establishing businesses, building institutions, and gaining respectability. Community leaders and members alike were thus reluctant to focus on "problems," "troublemakers," and "dirty" work.

By 2021, however, the Portuguese community had "made it." Like most liberal immigrant narratives, the public story of Portuguese immigration now emphasizes the overall success of life in Canada. Working-class Portuguese immigrants acquired a degree of material wealth that was not attainable in Portugal. They bought homes and raised children who either went on to university and professional careers or became very well paid tradespeople.[8] Today, Portuguese-run businesses proliferate in Toronto and there is a large professional class. The community boasts Portuguese Canadian city councillors as well as members of the Ontario Legislature and federal Parliament. And some of them are women. In the homeland, many left-wing governments have been elected since the 1974 Carnation Revolution. In January 2022, a socialist government came to power. In short, a great deal changed both in Portugal and in Toronto's Portuguese community in the almost fifty years since the 1974 wildcat strike at the TD Centre.

The speeches delivered at the unveiling ceremony by members of the broader Toronto political and labour community, as well as various segments of the Portuguese community, provide insight into how immigrant women cleaners are now perceived. Political representatives for the local Davenport riding, where the mural is located and where there is a large Portuguese population, reflected on the mural through both a political and personal lens. Invoking the familiar mantra of Canada as a "country of immigrants," Liberal MP Julie Dzerowicz spoke about the immigrants doing the jobs Canadians refused to do, a now popular theme that situates immigrants as nation builders. She also drew a connection between the Portuguese cleaners being honoured and her own experience as the daughter of a working-class Mexican immigrant woman who came to Canada in the 1970s. Dzerowicz's story speaks to how many Canadians, including Portuguese Canadians, can relate to the immigrant story of struggle and success. And that being a child of hard-working immigrants who persevered is now something to be celebrated. Calling the cleaners who fought for their rights women and workers "who got stuff done," NDP MPP Marit Stiles stressed how important it was for workers today to "continue the fight for decent work, for decent wages, for decent working conditions for all workers." Both speeches signal a shift in the broader public discourse around immigrants and labour activism: once-disparaged "troublemakers" have been renarrated as important actors in the city's history.

Andria Babbington, president of Toronto and York Region Labour Council, represented the labour community at the unveiling ceremony. A Jamaican-born woman who became a labour leader, Babbington reflected on her own experience as an eighteen-year-old immigrant doing the jobs that Canadians didn't want to do (an oft-repeated theme), including cleaning. In the most inspirational speech of the evening, she connected with the now elderly cleaners both emotionally and politically. In declaring that immigrant workers do not have to take the "disrespect" shown by their employers but have a right to struggle for dignity, she captured a sentiment central to the narratives of the many Portuguese cleaners featured in this book. Babbington herself represents an important intergenerational link between the past and present. A racialized woman and labour leader, she reflected on the changing demographics of the cleaning industry and its more ethnically heterogenous workforce, and thanked the Portuguese women whose past contributions to workplace activism were "paving the way for others" who continue to struggle for dignity in the workplace. Babbington ended by saying that, while she might be younger than the Portuguese cleaners, she proudly calls them her labour "sisters," the salutation underscoring her main approach to commemoration: seeing the usefulness of labour's past for today's struggles.

In light of past sins of omission, the speeches delivered by the community's political leaders and diplomatic representatives were certainly noteworthy, the presence of female leaders with a connection to the women all the more so. Did they reflect other approaches to the past? Or underscore the challenges of shaping public memory? As Craig Heron and other public historians observe, commemoration, or the shaping of public memory about the past, involves a process of inclusion and exclusion. Stephanie Yuhl puts it thus: "Cultural interest groups construct highly selective versions of history that generally purge less 'desirable' elements of the past in favor of articulating more flattering or 'useful' versions that serve group interests in the present." She notes, too, that the commemorative landscape is marked by the underrepresentation of militant and "radical political minorities." Even with the growing efforts of organizations like the Portuguese Canadian History Project, Myseum of Toronto, and the Workers Arts and Heritage Centre to redress the imbalance, Yuhl's observation certainly applies to Toronto, Ontario, and Canada. Also, commemoration can soften, even erase, both the violence inflicted on women by exploitative practices and dangerous workplaces and the women's participation in aggressive, and occasionally violent, confrontations. As for commemorating labour and radical histories, and women's militant histories in particular, the celebratory, even if heartfelt, pronouncements can gloss over troubling aspects of the past, such as the community's indifference to the women's plight. Also, the plaques and speeches might exaggerate the impact of the historical actors being celebrated. Or, alternatively, focus more attention on the interest groups than on the historical subjects of honour.[9]

What did community leaders and diplomatic representatives say? In her speech, Sousa Tavares, cultural attaché for the Portuguese Consulate, talked about knowing the artist, Vhils, personally and that she had been trying to get an installation by him in Toronto for a number of years. As a Portuguese immigrant herself, Deputy Mayor Bailão told those gathered in that parking lot that when Sousa Tavares approached her about the installation, she said she was most interested in a mural about the women "that have given so much for our families." Bailão's focus, then, was on the contribution these women have made through their work for the families, a central theme in the narratives of Portuguese women immigrants. During his address, José Carneiro Mendes, Portuguese consul-general in Toronto, portrayed the cleaners' workplace activism "as a case of human resistance" that contributed positively to Toronto's Portuguese community but also to the dissemination of *portugalidade*, roughly translated as a Portuguese essence, a mix of homeland and local identity, in Canada and globally. A term first used during the Estado Novo, *portugalidade* (or *lusophonie*) has been revived as a post-colonial term to encompass Portuguese culture in its many facets globally. The consul also thanked Vhils for his role in spreading Portuguese culture globally. Indeed, the mural attracted media attention in Portugal, bringing the cleaners' experience to an audience in their homeland for likely the first time.[10]

The two main actors at the event—the artist and one of his female subjects—were brief in their comments. Vhils said "the wall speaks for itself," meaning that his art conveys his message of the importance of the women's activism. In an interview, he did elaborate, saying "the idea of the mural is to portray the story, not that it's invisible . . . but to make it visible for people to discuss it, to talk about it and to feel proud about it."[11] From the sidelines, Vhils's crew of young artists, researchers, and videographers enthusiastically hooted their support for Vhils, and they were delighted to be invited to the podium to take their bows. Azevedo got up and thanked the crowd for being there and expressed her love for both Portugal and Canada. During her interviews with local Portuguese news stations earlier that day, she explained her workplace actions as a common sense strategy to ensure decent working conditions. In a more collectivist manner, she emphasized that she and her co-workers had acted to improve their workplaces despite being fearful of what might happen as a result. If Azevedo did not emphatically position herself as an activist in these public interviews, she has done so in the company of family and friends. She did not know about the mural until neighbours told her that someone was painting a large image of her face on a wall, but its completion and unveiling have reawakened feelings of pride and jubilation over the women's comradeship and the labour fights and victories of these years.[12]

A related challenge concerns the issue of who was not there and what was not said. None of the community workers and activists who supported Portuguese women in their job actions in the 1970s and 1980s spoke at the event, though some were in attendance. Marcie Ponte was there; she had been interviewed about her experiences working with Portuguese cleaners as part of the research conducted for the mural and the video. She brought Sidney Pratt, now living in Brazil, virtually through a video feed on her phone that allowed Pratt to watch the ceremony. Ponte and others loved the mural but were disappointed that the ceremony provided so little context and "storytelling" about Cleaners' Action and the women's many workplace actions. Except for Azevedo, there were no descriptions of the women in the mural or of the strike. Ponte had donated a duplicate of the Cleaners' Action street sign created by the Department of Public Memory that was installed near the mural, but no one mentioned it.[13] Also missing from the event was any nuanced history: no one pointed out that the actions of these labour heroines resulted in very few labour gains in what is still a cutthroat janitorial industry. Do such silences indicate a continuing discomfort in talking about a group of mostly Azorean working-class women who performed "dirty jobs"?

Whatever the answer, the ceremony was in essence more a celebration of bringing an internationally famous artist and his art to Toronto's Portuguese community. Even so, the mural provides a rare public "monument" that can inform the larger Portuguese and Toronto community about the history of cleaners' workplace activism, however superficially. And it publicly recognizes important features about these immigrant women: that they worked hard, supported their families, and fought for dignity and better working conditions alongside their small but committed group of supporters. We hope that those who walk by the mural

Epilogue

will want to learn more. Alas, the mural itself may not necessarily be a permanent installation. There is nothing to stop the owners from selling the house and it being demolished. Not that Vhils finds this unusual. As a creator of street art, he understands that creating art in a public space means that it may be painted over or demolished. Indeed, he says the art "belongs to the [evolving] city."[14]

Time will tell how much "storytelling" will come, but we certainly see our book as a telling tale about marginalized women who spoke truth to power. It affirms the value of the women's choices and underscores the importance of remembering their stories.

Old Defeats and Hopeful Options

The mural in Little Portugal celebrates the workplace actions of Portuguese women cleaners in 1970s and 1980s Toronto, but the two decades that followed saw little to celebrate. In terms of their twenty-year fight to secure successor rights in the industry, the building cleaners' story, and that of their community, feminist, union, and NDP allies, was largely one of defeat. Except for a two-year period (1993–95) under an NDP government, successor rights campaigns failed in the face of strong opposition from employers, the business community, and both Liberal and Progressive Conservative governments.

Over those twenty years, however, unions and social activists had become more interested in cleaners' issues. And they eventually realized that a focus on gaining or protecting successor rights, while a laudable goal, was a short-sighted one, as it did not help the majority of workers who were not unionized. They learned, too, that the labour movement achieved the most when it formed social justice coalitions with community groups, particularly those working with immigrants and women. New strategies were clearly needed.

In Canada, the SEIU had been under attack since the 1970s as part of a larger rejection of business unionism and American influences in the labour movement. Then, in the 1980s in the United States, the SEIU under the presidency of John Sweeney introduced new strategies to revitalize the union in response to the era's yet more anti-union climate. Tired of old-style labour bureaucrats, Sweeney hired young, educated, and committed leftists as labour organizers and gave them an intensive training in the field. A more militant SEIU was born. The building services had been the SEIU's historical base, but the union had lost ground to non-union competitors and made significant concessions to employers of unionized workers. By the mid-1980s, the national SEIU began to focus its attention back on these workers and the Justice for Janitors campaign emerged. The campaign adopted a new model for organizing cleaners, one that took on the increasing power and influence of contractors and the large corporations that hired them. The first offensive campaign appeared in Denver in 1986. It then arrived in Los Angeles, where, in the early 1990s, the SEIU had its largest and most publicized success. The janitors' struggles also inspired the Ken Loach 2000 film *Bread and Roses*. Within five years, the membership in LA had grown from 1,800 to 8,000 cleaners.[15]

J4J avoids site-by-site organizing, since building owners can easily terminate unionized contractors. Instead, the SEIU attempts to influence the local labour market as a whole. Workers are asked to identify with a movement, not just sign union cards. The goal of this "comprehensive campaign," or industry-wide approach, is to establish a master agreement that allows for standardization of the local labour market. Focused on building owners and managers, even though the official employers are the contractors, J4J's objective is to get them to agree to use union contractors paying union-scale wages. Through leafleting, press conferences, and public rallies, J4J publicly "shames" powerful corporations. The union stimulates worker support by acting as the de facto representative of workers employed by non-union contractors, filing unfair labour practice charges and representing workers in disputes with supervisors. It also develops co-operative and supportive relationships with the larger community, particularly the one from which their workers, overwhelmingly immigrants, hail. Churches and community organizations are central to cultivating worker support for the SEIU. While J4J has been perceived as a bottom-up campaign, it is also a top-down one, and the SEIU invests heavily in personnel and organizing. Indeed, im/migrant workers might have difficulty organizing without this investment, and the SEIU leadership devised many of the tactics used. Still, rank-and-file mobilization has been impressive. By 1990, more than 225,000 janitors in over thirty cities throughout the US and Canada have joined the SEIU.[16]

J4J did not come to Canada until 2007 in large part because Canadian SEIU officials were hesitant to take on US-style organizing tactics in a climate where Canadian nationalism was prevalent. But after the defeats of the 1980s and 1990s, it became a hopeful option. The reorganization of the SEIU in Canada made way for this campaign. Locals were reorganized by industry, and most janitors were brought under the new Local 2 banner in 2005. As of October 2022, the J4J website boasts that Local 2 represents 10,000 janitors, including members in Toronto, Ottawa, Vancouver, and Halifax.[17]

Recently, unionized cleaners with SEIU have been making advances in Toronto, Ottawa, and Vancouver. In December 2021, the union won victories for cleaners at the Vancouver International Airport and Metrotown, British Columbia's largest shopping centre. In April 2022, 2,500 cleaners employed by eleven companies in Toronto gained the biggest wage increase in the union's history, as well as improvements to benefits and the pension plan, which was established in 2019. In the summer of 2022, 2,800 unionized cleaners in the Ottawa area also gained the largest-ever wage increase. Successes have been spreading to office buildings, other malls, and university campuses.[18]

Large cleaning contractors that do not make a commitment to improving standards in the industry are shamed on the SEIU website and in other familiar ways. But the SEIU has a tough battle ahead. LiUNA is a competitor. And the workforce has changed, at least in Toronto. As the Portuguese who made up the large majority of downtown cleaners retired, the workforce became much more ethnically heterogeneous. Workers from around the world, including Latin America, Africa, and Asia, clean the downtown buildings, and language barriers and ethnic antagonisms often caused by employer strategies pose problems for solidarity. Still, the J4J campaign's reliance on community organizations for support and momentum exemplifies the importance of these networks for progressive labour activity.

Scholars have observed that the J4J campaign in Canada has not exhibited the same degree of confrontational tactics as in the United States. Our book instead documents the in-your-face tactics of Portuguese female cleaners in Toronto that preceded the US-based J4J campaigns. The politicized community organizers in Toronto in the 1970s and 1980s, and their influence in urging unions to take up the cleaners' cause, played a key role in the women's workplace actions, but the women's own deep-seated sense of outrage, their earthy militancy, and the hybrid culture they forged in Toronto also shaped their arresting and eye-catching behaviour. This history speaks to the potential for transformative action that arises at the grassroots level. In short, a respect for workers' culture and social justice coalitions are crucially important in new union movements.

The history of Portuguese female cleaners' activism speaks to the importance of progressive community work in transforming the lives of immigrants in Canada. Historically, immigrant interaction with Canadian institutions has been fraught with tension and condescension, but progressive community work offers the possibility of consciousness-raising around exploitation and equipping immigrants with the tools to effect change. Some community workers have lamented the waning since the 1980s of progressive community work, such as politicized ESL classes and community organizing. But most of the still active community organizers in this book continue to work in immigrant agencies that focus on gender, class, and ethnic exploitation.

Domestic Cleaning: Continuing Neglect?

Unlike the building-cleaning industry, daytime private housecleaning is unlikely in the near future to garner attention from unions or the state. While this informal work is a large portion of the economically active workforce in the Global south, the sector is not significant enough in Canada to become a target for organizing or regulation. And its gendered and racialized character does not help.[19] The demand for house cleaners will surely resume high levels post COVID-19 pandemic lockdowns as particularly women in middle- and high-range income occupations return to offices. As for the Portuguese cleaners, many are now in their eighties and have long retired, and some have passed away. Those still cleaning private homes in their sixties and early seventies find that their bodies are less able to withstand such strenuous labour. This immigrant generation of Portuguese cleaning ladies is not being replaced by new immigrants to nearly the same extent as they are in the building-cleaning industry. Private and informal work, with its lack of benefits, is unattractive to new immigrants who are less likely to see themselves as "sojourners," that is, workers who assume they will return home, rather than permanent settlers.

The rapid growth in recent decades of for-profit cleaning companies, like Molly Maid, which act as the intermediary between the private homeowner and cleaner, have given rise to new forms of domestic work and relationships between employers and cleaners.[20] For one month in 2006, Jan Wong, a reporter for the *Globe and Mail*, took an undercover job as a cleaner in Toronto with a company like Molly Maid to find out what it was like to live as a low-income Canadian. She chose cleaning because of the high demand for workers in the sector. The clients paid the company $28 an hour per cleaner, but Wong took home minimum wage, $7.75. She worked ten- and eleven-hour days and made about $50 a day (she was not paid for travel time between houses). On the rare occasion when she saw the people whose houses she cleaned, they hardly spoke to her. As she explained, "They're not interested in a relationship." The employers also issued frequent complaints about the work she and her partner did.

In going undercover as a cleaning lady in wealthy Toronto homes, Wong emulated the method used by journalist Barbara Ehrenreich for *Nickle and Dimed*, an attention-grabbing exposé on the working poor in 1990s America, but it is not difficult to understand why Wong chafed at how she was treated. Employers sometimes left days-old dog turds or overflowing toilets for her to clean up. She was not allowed to switch on the television, eat or drink, or use the clients' bathroom. She noted that the word "maid," which most cleaning companies use, spoke to conditions in the occupation. She developed rashes and carpal tunnel syndrome, and hated all the lifting (like vacuums) even more than cleaning toilets. Her (superficial) awareness of the Portuguese cleaning lady crept into her analysis. She noted, for example, that most Molly Maid cleaners were white and Canadian-born and quite unlike the "entrepreneurial cleaners" from Portugal who work alone, are paid in cash, and are treated like "one of the family."[21]

Even so, Wong's exposé pointed to a new phase of domestic work, one in which conditions were getting worse, not better. Changing immigration patterns and a new capitalist class of cleaning-company owners indicate that the occupation is continually in flux, which does not necessarily bode well for the cleaners themselves. In October 2022, the posted complaints of former employees of Molly Maid Canada franchises included the lack of any control over one's work regime, impossible workloads (too many houses in a day), and speed-ups (cutting corners), as well as managers quick to fire workers rather than investigate owner complaints and not being informed of the pay rate even when one is paid (no pay stubs). One complainant's post ends with advice with which the Portuguese private day cleaners featured here would likely agree. It reads: "You basically bust your butt for a non-liveable wage. They only give you a short time to do cleans, which ends up causing stress and short cuts. Not worth it for the back breaking labor. Also, almost none of the clients ever tipped. If you're going to clean, get your own clientele where you earn what you deserve."[22]

Elderly Cleaners

In the hustle and bustle of daily life, elderly Portuguese house cleaners, many of whom are caregivers for grandchildren, do not necessarily ruminate on their working lives in Canada. When they do talk about the past, many are matter of fact, asserting that they were just fighting for their rights, though some of them also emphatically stated, "I wasn't afraid." And some of the nervous energy of those years has subsided.

But they also speak with pride about their past struggles. They have learned a great deal about themselves too, including that, despite poverty, a poor education, and lack of English, they were able to face major hurdles with strength and courage. More than one explained, "If we want something, we have to fight for it." All of the women are proud of the contributions their work made to their families' economic mobility.

When a number of now elderly private house cleaners were asked whether they are happy they came to Canada, most said yes. Most important is that they were able to give their children a better life. "I think the best thing I ever did for my two kids," noted one woman, "was bringing them to this country" because "they had more options." But even these women are somewhat ambivalent about having chosen to emigrate to Canada. Some think they might have had a good life in Portugal after all, considering the socio-economic changes that have taken place there since the 1970s. Some still feel guilty about having left aging parents behind and not being there when their parents most needed them. Or about living apart from beloved siblings. Still others most remember the difficult early years of settlement, the alienation they felt, the double (or triple) day, and the difficult adjustment to the climate—and also crying a lot. Some women have kept links to Portugal over the years. They have gone on holidays to Portugal periodically, and a few have built houses there in anticipation of their retirement. But very few have in fact moved back permanently. At most, they might spend a few months a year there. Children and grandchildren have permanent ties to Canada, and with older age, and the wear and tear of their labour on their bodies, the women are dependent on the health care system here.[23]

As feminist labour and public historians, and as daughters of southern European working-class women who spent most of their adult lives in Canada working for wages, keeping house, and raising children, we want every working immigrant woman's story remembered. This book has devoted more attention to the labour struggle and activism of building cleaners than to the day cleaners who were less visible to employers and the public alike. But it is equally important to remember the stories of the women who not only laboured in private workplaces, but also transformed the conditions of their paid labour and helped to make the Portuguese cleaning lady a cultural marker of late-twentieth-century Toronto.

In addition to challenging the stereotypes of Portuguese immigrant women and giving them their rightful due as strong, brave, intelligent, and proud workers, our book offers insight into how employment relations shape resistance possibilities. Private cleaners were isolated and vulnerable to exploitation and oppression, with few collective ways to improve their working conditions. Women office cleaners faced formidable opposition from profit-driven employers and pro-business governments, and suffered the negative political and economic impacts of the contracting-out system. They were also undermined by business unions and top-down organizing practices and by the widespread prejudices that assumed they could not be organized or militant. In the context of 2022–26 Ontario, under a pro-business conservative government, and the general pro-business orientation of the federal governments of Canada, contracting out is one of the most effective ways of undermining worker power. The lessons of the Portuguese women cleaners offer important insights into potential ways of challenging government and employer efforts to make employment ever more precarious and, therefore, workers that much more subservient. In tracing how these women came to be active politically, we highlighted that they were motivated by pride in the work they did and a sense of injustice over their work not being recognized or valued. But also that their greatest success came when they were supported by community organizers who helped the workers self-organize and by coalitions with other activist groups, such as social justice, labour, and feminist groups. Equally important, the book makes a strong case for the importance of union organizing that starts from the concerns and knowledge of the workers involved and is linked by coalitions with other activist groups.

Notes

Preface

1 In the primary sources, the spelling of Cleaners' Action varies between the singular and plural versions of the name. The logo used the singular, Cleaner's Action. The editors of the newsletter that was launched in summer 1978 initially used the singular version but quickly shifted to the plural (by the fourth and final issue published in that first year) because it more accurately described the collective action involved. Unless citing a primary source with the singular spelling, we have used the plural version of Cleaners' Action for the same reason: it is more accurate.

2 The epilogue offers a detailed treatment of the mural, but see Gilberto Fernandes, "Collaboration with Vhils in Mural Honoring Cleaners' Action," 26 October 2021, gilbertofernandes.ca; Karen Longwell, "Famous Street Artist Etches Giant Face on Side of Toronto Building," *blogTO*, November 2021, blogto.com.

3 For more details about these women, and the interviews conducted by Susana Miranda, see chs. 3–4.

4 The few main publications on Portuguese women's working lives and labour activism in post-1960 Toronto are Susana Paula Miranda, "Working Women, 'Cleaning Ladies': Portuguese Immigrant Women and Domestic Day Cleaning in 1960s and 1970s Toronto," *Portuguese Studies Review* 11, no. 2 (Winter/Spring 2004): 89–108; and her "An Unlikely Collection of Union Militants?: Portuguese Cleaning Women Become Political Subjects in Postwar Toronto," *Atlantis: A Women's Studies Journal* 32, no. 1 (2007): 111–21, reprinted in *Sisters or Strangers: Immigrant, Ethnic, and Racialized Women in Canadian History*, 2nd ed., ed. Marlene Epp and Franca Iacovetta (Toronto: University of Toronto Press, 2016). See also Franca Iacovetta, *Before Official Multiculturalism: Women's Pluralism in Toronto, 1950s–1970s* (Toronto: University of Toronto Press, 2022), chs. 6 and 8. Feminist anthropologist Wenona Giles focused instead on women's domestic lives: see especially *Portuguese Women in Toronto: Gender, Immigration, and Nationalism* (Toronto: University of Toronto Press, 2002). Older studies that largely neglected women's paid work include Edite Noivo, *Inside Ethnic Families: Three Generations of Portuguese-Canadians* (Montreal/Kingston: McGill-Queen's University Press, 1997); Grace Anderson and David Higgs, *A Future to Inherit: The Portuguese Communities of Canada* (Toronto: McClelland and Stewart, 1976).

5 On the militancy of Portuguese and other immigrant garment workers in

postwar Montreal, see, for example, Carla Lipsig-Mummé, "Organizing Women in the Clothing Trades: Homework and the 1983 Garment Strike in Canada," *Studies in Political Economy* 22 (1987): 41–71, and ch. 6.; Leona Siaw, "Seam Stress: Garment Work and Gendered Labour Struggle in 1980s Montreal" (MA thesis, Concordia University, 2020). On Portuguese militant im/migrants and organizing hospitality workers in England: Gabriella Alberti, "The Hotel Workers Campaign in London: 'Community Unionism' and the Challenges of Organizing Transient Labor" (Leeds University, 2011, rev. 2014), research report for *Mobilizing against Inequality: Unions, Immigrant Workers, and the Crisis of Capitalism*, ed. Lee Adler, Maite Tapia and Lowell Turner (Ithaca: ILR Press, 2014), 5, archive.ilr.cornell.edu.

6   David Harvey, *A Brief History of Neoliberalism* (Oxford: Oxford University Press, 2005), 2, cited in Ethel Tungohan, "The Transformation and Radical Feminism of Grassroots Migrant Women's Movement(s) in Canada," *Canadian Journal of Political Science / Revue canadienne de science politique* 50, no. 2 (June / juin 2017): 484.

7   Details in chs. 5–7, but see Luis Aguiar, "Restructuring and Employment Insecurities: The Case of Building Cleaners," *Canadian Journal of Urban Research* 9, no. 1 (June 2000): 64–93; Luis L.M. Aguiar, "Janitors and Sweatshop Citizenship in Canada," in *The Dirty Work of Neoliberalism: Cleaners in the Global Economy*, ed. Luis L.M. Aguiar and Andrew Herod (Oxford: Blackwell, 2006).

8   See ch. 4.

9   Giles, *Portuguese Women in Toronto*; see especially our chs. 3 and 6.

10   The best treatment of this theme is Gilberto Fernandes, *This Pilgrim Nation: The Making of the Portuguese Diaspora in Postwar North America* (Toronto: University of Toronto Press, 2020). On the elites' recent embrace of the women they once shunned, see the epilogue.

11   On this theme, see especially ch. 4, but for general context, see Margaret Little, Lynne Marks, Marin Beck, Emma Paszat, and Liza Tom, "Family Matters: Immigrant Women Activists and Mainstream Feminists in Ontario and BC, 1960s–1980s, *Atlantis* 41, no. 1 (2021): 105–23; Meg Luxton, "Feminism as a Class Act: Working-Class Feminism and the Women's Movement in Canada," *Labour / Le Travail* 48 (Fall 2001): 63–88; Karen Charnow Lior, ed., *Making the City: Women Who Made a Difference* (Working Women Community Centre; Toronto and Halifax/Winnipeg: Fernwood, 2012); Joan Sangster, *Demanding Equality: One Hundred Years of Canadian Feminism* (Vancouver: UBC Press, 2021), esp. ch 10; Peter Graham with Ian McKay, *Radical Ambition: The New Left in Toronto* (Toronto: Between the Lines, 2019).

12   Ch. 4 focuses on the cleaners' closest (and less studied) community allies; the involvement of prominent (and better studied) union organizers and feminist legal and pay equity activists, as well as NDP politicians is addressed in chs. 5–7, but see Andrée Lévesques, ed., *Madeleine Parent: Activist* (Sumach Press, 2005); Sangster, *Demanding Equality*, ch. 10.

13   We address the theme in more detail in chs. 5–7, but for a different Toronto example, see Jeremy Milloy, "A Battle Royal: Service Work Activism and the 1961–1962 Royal York Strike," *Labour / Le Travail 58* (Fall 2006): 13–40.

14   A recent study is Nandita Sharma, *Home Economics: Nationalism and the Making of "Migrant Workers" in Canada* (Toronto: University of Toronto Press, 2006), but see

also Makeda Silvera, *Silenced: Caribbean Domestic Workers Talk with Makeda Silvera* (Toronto: Sister Vision Press, 1989); see our ch. 3.

15 Justice for Janitors, particularly in the American context, is also abbreviated JfJ. On building cleaners, Ruth Milkman, *L.A. Story: Immigrant Workers and the Future of the U.S. Labor Movement* (New York: Russell Sage Foundation, 2006), esp. ch. 4 co-authored with Kent Wong. Comparisons with Latina domestics arise in several chapters; see Mary Romero, *Maid in the USA* (New York: Routledge, 2002); Pierrette Hondagneu-Sotelo, *Doméstica: Immigrant Workers Cleaning and Caring in the Shadows of Affluence* (Berkeley: University of California Press, 2001).

16 James R. Barrett, "Americanization from the Bottom-Up: Immigration and the Remaking of the Working Class in the United States, 1880–1930," *Journal of American History* 79, no. 3 (December 1992): 996–1020; Milkman, *L.A. Story*; Luxton, "Feminism as a Class Act"; Jodi Giesbrecht, "Accommodating Resistance: Unionization, Gender and Ethnicity in Winnipeg's Garment Industry, 1929–1945," *Urban History Review* 39, no. 1 (2010): 5–19.

17 Chs. 5 and 6 provide a detailed discussion of the subject and scholarship, but a few examples include Julie Guard, "Authenticity on the Line: Women Workers, Native 'Scabs,' and the Multi-ethnic Politics of Identity in a Left-Led Strike in Cold War Canada," *Journal of Women's History* 15, no. 4 (Winter 2004): 117–40; Miranda, "Unlikely Collection of Union Militants?"; Donna Gabaccia, Franca Iacovetta, and Fraser Ottanelli, "Laboring across National Borders: Class, Gender and Militancy in the Proletarian Mass Migrations," *International Labor and Working-Class History* 66 (Fall 2004), esp. 70–71.

18 Comparisons to Justice for Janitors are drawn in chs. 5 and 6, and epilogue, but see Roger D. Waldinger et al., "Helots No More: A Case Study of the Justice for Janitors Campaign in Los Angeles" (Working Paper #15, Lewis Center for Regional Policy Studies, 1996); Milkman, *L.A. Story*.

19 On this literature, see, for example, the review essay (on work) by Lisa Pasoli and Julia Smith and (on immigrant, ethnic, and racialized women) by Marlene Epp and Franca Iacovetta, both in *Reading Canadian Women's and Gender History*, ed. Nancy Janovicek and Carmen Neilson (Toronto: University of Toronto Press, 2019).

20 The interviews (videos and transcripts) are posted on Rise Up! a digital archive of feminist activism, Women Unite: Feminist Activism in Toronto 1970s–1990s (hereafter Rise Up! Women Unite), riseupfeministarchive.ca.

21 Two key texts in what is also called feminist epistemology are Dorothy Smith, *The Everyday World as Problematic: A Feminist Sociology* (Boston: Northeastern University Press, 1987); Patricia Hill Collins, *Black Feminist Thought: Knowledge, Consciousness, and the Politics of Empowerment* (New York: Routledge, 1990).

22 Franca Iacovetta, *Such Hardworking People: Italian Immigrants in Postwar Toronto* (Montreal/Kingston: McGill-Queen's University Press, 1992). Earlier articles included "Primitive Villagers and Uneducated Girls: Canada Recruits Domestics from Italy, 1951–52," *Canadian Woman Studies* 7, no. 8 (Winter 1986): 14–18; "From Contadina to Woman Worker: Southern Italian Immigrant Working Women in Toronto, 1947–62," *Looking into My Sister's Eyes: An Exploration in Women's History*, ed. Jean Burnet (Toronto: Multicultural History Society of Ontario 1986), 195–222.

23 Both quotations from Introduction to *Beyond Women's Words: Feminisms and the*

Practises of Oral History in the 21st Century, ed. Katrina Srigley, Stacey Zembrzycki, and Franca Iacovetta (London and New York: Routledge, 2018), 1.

24 Sherna Berger Gluck and Daphne Patai, eds., *Women's Words: The Feminist Practice of Oral History* (New York: Routledge, 1991); Luisa Passerini, *Fascism in Popular Memory: The Cultural Experience of the Turin Working Class,* trans. Robert Lumley and Jude Bloomfield (Cambridge, UK: Cambridge University Press, 1987) cited in Introduction to Srigley et al., *Beyond Women's Words,* 1; on Indigenous oral history and decolonizing knowledge, see, for example, Introduction and especially the essays by Lianne C. Leddy, by Sue Anderson, Jaimee Hamilton, and Lorina L. Barker, by Penny Couchie and Muriel Miguel, and by Heather A. Howard in Srigley et al., *Beyond Women's Words.* On queer oral history, see, for example, Nan Alamilla Boyd and Horacio N. Roque Ramirez, eds., *Bodies of Evidence: The Practice of Queer Oral History* (New York: Oxford Press, 2023).

25 On this and related themes, see, for example, Lynn Abrams, *Oral History Theory,* 2nd ed. (New York: Routledge, 2016), ch. 4.

26 In regard to Miranda's positionality, being of a different generation and highly educated compared to the cleaners interviewed made her an "outsider," but the "insider" status derived from the fact that the women in her family are cleaners made both the women she already knew and those she did not more comfortable discussing their lives with her. Feminists have debunked the myth of the objective interviewer, but being an "insider" still made it difficult to address and intellectually assess painful matters like domestic violence. As an "insider," Miranda feels a certain pressure to "get the story right," but accepts that her story may be challenged. Also, the narrative differs among different people; some (more elite) community members did not want to discuss cleaners because of the association with servility and focused instead on "success" measured in terms of higher education and social standing. Wenona Giles discusses encountering similar sentiments when interviewing Portuguese cleaners in London in her "Clean Jobs, Dirty Jobs: Ethnicity, Social Reproduction and Gendered Identity," *Culture* 13, no. 2 (1993). Still, the close association of Portuguese immigrant women with cleaning in post-1960 Toronto means understanding, not ignoring, the stereotype.

27 This description draws on an extensive literature, but two texts that synthesize the debates are Abrams, *Oral History Theory* and Srigley et al., *Beyond Women's Words.*

Chapter 1. "I have always worked": Life in Portugal

1 Interview with Carolina Soares (pseudonym) by Susana Miranda, 2 June 2006.

2 Interviews by Susana Miranda with Carolina Soares (pseudonym), 2 June 2006, and Idalina Azevedo, 13 November 2006.

3 "Twentieth-Century Portugal: An Introduction" in *Modern Portugal,* ed. António Costa Pinto (Palo Alto: Society for the Promotion of Science and Scholarship, 1998), 2.

4 Costa Pinto, "Twentieth-Century Portugal," 2; Diamantino P. Machado, *The Structure of Portuguese Society: The Failure of Fascism* (New York: Praeger, 1991), 2.

5 Costa Pinto, "Twentieth-Century Portugal," 2–4; Machado, *Portuguese Society,* 43–44.

6   Costa Pinto, "Twentieth-Century Portugal," 3–6, 17; Machado, *Portuguese Society*, 44–47.

7   Salazar's sympathetic biographers painted him as a boy from an impoverished rural family, but his father was an estate manager and the family owned at least three houses. Machado, *Portuguese Society*, 49–51; Costa Pinto, "Twentieth Century Portugal," 23.

8   Quotation in Costa Pinto, "Twentieth-Century Portugal," 39.

9   Library and Archives Canada (LAC), Department of External Affairs, RG25, Vol. 7048, File: 7175–40, Part 3.1, Canadian Embassy, Lisbon, to Department of External Affairs (hereafter Canadian Embassy, Lisbon, to External Affairs), Re: The unreliability of OEEC reports on Portugal, 28 November 1958.

10   Machado, *Portuguese Society*, 54–56; see also entry on corporatism in *International Encyclopedia of Political Science*, ed. Bertrand Badie, Dirk Berg-Schlosser, and Leonardo Morlino (Los Angeles: Sage Publications, 2011).

11   For example, in 1965, only one-fifth of rural inhabitants belonged to *casas do povo*. Machado, *Portuguese Society*, 59–63 (statistic on p. 63).

12   Canadian Embassy, Lisbon, to External Affairs, Re: The Corporative State in Portugal, 17 November 1959.

13   Machado, *Portuguese Society*, 91.

14   Machado, *Portuguese Society*, 17–18; Fernandes, *This Pilgrim Nation*, 5–20, 187–288.

15   Machado, *Portuguese Society*, 88–89.

16   Ana Vicente, *Mulheres Portuguesas Vistas Por Viajantes Estrangeiros* (Lisboa: Gótica, 2001), 205.

17   City of Toronto Archives (CTA), SC484, St. Christopher House Fonds, Box 137061, File 4, Interview with Maria Vasconcelos (no date).

18   Costa Pinto, "Twentieth-Century Portugal," 35–36.

19   Machado, *Portuguese Society*, 5, 85.

20   Machado, *Portuguese Society*, 87.

21   Such as the Free Trade Association, the General Agreement on Tariffs and Trade, and the International Monetary Fund. Machado, *Portuguese Society*, 10–17.

22   Machado, *Portuguese Society*, 118.

23   Machado, *Portuguese Society*, 17–18.

24   Canadian Embassy, Lisbon, to External Affairs, Re: Portugal's two economic policies: the two faces of Dr. Salazar, 28 October 1958.

25   Machado, *Portuguese Society*, 20–21; Eugene K. Keefe et al., *Portugal: A Country Study* (Washington: Library of Congress, Federal Research Division, 1984), 81.

26   Canadian Embassy, Lisbon, to External Affairs, Re: Portugal's economic policy and her standard of living, 28 April 1960.

27   Gilberto Fernandes, "Moving the 'Less Desirable': Portuguese Mass Migration to Canada, 1953–74," *Canadian Historical Review* 96, no. 3 (2015): 339–74.

28   Herminio Martins, "Portugal," in *Contemporary Europe: Class, Status, and Power*, ed. Margaret Scotford Archer and Salvador Giner (London: Weidenfeld and Nicolson, 1971), 67; Machado, *Portuguese Society*, 22–23; Keefe, *Portugal*, 338.

29   Canadian Embassy, Lisbon, to External Affairs, Re: Agriculture in Portugal, 11 July 1958.

30   Martins, "Portugal," 84; Eric N. Baklanoff, *The Economic Transformation of Spain and Portugal* (New York: Praeger, 1978), 112; Machado, *Portuguese Society*, 24 and 11 (quotation).

31 David Birmingham, *A Concise History of Portugal* (Cambridge 1993), 130; interview with Maria Martins by Susana Miranda, 20 December 2009.

32 Keefe, *Portugal*, 111.

33 Statistic from Machado, *Portuguese Society*, 28; Martins, "Portugal," 84; Keefe, *Portugal*, 81. On the pattern, see, for example, John Bodnar, *The Transplanted: A History of Immigrants in Urban America* (Bloomington: Indiana University Press, 1985) and, for the post-1945 era, Fernandes, "Moving the 'Less Desirable'"; Noula Mina, "Taming and Training Greek 'Peasant Girls' and the Gendered Politics of Whiteness in Postwar Canada: Canadian Bureaucrats and Immigrant Domestics, 1950s–1960s," *Canadian Historical Review* 94, no. 4 (2013): 514–39; Iacovetta, *Such Hardworking People*, ch. 1.

34 The breakdown for the 1.3 million legal emigrants who left Portugal between 1950 and 1988 is as follows: France (25%); Brazil (23%), U.S. (14%); Germany (10%); Canada (10%); "other" (18%). Maria Ioannis B. Baganha, "Portuguese Emigration after World War II" in *Modern Portugal*, ed. Costa Pinto, 193.

35 Carlos Teixeira, "Portuguese," *Enyclopedia of Canada's Peoples* (Toronto: University of Toronto Press, 1999), 1076. The 2016 Canadian census lists 482,610 Portuguese Canadians in the country, statcan.gc.ca.

36 Baganha, "Portuguese Emigration after World War II," 191–92; Fernandes, "Moving the 'Less Desirable.'"

37 Baklanoff, *Economic Transformation of Spain and Portugal*, 130; Machado, *Portuguese Society*, 29–31; Fernandes, "Moving the 'Less Desirable.'"

38 Caroline Brettell, *Men Who Migrate, Women Who Wait: Population and History in a Portuguese Parish* (Princeton, NJ: Princeton University Press, 1986), 260.

39 Interview with Rita Ramos (pseudonym) by Susana Miranda, 16 June 2009.

40 Keefe, *Portugal*, 345.

41 Anderson and Higgs, *A Future to Inherit*, 21. The nine islands are São Miguel, Santa Maria, Faial, Pico, São Jorge, Graciosa, Terceira, Corvo, and Flores.

42 Baganha, "Portuguese Emigration after World War II," 195–96.

43 Anderson and Higgs, *A Future to Inherit*, 21.

44 Birmingham, *A Concise History of Portugal*, 172.

45 Costa Pinto, "Twentieth-Century Portugal," 40.

46 Machado, *Portuguese Society*, 129; on female resisters, Anne Cova and António Costa Pinto, "Women under Salazar's Dictatorship," *Portuguese Journal of Social Science* 1, no. 2 (2002): 129–46.

47 Birmingham, *Concise History of Portugal*, 178.

48 Vicente, *Mulheres Portuguesas*, 202; Cova and Costa Pinto, "Women under Salazar's Dictatorship," 130–31.

49 Virgínia Ferreira, "Engendering Portugal: Social Change, State Politics, and Women's Social Mobilization," in *Modern Portugal*, ed. Costa Pinto, 172–73.

50 Ferreira, "Engendering Portugal,"163.

51 Brettell documented these changes in northern Portugal. See her *Men Who Migrate*; Caroline Brettell, *We Have Already Cried Many Tears: The Stories of Three Portuguese Migrant Women* (Cambridge: Waveland, 1982).

52 Ferreira, "Engendering Portugal," 165.

53 Maria Manuela Stocker de Sousa and Maria Cristina Perez Dominguez, *Women in Portugal* (Brussels: Commission of European Communities, 1982), 21.

54 Machado, *Portuguese Society*, 26.

55 Joyce F. Riegelhaupt, "Saloio Women: An Analysis of Informal and Formal Political and Economic Roles of Portuguese Peasant Women," *Anthropological Quarterly* 40 (1967): 110.

56 Emilio Willems, "On Portuguese Family Structure," *International Journal of Comparative Sociology* 3 (1962): 65–79.

57 Brettell, *Men Who Migrate*; Brettell, *Cried Many Tears*.

58 Willems, "On Portuguese Family Structure," 69.

59 Fatimes Pires, "The Adjustment Problems of the Portuguese Mother," *Papers on the Portuguese Community* (Ottawa: Ministry of Culture and Recreation, 1976); Fernando Nunes, *Problems and Adjustments of the Portuguese Immigrant Family in Canada* (Porto: Secretaria de Estado das Comunidades Portuguesas, 1986). Wenona Giles's later scholarship did not examine women's roles in the homeland, but she, like us, notes that women came as workers even though not defined as such in immigration policy. Giles, *Portuguese Women in Toronto*, 33–36.

60 Ana Nunes de Almeida, "Trabalho feminine e estratégias familiars," *Análise Social* XXI (85), no. 1 (1985).

61 Interview with Mariana Batista (pseudonym) by Susana Miranda, 1 June 2006.

62 Interview with Carolina Soares (pseudonym) by Susana Miranda, 2 June 2006; interview with Rita Ramos (pseudonym) by Susana Miranda, 16 June 2009; Passerini, *Fascism in Popular Memory*.

63 Interview with Joaquina Gomes (pseudonym) by Susana Miranda, 20 June 2009.

64 Interview with Joana Soares (pseudonym) by Susana Miranda, 14 June 2006.

65 Interview with Lucia Ferreira by Susana Miranda, 20 May 2008.

66 Interview with Maria Martins by Susana Miranda, 20 December 2009.

67 Interview with Carolina Soares (pseudonym) by Susana Miranda, 2 June 2006; interview with Joana Soares (pseudonym) by Susana Miranda, 14 June 2006.

68 Interview with Idalina Azevedo by Susana Miranda, 13 November 2006.

69 Interview with Natalia Vilela by Susana Miranda, 15 July 2006.

70 Brettell, *Men Who Migrate*, 39.

71 Interview with Rita Ramos (pseudonym) by Susana Miranda, 16 June 2009.

72 Interview with Maria Martins by Susana Miranda, 20 December 2009.

73 Interview with Celia Filipe (pseudonym) by Susana Miranda, 10 June 2007.

74 Interview with Carolina Soares (pseudonym) by Susana Miranda, 2 June 2006; interview with Joana Soares (pseudonym) by Susana Miranda, 14 June 2006.

75 Interview with Emilia Silva by Susana Miranda, 14 July 2009.

76 Interview with Rosa Moreira (pseudonym) by Susana Miranda, 10 June 2007.

77 Interview with Joana Soares (pseudonym) by Susana Miranda, 14 June 2006.

78 Joan Wallach Scott and Louise A. Tilly, *Women, Work and Family* (New York: Routledge, 1978); de Almeida, "Trabalho feminine e estratégias familiars," 24–25; Lieve Meersschaert, "Alguns contributos para o estudo da identidade das empregadas domésticas em Portugal," *Análise Social* 22, no. 3–4 (1986): 92–93.

79 Interview with Mariana Batista (pseudonym) by Susana Miranda, 1 June 2006.

80 Interview with Natalia Vilela by Susana Miranda, 15 July 2006.

81 Interview with Joaquina Gomes (pseudonym) by Susana Miranda, 20 June 2009; Riegelhaupt, "Saloio Women," 118. See also Meersschaert, "Empregadas domésticas em Portugal," 92–93.

82 Interview with Fernanda Correia (pseudonym) by Susana Miranda, 22 January 2008.

83 Interview with Idalina Azevedo by Susana Miranda, 13 November 2006.

84 Interview with Sofia Bettencourt by Susana Miranda, 9 August 2006; Keefe, *Portugal*, 129–31.

85 Interview with Sofia Bettencourt by Susana Miranda, 9 August 2006.

86 It appeared in *Our Lives: Stories by Portuguese Women* (Toronto Board of Education, 1984), 24, an unpublished collection of stories by the Portuguese women in an ESL class in Toronto.

87 Interview with Joaquina Gomes (pseudonym) by Susana Miranda, 20 June 2009.

88 Interview with Maria Martins by Susana Miranda, 20 December 2009.

89 A tiny sample of the evolving scholarship includes Annie Phizacklea, ed., *One Way Ticket: Migration and Female Labour* (London: Routledge/Kegan Paul, 1983); Mirjana Morokvasic, Introduction, Special Issue: Women and Migration, *International Migration Review* 18, no. 4 (1984): 886–907; Katherine M. Donato et al., "A Glass Half Full?: Gender in Migration Studies," *International Migration Review* 40, no. 1 (2006): 3–26. See also Giles, *Portuguese Women in Toronto*, ch. 1.

90 Interview with Mariana Batista (pseudonym) by Susana Miranda, 1 June 2006.

91 Interview with Celia Filipe (pseudonym) by Susana Miranda, 10 June 2007.

92 Interview with Sofia Bettencourt by Susana Miranda, 9 August 2006; interview with Emilia Silva by Susana Miranda, 14 July 2009.

93 Iacovetta, *Before Official Multiculturalism*, ch. 8; Fernandes, *This Pilgrim Nation*, 17.

94 On this theme and that of economic restructuring, see also Giles, *Portuguese Women in Toronto*.

Chapter 2. Getting Settled

1 Case #560, which belongs to a sample of 2,450 confidential case files (1957 to 1974) featuring Portuguese clients created from Archives of Ontario (AO), International Institute of Metropolitan Toronto Fonds (IIMT), F884, Series E-3. The numbering of the case files in no way reflects where they are located in the collection. To ensure anonymity of all individuals, we have used pseudonyms (or no names at all) and modified some details.

2 Fernandes, *This Pilgrim Nation*, 51.

3 CTA, SC1135, Joe Pantalone Fonds, Box 141044, File 18, Linda Dunn to Commissioner Pirk, Department of Parks and Recreation, City Hall, 20 August 1984.

4 This ranged from help with translation, jobs, and applications for old age pensions to dealing with Workman's Compensation and Manpower services and family crises. LAC, Multiculturalism Directorate, Box 127, File: 3260-P2-2, Portuguese Community in Metropolitan Toronto, prepared by Solomon A. Nigosian for Citizenship Branch, Department of the Secretary of State, June 1971; Box 128, File: 3260-P2-190/P15, Notes for Minister on Portuguese Canadian Congress; John Medeiros, "A Model for Community Development and Organization in an Urban Setting" (MA Thesis, Environmental Studies, York University, 1975), 75–76.

5 AO, IIMT, MU6469, File: Branch Institute (Parkdale) 1962–63, Year-End Report 1 March 1962–1 March 1963. See also Edith Ferguson, *Newcomers in Transition*

(A Project of The International Institute of Metropolitan Toronto, 1962–64); Patricia J. O'Connor, *The Story of St. Christopher House, 1912–1984* (Toronto: Toronto Association of Neighbourhood Services, 1986). On activist work with cleaners, see ch. 4.

6   On the bulk orders involving early Polish veteran and Displaced Persons, Ninette Kelley and Michael Tribelcock, *Making of the Mosaic A History of Canadian Immigration Policy*, 2nd ed. (Toronto: University of Toronto Press, 2010), chs. 8–9; on Italians, Iacovetta, "Primitive Villagers and Uneducated Girls"; *Such Hardworking People*, ch. 2; on Greeks, Mina, "Taming and Training Greek 'Peasant Girls'; on Portuguese, Fernandes, "Moving the 'Less Desirable.'"

7   LAC, Department of Immigration, Immigration Branch, RG76, File: 568-3-23, Memorandum from O. Cormer, Officer-in-Charge, Paris, to Director (Att. Operations), Ottawa Re: Immigration from Portugal, Interim Report, 13 March 1954.

8   LAC, Department of National Health and Welfare, RG29, Vol. 3086, File: 854-3-11, Part 1, Report on Situation in the Azores and Madrid by L.A. Griffith, Medical Officer in Charge, Lisbon, 22 August 1961.

9   Intelligence tests were given to some prospective immigrants out of the Lisbon emigration office. LAC, RG29, Vol. 3086, File: 854-3-11, Part 1, Report on Recent Visit to Lisbon Office by Dr. W. G. Burrows, Psychiatric Consultant (Department of National Health and Welfare) to Dr. J.E. Grant, Chief Medical Officer, 4 April 1961 (quotation); Report on Situation in the Azores and Madrid by L.A. Griffith Medical Officer in Charge, Lisbon, 22 August 1961.

10 Quotation from Department of Citizenship and Immigration, RG26, Vol. 130, File: 3-33-27, Memorandum from Laval Fortier, Deputy Minister of Immigration to Director of Immigration, 25 October 1956; Anderson and Higgs, *A Future to Inherit*, 27; Domingos Marques and João Medeiros, *Portuguese Immigrants: 25 Years in Canada* (Toronto: West End YMCA, 1980); Fernandes, "Moving the 'Less Desirable.'"

11 This discussion draws on several sources, including LAC, RG76, Vol. 690, File 568-3-23, C.E. Smith, Director, Department of Citizenship and Immigration to Chief, Operations Division, 23 December 1952; Chief, Operations Division to Mr. E Beasley 24 February 1953; RG76, Vol. 722, File: 540-6-613, Part 3, D. Ross Fitzpatrick, Executive Assistant (Immigration-Secretariat) to Perry Ryan, MPP Toronto-Spadina, 10 December 1965; RG76, Vol. 900, File: 569-9613, Memo from Attache, Visa Office, Lisbon to Chief of Operations, 8 September 1964. For the comparative context, see Mina, "Taming and Training Greek 'Peasant Girls'" and Sedef Arat-Koc, "From Mothers of the Nation to Migrant Workers," in *Not One of the Family: Foreign Domestic Workers in Canada*, ed. Abigail Bakan and Daiva Stasiulis (Toronto: University of Toronto Press, 1997), 53–79.

12 Case #750.

13 Case #1000.

14 Iacovetta, "Primitive Villagers and Uneducated Girls," 17.

15 Case #250.

16 Case #561; Giles, *Portuguese Women in Toronto*, 31.

17 Varpu Lindström, *Defiant Sisters: A Social History of Finnish Immigrant Women in Canada*, 2nd ed. (Toronto: Multicultural History Society of Ontario, 1992), 91–93; Hondagneu-Sotelo, *Doméstica*, 54.

Chapter 2

18 On Portuguese single women migrating, Wenona Giles and Ilda Januario, "The Lone Woman: The Migration of Portuguese Single Women to Montreal and London," *Canadian Woman Studies* 8, no. 2 (Summer 1987).

19 Interview with Emilia Silva by Susana Miranda, 14 July 2009.

20 CTA, St. Christopher House Fonds, Box 137061, File 13, SCH Summer Report, 1966, Program Director.

21 Monica Boyd, "Immigrant Women in Canada," in *International Migration: The Female Experience,* ed. Rita James Simon and Caroline Brettell (Totowa, N.J.: Rowman & Allanheld, 1986).

22 AO, IIMT, MU6471, File: Cases 1960-62; Memo to Mrs. (Nell) West from Reception Centre, 20 October 1964; Reception Center Registration Forms, 1960-1963.

23 Case #101. When supplied in the text, the names of International Institute clients are pseudonyms.

24 Case #345; Case #444.

25 Case #104; Case #260; Case #40; Case #510. On the project and program (Programme Five of the Federal-Provincial Technical and Vocational Agreement), see Edith Ferguson, *Newcomers and New Learning* (International Institute of Metropolitan Toronto, 1964–66) (hereafter *NNL*); Iacovetta, *Before Official Multiculturalism,* ch. 6.

26 Giles, *Portuguese Women in Toronto,* 36; on Ferguson, AO, MU6470 (B436174), Parkdale Branch, 1962–1965, Ferguson, Report on Sewing Course Trainees, 18 September 1963; Ferguson, *NNL,* 59–62; Franca Iacovetta, *Gatekeepers: Reshaping Immigrant Lives in Cold War Canada* (Toronto: Between the Lines, 2006).

27 Case #160; Case #330.

28 Case #301; Case #120; Case #257; Ferguson, *NNL,* 22–29, 45–49, 75–77.

29 *Our Lives: Stories by Portuguese Women,* 31.

30 Giles, *Portuguese Women in Toronto;* see esp. our chs. 3, 5, and 6.

31 A detailed discussion of these themes is in Iacovetta, *Gatekeepers* and her *Before Official Multiculturalism,* Part 1.

32 AO, IIMT, Reception Center Registrations, 1960–63.

33 Anderson and Higgs, *A Future to Inherit,* 55; on Italian men, Iacovetta, *Such Hardworking People,* 52–76.

34 Case #589; Case #1300; Case #459; Iacovetta, *Gatekeepers,* ch. 5; Iacovetta, *Before Official Multiculturalism,* ch. 4.

35 AO, IIMT, Reception Center Registrations, 1961–63.

36 *Our Lives: Stories by Portuguese Women,* 27. (Only the first name of Lourdes is used).

37 Case #1001; Iacovetta, *Before Official Multiculturalism,* ch. 5.

38 Case #1024.

39 Case #689.

40 On the International Institute, Iacovetta, *Before Official Multiculturalism.*

41 "3 Casos," *Comunidade,* year 1, no. 8, 28 January 1976.

42 Interview with Emilia Silva by Susana Miranda, 14 July 2009.

43 Case #740; Case #870.

44 Case #950.

45 Case #620.

46 Case #360; interview with Mariana Batista (pseudonym) by Susana Miranda, 1 June 2006; Anderson and Higgs, *A Future to Inherit*, 43.

47 Interview with Carolina Soares (pseudonym) by Susana Miranda, 2 June 2006; interview with Joana Soares (pseudonym) by Susana Miranda, 14 June 2006.

48 CTA, St. Christopher House Fonds, Box 137061, File 13, Memo on Foster Day Care Project, 1967.

49 CTA, St. Christopher House Fonds, Box 137061, File 13, Monthly Report on Family Day Care, September to October 1967; Monthly Report on Family Day Care, November 1967.

50 CTA, St. Christopher House Fonds, Box 137061, File 13, Monthly Report on Family Day Care, September to October 1967.

51 "3 Casos," *Comunidade*.

52 For a history, see St. Stephen's Community House, "History," sschto.ca.

53 CTA, SC327, Dan Heap Fonds, Box 138447, File 32, Letter from Portuguese Parents Association, 722 College St., by Secretary Jose Santos Luz, 3 October 1973.

54 CTA, Dan Heap Fonds, Box 138447, File 32, SSCH Day Care Centre, 29 January 1977.

55 CTA, Dan Heap Fonds, Box 138447, File 32, St. Stephen's Community House, Co-operative Day Care Report, October 1973.

56 CTA, St. Christopher House Fonds, Box 137061, File 13, Memo on Foster Day Care Project, SCH, 1967.

57 Quotation from interview with Brenda Duncombe by Susana Miranda, 15 January 2008; CTA, Dan Heap Fonds, Box 138447, File 31, SSCH Day Care Centre, 29 January 1977.

58 CTA, St. Christopher House Fonds, Box 137061, File 15, A Family Life Project in a Downtown Neighbourhood, St. Christopher House, 1963.

59 CTA, St. Christopher House Fonds, Box 137032, File 9, Executive Director Report, John N. Haddad, The SCH Future Plans, Committee Topic No. 10, 1965; Franca Iacovetta and Valerie Korinek, "Jell-O Salads, One-Stop Shopping, and Maria the Homemaker: The Gender Politics of Food," in *Sisters or Strangers?: Immigrant, Ethnic, and Racialized Women in Canadian History*, ed. Marlene Epp, Franca Iacovetta, and Frances Swyripa (Toronto: University of Toronto Press, 2004).

60 Case #410. On the subject, see, for example, Fernando Nunes, "Portuguese-Canadian Youth and Their Academic Underachievement: A Literature Review," *Portuguese Studies Review* 11, no. 2 (Winter–Spring 2003), 41–87; Iacovetta, *Before Official Multiculturalism*, chs. 4 and 6.

61 Ferguson, *Newcomers in Transition*, ch 3.

62 Case #470.

63 Iacovetta, *Before Official Multiculturalism*, chs. 4 and 6.

64 Ferguson, *Newcomers in Transition*, 102, ch. 3.

65 Our detailed treatment is in chs. 4-6, but see Anderson and Higgs, *A Future to Inherit*, 162–74; CTA, Joe Pantalone Collection 1135, Box 14103, File 1, Keynote speech by Rev. Eduardo Couto at Portuguese Interagency Network Conference, May 1982, in The Portuguese Community of Toronto: Needs and Services Report. On elites and community building, see especially Fernandes, *This Pilgrim Nation*.

Chapter 2

Chapter 3. The Work of Cleaning, Workplace Control, and the Cleaner's Body

1   *Toronto Star*, 23 August 1972; "Davenport's Mario Silva Paves Way to Parliament Hill," *Toronto Star*, 12 July 2004.

2   Interview with Beatrice Pinto (pseudonym) by Susana Miranda, 29 June 2007.

3   For just two examples, see Margaret Lynch-Brennan, *The Irish Bridget: Irish Immigrant Women in Domestic Service in America, 1840–1930* (Syracuse: Syracuse University Press, 2009); Ruth Frager, *Sweatshop Strife: Class, Ethnicity and Gender in the Labour Movement of Toronto, 1900–1939* (Toronto: University of Toronto Press, 1992).

4   The same pattern obtained for women in Portugal who migrated from the countryside to the cities. See de Almeida, "Trabalho feminine e estratégias familiars."

5   This discussion draws on several files and interviews, including Case #590; Case #888; Case #777; interview with Celia Filipe (pseudonym) by Susana Miranda, 10 June 2007.

6   AO, Ontario Ministry of Labour, Correspondence of Director of Women's Bureau, RG 7-92, Box 6, File-0-210, Women's Bureau, Report: Overview of Domestic Workers in Ontario, November 1976 (hereafter WB Report: Overview of Domestic Workers).

7   AO, Ontario Ministry of Labour, Minister's Correspondence and Subject Files, RG 7-1, Box 220786, File: Employment Standards Act—Domestics Coverage 1979-80, Explanatory Notes (n.d.); Judy Fudge, "Little Victories and Big Defeats: The Rise and Fall of Collective Bargaining Rights for Domestic Workers in Ontario," in *Not One of the Family*, ed. Bakan and Stasiulis, 119–46.

8   Case #85; Case #369.

9   Case #164.

10 Case #782.

11 Cited in "Office Cleaning: Big Business or an Evil Industry?," *Toronto Star*, 27 September 1975.

12 Case #1060; Case #1213.

13 Anderson and Higgs, *A Future to Inherit*, 56; Manuel Armando Oliveira, "Azorean Diaspora and Cultural Retention in Montreal and Toronto," in *The Portuguese in Canada: Diasporic Challenges and Adjustment*, ed. Carlos Teixeira and Victor M.P. Da Rosa (Toronto: University of Toronto Press, 2009), 98.

14 Lily McQueen, "Why You Can't Get Domestic Help," *Chatelaine*, November 1967.

15 Cynthia Steers, "What You Should Know about Your Cleaning Woman," *Chatelaine*, October 1959.

16 Labour force statistics for 1961 record that 57 percent of Canada's employed Italian women worked in manufacturing, and 28 percent in service jobs, including in laundries, and as cleaners in homes and buildings. Iacovetta, *Such Hardworking People*, 93.

17 AO, IIMT, MU6469, File: Branch Institute 1962–63, Parkdale Branch, Year-End Report, 1 March 1962–1 March 1963.

18 AO, RG7-92-0-305, Box 225058, File: RG7-92, SFWP—Survey of Female Clients May–July 1969 inclusive, by Rosalind Harley, Women's Bureau Career Counsellor; MU6504, Register of Job Opportunities (hereafter Job Register), October 1964–March 1966; Job Book, November 1970–March 1973.

19 AO, RG 7-92, Box 225058, File: SFWP, Rosalind Harley, Women's Bureau Career Counsellor, Survey of Female Clients, May–July 1969.

20 Job Register, October 1964–March 1966; MU6493, Index of Occupations, 1973–74.

21 Interview with Irene Sousa (pseudonym) by Susana Miranda, 1 August 2007. (Miranda conducted all thirteen interviews.)

22 This discussion draws on several interviews by Susana Miranda with day cleaners.

23 Examples from Institute Job Register, October 1964–March 1966.

24 Michele A. Johnson, "'Problematic Bodies': Negotiations and Terminations in Domestic Service in Jamaica, 1920–1970," *Left History* 12, no. 2 (Fall/Winter 2007): 89, 104.

25 Case #761.

26 Case #807; Case #1111.

27 Case #497.

28 Johnson, "Problematic Bodies," 92.

29 For more details on buildings and strikes, see chs. 5 and 6.

30 Walter P. Reuther Library of Labor and Urban Affairs, Wayne State University, (hereafter LLUA), Service Employees International Union (SEIU) Fonds, Box 4, Research Department Collection Part I, File 8: Report 40: Cleaning Industry Data, November 1974.

31 Job Register, October 1964–March 1966.

32 Interview with Isabel de Almeida by Susana Miranda, 14 October 2008.

33 Estimates cited are in several sources, including: Rusty Neal and Virginia Neale, "'As Long as You Know How to do the Housework': Portuguese-Canadian Women and the Office Cleaning Industry in Toronto," *Resources for Feminist Research* 16, no. 1 (1987): 39–41; Wendy Iler, "A Look at the Cleaning Industry," *Canadian Woman Studies* 4, no. 2 (Winter 1982): 70–71; Luis Aguiar, "Restructuring and Employment Insecurities: The Case of Building Cleaners," *Canadian Journal of Urban Research* 9, no. 1 (June 2000): 69–71; Susana Miranda, personal communication with Allen Ferens (SEIU), 16 October 2009; interview with Albert Walker by Susana Miranda, 27 November 2009.

34 Case #444; WB Report: Overview of Domestic Workers; Statistics Canada: average weekly salaries for selected office occupations by city, 1956–1975 (hereafter SC: average weekly salaries), statcan.gc.ca (CSV Version).

35 WB Report: Overview of Domestic Workers; SC: average weekly salaries.

36 Case #999; Iacovetta, *Gatekeepers*, ch. 6; Iacovetta and Korinek, "Jell-O Salads, One-Stop Shopping, and Maria the Homemaker."

37 This discussion draws on interviews by Susana Miranda with several women.

38 Interviews by Susana Miranda with Sofia Bettencourt, 9 August 2006, and Joaquina Gomes (pseudonym), 20 June 2009. On resentment, Romero, *Maid in the USA*, ch. 5.

39 "Office Cleaning: Big Business or an Evil Industry?," *Toronto Star*, 27 September 1975; and n.41.

40 "The Women Who Clean while the City Sleeps," *Globe and Mail*, 26 July 1962.

41 Luis Aguiar, "The 'Dirt' on the Contract Building Cleaning Industry in Toronto: Cleanliness and Work Reorganization" (PhD thesis, York University, 2001), 172; interview with Albert Walker by Susana Miranda, 27 November 2009.

42 Gordon A. MacEachern cited in "The Women Who Clean," *Globe and Mail*.

Chapter 3

43 AO, Ontario Human Rights Commission (OHRC), RG 76-5, Modern Building Cleaning Division memo from Stewart G. Paul, Vice-President, Services to Senior Executives, 23 April 1971. In 1972, Canada signed the International Labour Organization's 1951 Convention 100, which codified the principle of equal pay for equal work. Promoted by the 1970 Royal Commission on the Status of Women, the principle was enshrined in the Canadian Human Rights Act in 1977, but it required women in female-dominated jobs to complain to the Human Rights Commission and to establish discrimination. Proactive legislation, which places the onus on employers to institute pay equity, was implemented by six provinces beginning in 1985. Rosemary Warkett, "Political Power, Technical Disputes, and Unequal Pay: A Federal Case," in *Just Wages: A Feminist Assessment of Pay Equity*, ed. Judy Fudge and Patricia McDermott (Toronto: University of Toronto Press, 1991), 176–80.

44 In his 2009 interview with Miranda, Walker said the profit margins went from being in the double digits in the 1980s to 0 percent–5 percent.

45 "The Women Who Clean," *Globe and Mail*.

46 Mark P. Thomas, "Regulating Flexibility: The Ontario Employment Standards Act and the Politics of Flexible Production" (PhD thesis, York University, 2003), 161.

47 "Tory MPP Says Equal Pay Struggle Is up to Women," *Globe and Mail*, 14 January 1975.

48 "Government Still Guilty of Sex Bias, Unionist Says," *Toronto Star*, 15 May 1975; AO, Correspondence of Ontario Assistant Deputy Minister of Labour, RG 7-22, Box 354637, File RG7-22-0-84, Memorandum: Government Tendering of Contracts and Implications for Labour Policy (C. Backhouse) to Ministry of Labour, 25 March 1976 (hereafter Government Tendering of Contracts 1976).

49 Workplaces of less than 10 workers are excluded from the Act; those with 10 to 99 employees are not obliged but may develop pay equity plans. Unionized companies with over 100 workers have had the most success with implementing pay equity plans because unions have the resources to pursue remedies under the Act. Non-unionized workers face a greater challenge in pursuing pay equity. Carl C. Cuneo, "The State of Pay Equity: Mediating Gender and Class through Political Parties in Ontario," in *Just Wages*, ed. Fudge and McDermott, 43–45.

50 Aguiar, "The 'Dirt,'" 114.

51 Interview with Albert Walker by Susana Miranda, 27 November 2009. On the campaign, see interview with Mary Cornish and Laurell Ritchie by Sue Colley for Rise Up! Women Unite, Winning Equal Pay for Work of Equal Value in Ontario, riseupfeministarchive.ca.

52 Steers, "What You Should Know."

53 The evolution from live-in to live-out domestic work remains hazy for Canada, but for the United States, Alana Erickson Coble, *Cleaning Up: The Transformation of Domestic Service in Twentieth Century New York City* (New York: Routledge, 2006), 23–67, cites World War I and the Depression as key turning points in the process.

54 Interview with Martha Ocampo, Cenen Bagon, Anita Fortuno, Genie Policarpio by Franca Iacovetta for Rise Up! Women Unite, Filipina Activists / Organizing Domestic Workers: Intercede; and interview with Judith Ramirez by Franca Iacovetta, Founding of Toronto Wages for Housework, 1975, both at riseupfeministarchive.ca; Silvera, *Silenced*.

55 Fudge, "Little Victories, Big Defeats" and other essays in *Not One of the Family*, ed. Bakan and Stasiulis.

56 On union organizing efforts in Vancouver, see Rachel Epstein, "Domestic Workers: The Experience in B.C," in *Union Sisters: Women in the Labour Movement*, ed. Linda Briskin and Lynda Yanz (Toronto: Women's Press, 1993).

57 Interview with Martha Ocampo, Cenen Bagon, Anita Fortuno and Genie Policarpio, by Franca Iacovetta for Rise Up! Women Unite, Filipina Activists / Organizing Domestic Workers: Intercede; and interview with Judith Ramirez (Founding of Toronto Wages for Housework, 1975) both at riseupfeministarchive.ca. See also Silvera, *Silenced*.

58 Interview with Joana Soares (pseudonym) by Susana Miranda, 14 June 2006.

59 Interview with Carolina Soares (pseudonym) by Susana Miranda, 2 June 2006.

60 Steers, "What You Should Know."

61 Case #432.

62 Interview with Carolina Soares (pseudonym) by Susana Miranda, 2 June 2006.

63 Interview with Carolina Soares (pseudonym) by Susana Miranda, 2 June 2006.

64 AO, IIMT, MU6474, File: Meetings—Reception Centre, Minutes of Meeting, 16 January 1963.

65 Job Register, October 1964–March 1966 and October 1964–March 1966; Job Book, November 1970–March 1973.

66 Synthetic overviews of the many detailed historical case studies of immigrant domestics include Marilyn Barber, *Immigrant Domestic Servants in Canada* (Ottawa: Canadian Historical Association, 1991); Sedef Arat-Koc, "From 'Mothers of the Nation' to Migrant Workers,'" in *Not One of the Family*, ed. Bakan and Stasiulis.

67 Interview with Carolina Soares (pseudonym) by Susana Miranda, 2 June 2006.

68 Interview with Rita Ramos (pseudonym) by Susana Miranda, 16 June 2009.

69 Joy Parr, *Domestic Goods: The Material, The Moral, and the Economic in the Postwar Years* (Toronto: University of Toronto Press, 1999), 219.

70 Interview with Natalia Vilela by Susana Miranda, 15 July 2006.

71 Interviews by Susana Miranda with Joana Soares (pseudonym), 14 June 2006, and with Joaquina Gomes (pseudonym), 20 June 2009.

72 Susan Strasser, *Never Done: A History of American Housework* (New York: Macmillan, 1982), 89; Ruth Schwartz Cowan, *More Work for Mother: The Ironies of Household Technology from the Open Hearth to the Microwave* (New York: Basic Books, 1983), 11–12; Caroline Davidson, *A Woman's Work Is Never Done: A History of Housework in the British Isles, 1650–1950* (London: Chatto & Windus, 1982), 125.

73 With the suction motor and bag built into a central location and vacuum inlets provided throughout a building, only the (usually 8-metre) hose and the pickup head of a central vacuum is carried from room to room, allowing for a large range of movement without changing inlets.

74 Interview with Joaquina Gomes (pseudonym) by Susana Miranda, 20 June 2009, among other interviews.

75 Interviews by Susana Miranda with Joana Soares (pseudonym) 14 June 2006, and with Rita Ramos (pseudonym), 16 June 2009.

76 Interview with Lucia Ferreira by Susana Miranda, 20 May 2008; "Raise Is Raw Deal, Cleaning Women Say," *Globe and Mail*, 7 February 1976; interview with Idalina Azevedo by Susana Miranda, 13 November 2006.

Chapter 3

77 Interview with Albert Walker by Susana Miranda, 27 November 2009.

78 Government Tendering of Contracts 1976.

79 Aguiar, "The 'Dirt,'" 9–11.

80 "Raise Is Raw Deal," *Globe and Mail*; interview with Lucia Ferreira by Susana Miranda, 20 May 2008.

81 CAW Local 40, First Canadian Place Files, Food and Service Workers of Canada Collection (hereafter FASWOC), Commercial Building Services Notice to Employees, by Jose Martins, Manager, 5 January 1989.

82 AO, Ontario Ministry of Labour, Awards of Arbitration, RG 7-40, Confidential File, 22 September 1981; CAW Local 40, First Canadian Place Files, FASWOC, Memo from FASWOC: Labour School, 12 November 1981.

83 On infrequent employee theft at First Canadian Place, see Ontario Labour Relations Board (OLRB) Reports, *Food and Service Workers of Canada vs Federated Building Maintenance Company Limited and Olympia and York Developments Limited*, November 1985. Online, see *Food and Service Workers of Canada* v. *Federated Building Maintenance Company*, 1985 CanLII 1096 (ON LRB), canlii.ca.

84 CAW Local 40, First Canadian Place Files, FASWOC, Letter to Mr. F. Berbereia from Antonio Meneses, 25 October 1989; Notes from negotiations, 16 February 1988.

85 Sjaak van der Velden, "Strikes, Lockouts, and Informal Resistance," in *Handbook Global History of Work*, ed. Karin Hoffmeester and Marcel van der Linden (Berlin/ Boston: Walter De Gruyter, 2018), 539.

86 Romero, *Maid in the USA*, 15.

87 Hondagneu-Sotelo, *Doméstica*, 201.

88 Interviews by Susana Miranda with several women, including with Joaquina Gomes (pseudonym), 20 June 2009.

89 Coble, *Cleaning Up*, 112, 131; Little, Marks, et al. "Family Matters."

90 This discussion draws on interviews by Susana Miranda with Carolina Soares, Mariana Batista, Rosa Moreira (pseudonyms), and Lucia Ferreira.

91 Craig Heron, *The Canadian Labour Movement: A Short History*, 2nd ed. (Toronto: James Lorimer & Company, 1996), 4.

92 Aguiar, "The 'Dirt,'" 46–47. On this theme, see also Mason Godden, "Contesting Big Brother: Legal Mobilization against Workplace Surveillance in the Puretex Knitting Company Strike, 1978–1979," *Labour / Le Travail* 86 (2020): 71–98.

93 CAW Local 40, First Canadian Place Files, FASWOC, Memo from FASWOC: The Lights, 12 November 1981; Iler, "A Look at the Cleaning Industry."

94 OLRB Reports, *Food and Service Workers of Canada vs. Federated Building Maintenance Company Limited and Olympia and York Developments Limited*, November 1985.

95 Interview with Emilia Silva by Susana Miranda, 14 July 2009.

96 Interview with Idalina Azevedo by Susana Miranda, 13 November 2006.

97 AO, OHRC, RG-76-5, Investigation Report by Fern Gaspar, Human Rights Officer, 3 August 1979.

98 Interview with Albert Walker by Susana Miranda, 27 November 2009.

99 CAW Local 40, First Canadian Place Files, FASWOC, Gina Martins, CTCU to J. Martins, Federated Building Maintenance, 4 April 1989 (first quotation); Gina Martins to Mr. J. Martins, 24 March 1988; Gina Martins, CTCU to Ted Christian, Federated Building Maintenance, 6 December 1989 (second quotation).

100 Case #1002; Case #965. On women and occupational health, see, for example,

Karen Messing, *Bent Out of Shape: Shame, Solidarity and Women's Bodies at Work* (Toronto: Between the Lines, 2021).

101 Interview with Rita Ramos (pseudonym) by Susana Miranda, 16 June 2009.

102 Case #666.

103 Case #1211; Case #533.

104 Interview with Rita Ramos (pseudonym) by Susana Miranda, 16 June 2009.

105 Interview with Joaquina Gomes (pseudonym) by Susana Miranda, 20 June 2009.

106 AO, Ontario Ministry of Labour, Standards and Programs, RG 7-125, Box 392528, File: Domestic, Janitors, Cleaners—Extended Coverage 1978, Report: Background Material on Inclusion of Janitors, Charpersons and Cleaners under Universal Coverage Amendment to Bill 70, Ministry of Labour, 12 April 1970.

107 CAW Local 40, First Canadian Place Files, FASWOC, Notice from CUPE Local 2295 to cleaning staff, 23 January 1985.

108 CAW Local 40, First Canadian Place Files, FASWOC, Gina Martins to J. Martins, 17 May 1989.

109 Interview with Maria Rodrigues by Susana Miranda, 12 May 2009; "Cleaning Substances and Your Health," *Cleaners' Action Newsletter*, year 2, no. 2 (July 1979).

110 CAW Local 40, First Canadian Place Files, FASWOC, Notes from negotiations, 16 February 1988; Letter to Delia from Workers' Compensation Board, 15 November 1988.

111 Heron, *Canadian Labour Movement*, 149; CAW Local 40, First Canadian Place Files, Wendy Iler to T. Kavanagh, Re: Health and Safety Committee, 30 October 1980, Report 13; A Guide for Union Representatives, Health and Safety in the Building Service Industries, June 1981; LLUA SEIU Fonds, Box 1, File 46, Research Department Collection Part Two.

112 Interview with Joaquina Gomes (pseudonym) by Susana Miranda, 20 June 2009.

113 Interview with Joaquina Gomes (pseudonym) by Susana Miranda, 20 June 2009.

114 Interview with Joana Soares (pseudonym) by Susana Miranda, 14 June 2006.

115 Interview with Mariana Batista (pseudonym) by Susana Miranda, 1 June 2006; employers' comments in Job Register, March 1966–August 1967.

116 Interview with Elena Afonso (pseudonym) by Susana Miranda, 3 November 2009.

117 Women's Movement Archives (WMA), University of Ottawa, Working Women Community Centre Collection (WWCCC), SR-X10-29-24, File: Employment options for women, Interview with Portuguese Woman, July 1975.

118 Interview with Celia Filipe (pseudonym) by Susana Miranda, 10 June 2007.

119 Interview with Joaquina Gomes (pseudonym) by Susana Miranda, 20 June 2009.

120 Interview with Joaquina Gomes (pseudonym) by Susana Miranda, 20 June 2009.

121 WMA, SR-X10-29-24, WWCCC, File: Employment options for women, Interview with Portuguese Woman, July 1975. Emphasis added.

122 Interviews by Susana Miranda with Joaquina Gomes (pseudonym), 20 June 2009, and with Celia Filipe (pseudonym), 10 June 2007.

Chapter 3

123 Interviews by Susana Miranda with several women, including Rosa Moreira (pseudonym) and with Joaquina Gomes (pseudonym), 20 June 2009.

124 Interview with Carolina Soares (pseudonym) by Susana Miranda, 2 June 2006.

125 Interview with Joaquina Gomes (pseudonym) by Susana Miranda, 20 June 2009.

Chapter 4. Forging Alliances with Radical Community Workers in 1970s Toronto

1 The "Sweep and Say Union" song and narrative came to us from Marcie Ponte, who was given it by Sidney Pratt, who had been given a copy by Deborah Brandt. Our thanks to them for sharing this wonderful document.

2 See, for example, Iacovetta, *Gatekeepers*.

3. A small sample of the now extensive and growing literature includes Graham and McKay, *Radical Ambition*; Lara Campbell, Dominique Clement, and Gregory Kealey, eds., *Debating Dissent: Canada and the 1960s* (Toronto: University of Toronto Press, 2012); Scott Rutherford, *Canada's Other Red Scare: Indigenous Protest and Colonial Encounters during the Global Sixties* (Montreal/Kingston: McGill-Queen's University Press, 2020); Doug Owram, *Born at the Right Time: A History of the Baby Boom Generation* (Toronto: University of Toronto Press, 1996); Alvin Finkel, *Our Lives: Canada after 1945* (Toronto: James Lorimer & Company, 1997); Magda Fahrni and Robert Rutherdale, eds., *Creating Postwar Canada: Community, Diversity, and Dissent, 1945–75* (Vancouver: UBC Press, 2008). See also Heron, *Canadian Labour Movement*.

4 See Saul Alinsky, *Reveille for Radicals* (Chicago: Penguin Random House, 1946); Saul Alinsky, *Rules for Radicals: A Practical Primer for Realistic Radicals* (New York: Discover Books, 1971); Sanford D. Horwitt, *Let Them Call Me Rebel: Saul Alinsky, His Life and Legacy* (New York: Alfred A. Knopf, 1989).

5 Hugh McLeod, *The Religious Crisis of the 1960s* (Oxford: Oxford University Press, 2007), 89, 97; Hugh McLeod, ed., *The Cambridge History of Christianity, Vol. 9: World Christianities c. 1914–2000* (Cambridge: Cambridge University Press, 2006); Terrence Murphy and Roberto Perin, eds., *A Concise History of Christianity in Canada* (Toronto: Oxford University Press, 1996), 363–65. On early-twentieth-century Canada, see Ramsay Cook, *The Regenerators: Social Criticism in Late Victorian English Canada* (Toronto: University of Toronto Press, 1985); Mariana Valverde, *The Age of Light, Soap, and Water: Moral Reform in English Canada, 1885–1925* (Toronto: University of Toronto Press, 1991).

6 Peter Mayo, *Gramsci, Freire and Adult Education: Possibilities for Transformative Action* (London/New York: Zed Books, 1999), 58–74; Paulo Freire, *Pedagogy of the Oppressed* [1968], 30th anniversary ed., trans. Myra Bergman Ramos (NYC: Continuum International, 2005); Rosemary Donegan, Anita Shilton Martin, D'Arcy Martin, and consultant Paulo Freire, *Starting from Nina: The Politics of Learning* (Development Education Centre, Toronto, and Icarus Films, New York, 1978), riseupfeministarchive.ca.

7 Luxton, "Feminism as a Class Act." Other examples include Sangster, *Demanding Equality*, ch. 10.

8 Racial tensions in Windsor led to a second office being opened there in July 1971; it served Portuguese, Italian, Greek and other European immigrants, Caribbean immigrants, and American Blacks from Detroit.

9 AO, Correspondence of Ontario Deputy Minister of Labour, RG 7-12, Box 363754, File RG 7-12-0-4170, A Research Evaluation of Services for Working People [SFWP], Interim Report, October 1970, prepared by Albert Rose, PhD and John M. Gandy (hereafter SFWP Interim Report, October 1970); Box 354078, File RG 7-12-0-4103, SFWP Report—Services for Working People (n.d.) (hereafter SFWP Report n.d.); AO, Ontario Human Rights Commission (OHRC), RG-76-3, Box 44, File RG76-3-0-765, Report by Robert V. Marino, 3 April 1970.

10 AO, OHRC, RG76-3, Box 44, File RG-76-3-0-924, David V. Trotman Report, Blacks and Portuguese in Downtown Toronto, Summer 1971.

11 Between 1969 and 1971, the average monthly intake jumped from 210 to 1,140 persons. SFWP Report n.d.

12 For example, the Portuguese represented 52 percent of the total client base in October 1970. SFWP Interim Report, October 1970.

13 SFWP Interim Report, October 1970.

14 Quotation from AO, RG 7-92, Box 225058, File: RG 7-92-0-305, Rosalind Harley, WB Career Counsellor, SFWP—Survey of Female Clients (hereafter, SFWP Survey Female Clients), May–July 1969. On the Bureau, see Joan Sangster, "Women Workers, Employment Policy and the State: The Establishment of the Ontario Women's Bureau, 1963–1970," *Labour / Le Travail* 36 (Fall 1995): 119–120.

15 Franca Iacovetta, "Making 'New Canadians': Social Workers, Women, and the Reshaping of Immigrant Families," in Franca Iacovetta, Paula Draper, and Robert Ventresca, *A Nation of Immigrants: Women, Workers, and Communities in Canadian History, 1940s–1960s* (Toronto: University of Toronto Press, 1998), 507; Sangster, "Women Workers, Employment Policy and the State," 129; SFWP Survey Female Clients, May–July 1969.

16 SFWP Survey Female Clients, May–July 1969.

17 SFWP Survey Female Clients, December 1969.

18 SFWP Survey Female Clients, May–July 1969.

19 SFWP Survey Female Clients, August–September 1969.

20 SFWP Interim Report, October 1970.

21 Quotation from RG7-22, Box 354637, File RG7-22-0-84, Memorandum re: Modern Building Cleaners Ltd, Ian Hunter, Faculty of Law, University of Western Ontario to George A. Brown, Ontario Human Rights Commission, 9 March 1976 (hereafter Memo—Modern Building 1976); Government Tendering of Contracts 1976.

22 Government Tendering of Contracts 1976; "Mulheres Portuguesas Lutam Contra a Discriminação," *Comunidade*, year 2, no. 1 (20 July 1976); interview with Michelle Swenarchuk by Susana Miranda, 5 September 2007; *Madeleine Parent: Activist*, ed. and trans. Andrée Lévesque (Toronto: Sumach Press, 2005). On Swenarchuk, see also ch. 5.

23 Government Tendering of Contracts 1976; RG-76-5, Ontario Human Rights Commission, Naison Mawande, Supervisor, Community Relations to J.M. Horgan, Branch Manager, Modern Building, 30 April 1976.

24 Quotation from RG 7-22, Box 354637, File RG7-22-0-84, Ministry of Labour, Government Contracts and Labour Policy Implications, 7 April 1976.

25 CTA, St. Christopher House Fonds, Box 137040, File 35, Free Interpreter Service, Statistical Survey, 1 December 1971–31 January 1972.

26 St. Christopher House, Box 137040, File 36, "A proposal for a new model of

Chapter 4 217

service in the Portuguese Community," 3 July 1974 (hereafter "A proposal, 1974"); interview with Isabel de Almeida by Susana Miranda, 14 October 2008.

27 Interview with Judith Ramirez by Franca Iacovetta for Rise Up! Women Unite, Founding of Toronto Wages for Housework, 1975, riseupfeministarchive.ca.

28 Susana Miranda email correspondence with Sidney Pratt, 2 June 2007.

29 Susana Miranda email correspondence with Sidney Pratt, 28 November 2009

30 Susana Miranda email correspondence with Sidney Pratt, 2 June 2007.

31 May Hobbs, *Born to Struggle* (London: Quartet Books Limited, 1973). See also Sarah Taylor's portrait of Hobbs in East End Museum, "May Hobbs and the Night Cleaners' Campaign," eastendwomensmuseum.org and Sheila Rowbotham's more critical "Cleaners' Organizing in Britain from the 1970s: A Personal Account," in *The Dirty Work of Neoliberalism*, ed. Aguiar and Herod, 177–94.

32 Susana Miranda email correspondence with Pratt, 2 June 2007; interview with Sidney Pratt by Susana Miranda, 18 June 2007.

33 "A proposal, 1974."

34 Sidney Pratt had read Alinsky's book and knew some of the people who worked with him. Susana Miranda email correspondence with Sidney Pratt, 28 November 2009.

35 She later moved to British Columbia to teach at a Catholic primary school funded by the community. Interview with Claire Richard by Susana Miranda, 30 July 2008. On The Grail (est. in Holland in 1921), which today includes other Christians as well as non-Christians, and has branches in two dozen countries, see grail-us.org.

36 CTA, St. Christopher House Fonds, Box 137057, File 13, Programme Package on PISEM, August 1977.

37 Interview with Claire Richard by Susana Miranda, 30 July 2008. For wider Toronto contexts, see Graham and McKay, *Radical Ambition*.

38 Birmingham, *A Concise History of Portugal*, 174–75; CTA, Joe Pantalone Collection 1135, Box 14103, File 1, The Portuguese Community of Toronto: Needs and Services Report, Rev. Eduardo Couto, keynote speech at Portuguese Interagency Network Conference, May 1982; interview with Sidney Pratt by Susana Miranda, 18 June 2007.

39 CTA, St. Christopher House Fonds, Box 137057, File 13, Programme Package on PISEM, August 1977 (hereafter Programme Package on PISEM August 1977).

40 Programme Package on PISEM August 1977.

41 Quotation from Programme Package on PISEM August 1977; Pratt quotation from interview with Sidney Pratt and Marcie Ponte by Franca Iacovetta for Rise Up! Women Unite, Portuguese Cleaners / Birth of Cleaners' Action 1975, riseupfeministarchive.ca.

42 Programme Package on PISEM August 1977.

43 Interview with João Medeiros by Susana Miranda, 12 June 2006. Medeiros completed a master's in Environmental Studies at York University in 1975. His major research paper, entitled "A Model for Community Development and Organization in an Urban Setting," was based on the Portuguese community.

44 Domingos Marques, who arrived in Canada in 1968 at age 19, had attended a seminary in Portugal so was well educated.

45 Domingos Marques Personal Files, Domingos Marques and João Medeiros, Media Workshop: Filling the Gap in Information.

46 Interview with Brenda Duncombe by Susana Miranda, 15 January 2008.

47 See entries by Pratt and others in Duncombe's obituary, legacy.com.

48 John R. Graham, "The Downtown Churchworkers' Association: The Emergence of a Social Welfare Ethos in the Anglican Diocese of Toronto, 1912–1988," in *Social Welfare in Toronto: Two Historical Papers* (Toronto: Faculty of Social Work, University of Toronto, 1991).

49 Susana Miranda email correspondence with Sidney Pratt, 28 November 2009; Heron, *Canadian Labour Movement*, 148.

50 CTA, St. Christopher House Fonds, Box 137057, File 13, Community Development and Education: An Experience in Literacy 1977–78.

51 *Literacy: Charitable Enterprise or Political Right?*, prepared by Literacy Working Group, St. Christopher House, Toronto, 1977. Co-written by Sidney Pratt, Naldi Nomez, and Patricio Urzua. Available on greedymouse.ca.

52 CTA, St. Christopher House Fonds, Box 137057, File 13, Community Development and Education: An Experience in Literacy 1977–78; Box 137061, File 1, Literacy Content Analysis (no date); Iacovetta interview with Pratt and Ponte, Rise Up! Women Unite; Franca Iacovetta email correspondence with Sidney Pratt, 19 September and 24 October 2022.

53 Pratt, Nomez, and Urzua, *Literacy: Charitable Enterprise or Political Right?*

54 Donegan et al., *Starting from Nina*; on *Writers Ink*, West Neighbourhood (formerly St. Christopher) website, "Our History," westnh.org.

55 Interview with Jean Connon Unda by Susana Miranda, 25 September 2007.

56 Interview with Sidney Pratt by Susana Miranda, 18 June 2007; Hobbs, *Born to Struggle*; Taylor, "Hobbs and the Night Cleaners' Campaign." On broader efforts, see Rowbotham, "Cleaners' Organizing in Britain from the 1970s."

57 Marcie Ponte (first quotation) and Sidney Pratt (second and third quotations) from interview by Franca Iacovetta for Rise Up! Women Unite, Portuguese Workers / Birth of Cleaners' Action 1975, riseupfeministarchive.ca.

58 Interview with Marcie Ponte (and Sidney Pratt) by Franca Iacovetta for Rise Up! Women Unite, Portuguese Workers / Birth of Cleaners' Action 1975, riseupfeministarchive.ca.

59 *Cleaner's Action Newsletter*, year 1, no. 1 (Summer 1978). On spelling, see Preface n.1.

60 *Cleaner's Action Newsletter*, year 1, no. 1 (Summer 1978).

61 Pratt interviewed by Miranda, 18 June 2007. On feminist and immigrant women's activism, see, for example, Little, Marks, et al., "Family Matters"; Luxton, "Feminism as a Class Act"; Karen Charnow Lior, *Making the City: Women Who Made a Difference* (Working Women Community Centre) (Halifax/Winnipeg: Fernwood, 2012).

62 Quotation from entry, "Economic Nationalism," by Abraham Rotstein, *Canadian Encyclopedia* (2006; 2015), thecanadianencyclopedia.ca.

63 "Government Office Cleaners Complain of New Pay Contract," *Toronto Star*, 10 February 1976.

64 Details from CTA, St. Christopher House Fonds, Box 137060, File 53, Minutes of Meeting of St. Christopher House Adult Services Review Committee, 15 May 1979; Draft Report of Adult Services Review Committee; Box 137041, File 102; Report of Adult Services Review Committee, September 1979.

65 By the later 1970s and early 1980s, WWCC aided on average two hundred Spanish and Portuguese-speaking women per month. Women's Movement

Chapter 4

Archives (WMA), University of Ottawa, Box 949, Working Women Community Centre, Files X10-29, 20th Anniversary Commemorative Issue on WWCC) 1976–1996; Immigrant Settlement Statistics for 1970–83; Lior, *Making the City*, 13–18; interview with Marcie Ponte by Sue Colley for Rise Up! Women Unite, Immigrant Women Create the Working Women Community Centre, riseupfeministarchive.ca.

66 Susana Miranda email correspondence with Marcie Ponte, 29 April 2010.

67 Quotation from 20th Anniversary Commemorative Issue, WWCC 1976–1996; interview with Marcie Ponte by Susana Miranda, 3 July 2007; Miranda email correspondence with Marcie Ponte, 29 April 2010.

68 Tania Das Gupta, *Learning from Our History: Community Development by Immigrant Women in Ontario, 1958–1986* (Toronto: Cross Cultural Community Centre, 1986), 62–63.

69 Portuguese Women's Group, File: Portuguese Daily Statistics, Box 945, Working Women Community Centre Files X10-29, WMA; Interview with Marcie Ponte by Sue Colley for Rise Up! Women Unite, Immigrant Women Create the Working Women Community Centre, 1975, riseupfeministarchive.ca.

70 Das Gupta, *Learning from Our History*, 72–73; interview with Lina Costa by Susana Miranda, 6 February 2008; on earlier social workers, Iacovetta, *Gatekeepers*.

71 Interview with Lina Costa by Susana Miranda, 6 February 2008.

72 CTA, St. Christopher House Fonds, Box 137061, File 19, Memo on "Battered Immigrant Women's Group," 1983.

73 Interview with Lina Costa by Susana Miranda, 6 February 2008.

74 Interview with Lina Costa by Susana Miranda, 6 February 2008.

75 *Cleaners' Action Newsletter*, year 5, no. 2 (July 1982).

76 Interview with Lina Costa by Susana Miranda, 6 February 2008.

77 CTA, St. Christopher House Fonds, Box 137068, File 12, Adult Services—Domestic Violence 1983.

78 CTA, St. Christopher House Fonds, Box 137068, File 12, Adult Services—Domestic Violence 1983, St. Christopher Neighbourhood House, "We Are Not Born to Suffer: Six Portuguese Women Tell Their Stories" (Toronto, 1991), 4–5. Only the first name of Ana is used.

79 CTA, St. Christopher House Fonds, File 12, Box 137068, Domestic Violence Group Project, 1982–83.

80 St. Christopher Neighbourhood House, "We Are Not Born to Suffer," xi.

81 Susana Miranda email correspondence with Sidney Pratt, 2 June 2007.

82 Barrett, "Americanization from the Bottom Up"; see also Milkman, *L.A. Story*, ch. 3; Giesbrecht, "Accommodating Resistance."

83 Interview with Brenda Duncombe by Susana Miranda, 15 January 2008.

Chapter 5. Battling Corporate Giants: Union Activism in the 1970s

1 Christopher Hume, "When Mies's Towers Scraped the Sky," *Toronto Star*, 28 May 2007; Jaren Kerr, "TD Centre Marks 50th Anniversary with Minimalist Message in the Sky," *Toronto Star*, 4 September 2017, thestar.com.

2 CTA, Dan Heap Fonds, Box 138426, File 19, Dan Heap, Alderman Ward 6, to Local Board of Health re: Cleaners, T-D Centre, 9 June 1974 (quotation); G.W.O Moss, Medical Officer of Health, City of Toronto, Department of Public Health, to Alderman Dan Heap re: Fairview Corp. Ltd, T-D Centre, 28 May 1974.

3   Interview with Idalina Azevedo by Susana Miranda, 13 November 2006.
4   Some examples of historical work on immigrant women and unions for an earlier period include Frager, *Sweatshop Strife*; Joy Parr, *The Gender of Breadwinners: Women, Men, and Change in Two Industrial Towns, 1880–1950* (Toronto: University of Toronto Press, 1990); and Giesbrecht, "Accommodating Resistance"; and for the post-1945 era, Lipsig-Mummé, "Organizing Women in the Clothing Trades"; Joan Sangster, *Transforming Labour: Women and Work in Post-war Canada* (Toronto: University of Toronto Press, 2010), ch. 2; Guard, "Authenticity on the Line"; and Godden, "Contesting Big Brother."
5   More recent work includes Fernandes, *This Pilgrim Nation*; Miranda, "Working Women, 'Cleaning Ladies'" and her "An Unlikely Collection of Union Militants?"; Giles, *Portuguese Women in Toronto*. Older studies include Noivo, *Inside Ethnic Families*; Anderson and Higgs, *A Future to Inherit*.
6   Heron, *Canadian Labour Movement*, chs. 4–5; David Camfield, "Renewing the Study of Public Sector Unions in Canada," in *Public Sector Unions in the Age of Austerity*, ed. Stephanie Ross and Larry Savage (Fernwood, 2013), 55–72; Luxton, "Feminism as a Class Act."
7   There are social hierarchies within the service sector, with cleaners ranking near the bottom of the hierarchy. Examples of the activism of such workers include: Annelise Orleck, *"We Are All Fast-Food Workers Now": The Global Uprising against Poverty Wages* (Boston: Beacon Press, 2018); Dorothy Sue Cobble, *Dishing It Out: Waitresses and Their Unions in the Twentieth Century* (University of Illinois, 1992); Waldinger et al., "Helots No More"; Milkman, *L.A. Story*; and for post-1945 Toronto, Jeremy Milloy, "A Battle Royal: Service Work Activism and the 1961–1962 Royal York Strike," *Labour / Le Travail* 58 (Fall 2006): 13–40. Union drives among other service workers, such as office employees, bank tellers, and salesclerks, have in some cases been both inspiring and notoriously difficult.
8   Interview with Idalina Azevedo by Susana Miranda, 13 November 2006.
9   Examples include Parr, *Gender of Breadwinners*; Joan Sangster, *Earning Respect: The Lives of Wage-Earning Women in Small Town Ontario, 1920–60* (Toronto: University of Toronto Press, 1994); Pamela Sugiman, *Labour's Dilemma: The Gender Politics of Auto Workers in Canada, 1937–1979* (Toronto: University of Toronto Press, 1994).
10   Guard, "Authenticity on the Line," 118. A small sample of this now extensive literature includes Rhonda L. Hinther, *Perogies and Politics: Canada's Ukrainian Left, 1891–1991* (Toronto: University of Toronto Press, 2018); Jennifer Guglielmo, "Italian Women's Proletarian Feminism in the New York City Garment Trades, 1890s–1940s"; Caroline Merithew [Waldron], "Anarchist Motherhood: Toward the Making of a Revolutionary Proletariat in Illinois Coal Towns"; José Moya, "Italians in Buenos Aires' Anarchist Movement: Gender Ideology and Women's Participation, 1890–1910," all in *Women, Gender and Transnational Lives: Italian Workers of the World*, ed. Donna Gabaccia and Franca Iacovetta (Toronto: University of Toronto Press, 2002); Robert Ventresca, "Cowering Women, Combative Men?: Femininity, Masculinity, and Ethnicity on Strike in Two Southern Ontario Towns, 1964–66," *Labour / Le Travail* 39 (Spring 1997): 125–58; and Ardis Cameron, *Radicals of the Worst Sort: Laboring Women in Lawrence, Massachusetts, 1890–1912* (Urbana: University of Illinois Press, 1993), which also documents how the women's critics drew on middle-class expectations of

Chapter 5   221

feminine propriety to label such women (including the wives of strikers who engaged in aggressive behaviour) as unruly and unfeminine. See also ch. 6.

11 Here, we borrow from and apply to rank-and-file workers Janet Zandy's evocative discussion of leading radical women in "Dangerous Working-Class Women: Mother Jones, Lucy Parsons, and Elizabeth Gurley Flynn," *DQR Studies in Literature* 45, no. 1 (January 2010): 41–62. On the earthy militancy of southern European women workers, see, for example, Donna Gabaccia and Franca Iacovetta, eds., Introduction to *Women, Gender, and Transnational Lives: Italian Workers of the World* (Toronto: University of Toronto Press, 2002) and the references in the next note.

12 Gabaccia, Iacovetta, and Ottanelli, "Laboring across National Borders," 70–71. On decentring, Miranda, "Unlikely Collection of Union Militants?"; Franca Iacovetta, "Feminist Transnational Labour History and Rethinking Women's Activism and Female Militancy in Canadian Contexts: Lessons from an International(ist) Project," paper presented at annual meeting of the Canadian Historical Association, June 2004.

13 Jennifer Guglielmo, *Living the Revolution: Italian Women's Resistance and Radicalism in New York City, 1880–1945* (University of North Carolina Press, 2010); Waldinger et al., "Helots No More"; Milkman, *L.A. Story*, esp. ch. 3; Guard, "Authenticity on the Line."

14 Heron, *Canadian Labour Movement*, chs. 4–5.

15 Heron, *Canadian Labour Movement*, 75–84; on its uneven impact, see Sangster, *Transforming Labour*.

16 Approximately 10 percent of cleaners were organized. LAC, Confederation of Canadian Union Fonds, R7115, File 37-9, FASWOC Submission to Hon. David Peterson and Hon. William Wrye, 6 February 1986.

17 Albert G. Hearn, *Building a Dream: The History of a Union for Canadian Service Workers 1943–1988* (1988), 6–10, 33.

18 Hearn, *Building a Dream*, 39.

19 LLUA, SEIU Fonds, Box 67, Executive Office Files: George Hardy Collection, Summary of potential organizing by Al Hearn, 27 May 1971.

20 The William Ready Division of Archives and Research Collections (hereafter WRDARC), McMaster University, Series 8, Service Employees International Union (SEIU) Fonds, File: Newspaper clippings 1964–1966; Albert G. Hearn, "A View from the Basement: How the Union Looks at the Case for the Building Employee," *Building Management* 3, no. 8 (August 1964).

21 WRDARC, SEIU Fonds, Series 2, Box 5, File: Minute Book, July 1966 to January 1967, Minutes of General Meeting of Local 204, BSEIU, 11 May 1966; Report to Executive Board submitted by Brother Hearn Re: Toronto Dominion Centre.

22 WRDARC, SEIU Fonds, Series 2, Box 5, Minutes of Executive Board Meeting of SEIU Local 204, 4 May 1972.

23 LLUA, SEIU Fonds, "204 Leadership for City's New Canadians," *Canadian Service Employee* 1, no. 8 (August 1972).

24 Barrett, "Americanization from the Bottom-Up," 996–1020. See also Milkman, *L.A. Story*, ch. 3; Giesbrecht, "Accommodating Resistance."

25 "204 Leadership for City's New Canadians," *Canadian Service Employee*.

26 Portuguese hotel cleaners in England formed a Portuguese branch of the Transport and General Workers' Union in 1972; soon afterwards, it was opened to

workers of other nationalities and renamed the International Workers' Branch. See Alberti, "Hotel Workers Campaign in London"; University of Warwick, Modern Records Centre, Transport and General Workers' Union International Workers' Branch: Papers of Alvaro de Miranda, mrc-catalogue.warwick.ac.uk.

27 This description draws on several sources, including CTA, Dan Heap Fonds, Box 138426, File 19, Dan Heap, Alderman Ward 6 to Chairman and Members of Local Board of Health re: Cleaners, TD Centre, 19 June 1974; G.W.O Moss, Medical Officer of Health, City of Toronto, Department of Public Health to Heap re: Fairview Corp. Ltd, T-D Centre, 28 May 1974.

28 Interview with Idalina Azevedo by Susana Miranda, 13 November 2006; CTA, Dan Heap Fonds, Box 138426, File 19, Dan Heap, Alderman Ward 6 to Chairman and Members of the Local Board of Health re: Cleaners, TD Centre, 19 June 1974.

29 CHIN radio interview with Idalina Azevedo, October 2021.

30 On the complex, see *Toronto Modern: Documenting Modernist Architecture in Toronto* (blog), "Conserving a Hideo Sasaki landscape," by Toronto Modern Architecture, 13 August 2015, robertmoffatt115.wordpress.com; and The Cultural Landscape Foundation, "Queen's Park Complex," tclf.org.

31 Michelle Swenarchuk, "Portuguese Women Organize," *Law Union News* 3, no. 2 (February 1976). The male differential was $2.50–$3.00 versus $4.62 an hour.

32 CTA, Dan Heap Fonds, Box 138443, File 3, "Practical Politics," *The Kensington*, October 1976.

33 João Medeiros, "Origem Da Luta Das Mulheres de Limpeza," *Comunidade*, year 1, no. 5 (November 1975): 1, 10.

34 Interview with Elena Afonso (pseudonym) by Susana Miranda, 3 November 2009.

35 Milkman, *L.A. Story*.

36 For just one example, Guglielmo in "Italian Women's Proletarian Feminism in the New York City Garment Trades."

37 Medeiros, "Origem Da Luta Das Mulheres de Limpeza."

38 Swenarchuk, "Portuguese Women Organize."

39 Quotation from AO, OHRC, RG76-3, Box 55, File RG 76-3-0-1261, Services for Working People, 1974 Narrative; interview with Michelle Swenarchuk by Susana Miranda, 5 September 2007.

40 Interview with Elena Afonso (pseudonym) by Susana Miranda, 3 November 2009.

41 Swenarchuk, "Portuguese Women Organize."

42 Heron, *Canadian Labour Movement*, 91.

43 "Asked for Higher Pay, 97 Cleaning Workers Get Dismissal Notices," *Globe and Mail*, 17 September 1975.

44 Swenarchuk, "Portuguese Women Organize."

45 "Governo nada fez pelas mulheres de limpeza," *Comunidade*, year 1, no. 4 (October 1975).

46 "Asked for Higher Pay," *Globe and Mail*.

47 Services for Working People, 1974 Narrative.

48 Mercedes Steedman, *Angels of the Workplace: Women and the Construction of Gender Relations in the Canadian Clothing Industry, 1890–1940* (Toronto: University of Toronto Press, 1997).

49 LLUA, SEIU Fonds, Box 22, File 22-8, John J. Sweeney to George Hardy Re:

Chapter 5   223

Request for Separate Charter by employees at the University of Toronto Local 204.

50 CTA, Dan Heap Fonds, Box 138427, File 19, Dan Heap, Alderman Ward 6, to Neil Wood, President, Cadillac Fairview Corp. Ltd., 21 March 1978; Albert G. Hearn, International VP SEIU, to Alderman Dan Heap, 27 March 1978; J.R. Stanley, Manager, Cleaning Services, Modern Building Cleaning to Miss June Nobuoka, Executive Assistant, Cadillac Fairview Corp, 29 March 1978. See also "T.D. Cleaners Remove American Union," *Cleaners' Action Newsletter*, year 2, no. 1 (May 1979).

51 Quotation from Pratt in Interview by Franca Iacovetta with Sidney Pratt and Marcie Ponte, Birth of Cleaners' Action, for Rise Up!, riseupfeministarchive.ca.

52 Quotation from WRDARC, SEIU Fonds, Series 2, Box 6, File: Executive Board and Council Minutes, May 1974–10 July 1974, Business Agent's Report for May 1974; CTA, St. Christopher House Fonds, Box 137060, File 53, Minutes of Meeting of St. Christopher House Adult Services Review Committee, 16 May 1979; interview with Sidney Pratt by Susana Miranda, 18 June 2007; "T.D. Cleaners Remove American Union," *Cleaners' Action Newsletter*.

53 Interview with Michelle Swenarchuk by Susana Miranda 5 September 2007. On the larger theme, see, for example, Heron, *Canadian Labour Movement*, 134–43. See also ch. 4.

54 "Cleaners Do T.D. Center Expulsam Sindicato Incompetente," *Comunidade*, year 5, no. 1 (29 June 1979).

55 "Cleaners Do T.D. Center Expulsam Sindicato Incompetente," *Comunidade*.

56 LAC, Confederation of Canadian Union Fonds (CCU), R 7115, File: 23-10, Wendy Iler to Peter Quinn, President, CFASU, 1 November 1978.

57 "T.D. Cleaners Remove American Union," *Cleaners' Action Newsletter*.

58 See Stephanie Ross, "The Making of CUPE: Structure, Democracy and Class Formation" (Ph.D. diss., York University), esp. 255–56.

59 LLUA, SEIU Fonds, Series 1, Box 21, File 2151, Albert G. Hearn, 2nd International Vice President to Donald MacDonald, President Canadian Labour Congress, Ottawa, 30 March 1970, Re: CUPE and SEIU Local 204 and Metropolitan Toronto Separate School Board.

60 Heron, *Canadian Labour Movement*, 98; "Cleaners Choose a New Union," *Cleaners' Action Newsletter*, year 2, no. 2 (July 1979).

61 Interview with Humerto Da Silva by Susana Miranda, 12 December 2006.

62 On CFASU, see UBC Library, Fonds RBSC-ARC-1197, Food and Service Workers of Canada Union fonds, prepared by Diane Rodgers and Michael Carter, 7 December 1992, rbscarchives.library.ubc.ca.

63 Mine-Mill hosted the founding convention in Sudbury in July 1969. Besides Mine-Mill and Canadian Textile and Chemical Union (formerly Canadian Textile Council), other early affiliates consisted of unions that had broken away from US internationals in the 1960s, such as the Pulp and Paper Workers of Canada, the Canadian Association of Industrial, Mechanical and Allied Workers, the Bricklayers, Masons Independent Union of Canada, the Canadian Union of Operating Engineers, and the Canadian Electrical Workers Union.

64 Interview with John Lang by Susana Miranda, 13 March 2007. Heavily immigrant workplaces included Artistic Woodwork, Puretex Knitting, and McGregor Hosiery Mills. CAW Local 40, First Canadian Place Files, FASWOC, Canadian Textile and Chemical Union: A Brief History.

65 CTA, St. Christopher Fonds, Box 137061, File: Visits, Organizers Meeting, 23 September 1977; Instructions for Visits (n.d.); Canadian Food and Associated Services Union Flyer, "Does 5 Cents Give Us Job Security?"; "Mulher Portuguesa Exigiu Direitos," *Comunidade*, year 2, no. 6 (25 November 1976).

66 Interview with Wendy Iler by Susana Miranda, 16 August 2006; interview with Emilia Silva by Susana Miranda, 14 July 2009.

67 Interview with Lucia Ferreira by Susana Miranda, 20 May 2008.

68 Interview with Emilia Silva by Susana Miranda, 14 July 2009.

69 LAC, CCU Fonds, R 7115, File: 23-9, *inDIGESTion* (Canadian Union for Restaurant, Hotel and Hospitality Industry Workers—CCU).

70 Interview with Emilia Silva by Susana Miranda, 14 July 2009.

71 On this theme, see, for example, Luxton, "Feminism as Class Act"; Lévesques, ed., *Madeleine Parent: Activist*, especially editor's Introduction and chapters by John Lang and by Lynn Kaye and Lynn McDonald; interview with Mary Cornish and Laurell Ritchie by Sue Colley for Rise Up! Women Unite, Winning Equal Pay for Work of Equal Value in Ontario, riseupfeministarchive.ca; Sangster, *Demanding Equality*, ch. 10; Godden, "Contesting Big Brother"; and ch. 4.

72 CAW Local 40, First Canadian Place Files, FASWOC, Memo from Federated Building Maintenance, Housekeeping Manager Re: Wages and Benefits, 4 May 1978.

73 Including at this time at the Royal Bank and Commerce Court buildings. CAW Local 40, First Canadian Place Files, FASWOC, Notes by Ted Kavanagh (Federated) to Local 51 FASWOC office (n.d.).

74 "Chars Clean Up—on the Boss," *Toronto Star*, 3 October 1979.

75 Ontario Labour Relations Board Report (OLRB), Canadian Food and Associated Services Union vs. Federated Building Maintenance Company Limited, October 1979.

76 Interview with Michelle Swenarchuk by Susana Miranda, 5 September 2007.

77 The first collective agreement came into effect on 13 April 1980. A second one was executed in 1982 for another two-year term. OLRB Report, *Canadian Food and Associated Services Union vs. Federated Building Maintenance Company Limited*, October 1979; OLRB, November 1985.

Chapter 6. "We are women and immigrants but we can fight": First Canadian Place Strike, 1984

1 Tim Harper, "Four Arrested for Trespassing at Cleaners' Picket Line," *Toronto Star*, 28 June 1984, A3.

2 See, for example, Waldinger et al., "Helots No More"; Milkman, *L.A. Story*.

3 Fatima Rocchia (her married name) was one of the founders of the Action Committee for Garment Workers (CATV), which helped to mobilize the heavily female, diverse, and militant immigrant garment workers with the US-based International Ladies Garment Workers Union (ILGWU) to protest worsening conditions by launching an industry-wide strike (known as "la greve de la fiertes" / "the strike of pride") in Montreal in 1983. In a recent interview (2017) with Leona Siaw, Rocchia, writes Siaw, "openly marveled at her own pluck, repeatedly calling herself a '*brasseuse de merde*.'" Leona Siaw, "Seam Stress: Garment Work and Gendered Labour Struggle in 1980s Montreal" (MA thesis, Concordia University, 2020), 15–19, quotation on 16. See also Lipsig-Mummé,

"Organizing Women in the Clothing Trades"; Lauren Laframboise, "Gendered Labour, Immigration, and Deindustrialization in Montreal's Garment Industry" (MA thesis, Concordia University, 2021).

4   Barrett, "Americanization from the Bottom-Up"; Giesbecht, "Accommodating Resistance." We thank Meg Luxton for reminding us to emphasize the second point, and see, for example, her "Feminism as a Class Act."

5   CAW Local 40, First Canadian Place Files, FASWOC, FASWOC National Vice President was Wendy Iler, and the union rep was Michael Schuster. "Police Accused of Helping 'Scabs': Tension Rises on Cleaners' Picket Line," *Globe and Mail*, 6 June 1984.

6   Heron, *Canadian Labour Movement*, 111.

7   "Strike Wins Women Better Deal," *Toronto Star*, 14 July 1984.

8   Ontario Labour Relations Board Report, *Canadian Food and Associated Services Union vs. Federated Building Maintenance Company Limited*, October 1979.

9   "Cleaning Ladies Fight Goliath," *Paranoia* (CEIU) 2, no. 5 (July–August 1984).

10   Wendy Iler interviewed by Susana Miranda, 16 August 2006; Stuart Crombie, "Cleaners on Line," *NOW*, 21 June 1984.

11   Suzanne Goldenberg, "Cleaners Vow They Won't Quit Despite Hardships of Walkout," *Globe and Mail*, 30 June 1984 (Estrela misspelled as Estrella); profile from FCPF/FASWOC, Job Applications, various dates.

12   Tim Harper, "Cleaners' Strike Shakes Dream of a Better Life," *Toronto Star*, 11 July 1984, A1.

13   For Ybor City, see Gary R. Mormino and George E. Possetta, *The Immigrant World of Ybor City, Italians and Their Neighbors in Tampa, 1885–1985* (Gainesville: University Press of Florida, 1998); Nancy A. Hewitt, *Southern Discomfort: Women's Activism in Tampa, Florida, 1880s–1920s* (Champaign, IL: University of Illinois Press, 2001). For an early Canadian example, see Allen Seager, "Class, Ethnicity, and Politics in the Alberta Coalfields, 1905–45," in *Struggle a Hard Battle: Essays on Working Class Immigrants*, ed. Dirk Hoerder (Dekalb, Illinois: Northern Illinois Press, 1986), 304–24.

14   Interview with Wendy Iler by Susana Miranda, 16 August 2006; Crombie, "Cleaners on Line."

15   For example, see Manuel Armando Oliveira, "Azorean Diaspora and Cultural Retention in Montreal and Toronto," in *The Portuguese in Canada: Diasporic Challenges and Adjustment*, 2nd ed., ed. Carlos Teixeira and Victor M.P. Da Rosa (Toronto: University of Toronto Press, 2009).

16   Harper, "Cleaners' Strike Shakes Dream" (Gouveia mispelled as Goveia).

17   CAW Local 40, First Canadian Place Files, FASWOC, Emilia Silva, president, Local 51 FASWOC, to Albert Reichmann, president, Olympia and York Developments Ltd., 30 June 1984. On Reichmanns, see, for example, *Canadian Encyclopedia*, entry by Jorge Niosi, "Reichmann Family" (last ed. 16 December 2013) at thecanadianencyclopedia.ca, and by John Schofield, "Reichmanns Rebound" (last ed. 4 March 2015) at thecanadianencyclopedia.ca.

18   Crombie, "Cleaners on Line."

19   On this theme, see, for example, Aya Fujiwara, *Ethnic Elites and Canadian Identity: Japanese, Ukrainians, and Scots, 1919–1971* (Winnipeg: University of Manitoba Press, 2012); Carmela Patrias and Ruth Frager, "'This Is Our Country, These Are

Our Rights': Minorities and the Origins of Ontario's Human Rights Campaigns," *Canadian Historical Review* 82, no. 1 (March 2001): 1–35.

20 For example, see Carmela Patrias, *Relief Strike: Immigrant Workers and the Great Depression in Crowland, Ontario, 1930–1935* (Toronto: New Hogtown Press, 1990); on children in ethnic women's protest movements and cultures, see Julie Guard, *Radical Housewives: Price Wars and Food Politics in Mid-Twentieth-Century Canada* (Toronto: University of Toronto Press, 2019); Hinther, *Perogies and Politics*; Ester Reiter, "Secular Yiddishkait: Left Politics, Culture, and Community," *Labour / Le Travail* 49 (Spring 2002): 121–46.

21 Goldenberg, "Cleaners Vow They Won't Quit," 19.

22 Interview with Emilia Silva by Susana Miranda, 14 July 2009.

23 Donegan et al., *Starting from Nina.*

24 Portuguese Canadian History Project (est. 2008 by Gilberto Fernandes and Susana Miranda), "City Builders: A History of Immigrant Construction Workers in Postwar Toronto," toronto-city-builders.org; Iacovetta, *Such Hardworking People*, chs. 3 and 7.

25 Harper, "Cleaners' Strike Shakes Dream."

26 Harper, "Cleaners' Strike Shakes Dream."

27 Crombie, "Cleaners on Line"; Franca Iacovetta, "Immigrant Gifts, Canadian Treasures, and Spectacles of Pluralism, The International Institute of Toronto in North American Context, 1950s–70s," *Journal of American Ethnic History* 31, no. 1 (Fall 2011): 34–73.

28 Gabaccia, Iacovetta, and Ottanelli, "Laboring across National Borders," 70–72.

29 Striker cited in Harper, "Cleaners' Strike Shakes Dream."

30 Interview with Emilia Silva by Susana Miranda, 14 July 2009; interview with Lucia Ferreira by Susana Miranda, 20 May 2008. On the bird dance, "The Bird Dance: Canada's Connection to the Enduring Poultry Polka," youtu.be/IhSNgEWK--M.

31 Interview with Lucia Ferreira by Susana Miranda, 20 May 2008.

32 "250 Striking Cleaners Expect Strike-Breakers," *Globe and Mail*, 9 June 1984.

33 CAW Local 40, First Canadian Place Files, FASWOC, FASWOC Booklet of Songs, 1984; Duncan McMonagle, "250 Striking Cleaners Expect Strike-Breakers," *Globe and Mail*, 9 June 1984, 19; António Costa Pinto, *Contemporary Portugal: Politics, Society and Culture*, 2nd ed. (New York: SSM-Columbia University Press, 2011); Gil Green, *Portugal's Revolution* (New York: International Publishers, 1976).

34 Ian Radforth, *Expressive Acts: Celebrations and Demonstrations in the Streets of Victorian Toronto* (Toronto: University of Toronto Press, 2023).

35 Quotation from John Deverell, "Bravo! Pasta Strikers Hail Norma Rae [Michelina Mior]," *Toronto Star*, 29 May 1979. Other media coverage includes "Greve na Lancia-Bravo," *Comunidade*, year 4, no. 11 (30 March 1979); Naomi Wall, "Spirited Strike against Lancia-Bravo," *Union Woman*, 2–5 May 1979; "Strike Ends at Food Plant after 10 Weeks," *Globe and Mail*, 30 May 1979; "Greve na Lancia-Bravo Acaba Com Bons Ganhos," *Comunidade*, year 4, no. 13 (31 May 1979).

36 Cited in Harper, "Cleaners' Strike Shakes Dream"; interview with Emilia Silva by Susana Miranda, 14 July 2009.

37 "Picketing Cleaners Tackle Bay St. Giant," *Toronto Star*, 6 June 1984; "Cleaning Ladies Fight Goliath," *Paranoia* (CEIU) 2, no. 5, July–August 1984; "Cleaning Women Battle Corporate Giant," *Catholic New Times*, 8 July 1984.

38 "Tension Rises on Cleaners' Picket Line: Police Accused of Helping 'Scabs,'" *Globe and Mail*, 6 June 1984; interview with Emilia Silva by Susana Miranda, 14 July 2009.

39 Interview with Wendy Iler by Susana Miranda, 16 August 2006; Eric Solsten, "The Lower Class," in *Portugal: A Country Study* (Washington: Library of Congress, 1993), countrystudies.us.

40 Serafin cited in Harper, "Four Arrested for Trespassing." The phrase "neither ladylike nor deferential" is from Ellen Ross's pioneering article on poor and working-class women's rough language, "Fierce Questions and Taunts: Married Life in Working-Class London, 1870–1914," *Feminist Studies* 8, no. 3 (Autumn, 1982): 575–602.

41 CAW Local 40, First Canadian Place Files, FASWOC, Notes by Medeiros' lawyer; Mary Ellen Nettle, "Immigrant Women Clean Up!," *Hysteria* 3, no. 3 (Fall 1984): 7.

42 Cited in Harper, "Cleaners' Strike Shakes Dream."

43 Cited in Harper, "Cleaners' Strike Shakes Dream"; on Portuguese Canadian elites, see Fernandes, *This Pilgrim Nation*; see also ch. 2.

44 Parr, *Gender of Breadwinners*; Sangster, *Earning Respect*. See also Sugiman, *Labour's Dilemma*.

45 Other examples include Ventresca, "'Cowering Women, Combative Men?'"; Guard, "Authenticity on the Line"; see also ch. 5. On in-your-face tactics in Justice for Janitors struggles in Los Angeles, see Waldinger et al., "Helots No More"; Milkman, *L.A. Story*, esp. ch. 4 (with Kent Wong).

46 International Women's Day Committee Newsletter, September 1984 (Double Issue), "Women Strike Again," 22, Rise Up! a digital archive of feminist activism, riseupfeministarchive.ca.

47 *Union Woman*, September–October 1984, Rise Up! a digital archive of feminist activism, riseupfeministarchive.ca; on OWW, interviews with Barbara Cameron, Holly Kirkconnell, Wendy Cuthbertson, and Margaret McPhail by Franca Iacovetta, Rise Up! Women Unite, for Organized Working Women and for Fleck Strike and Feminist Solidarity, both at riseupfeministarchive.ca. On Red Berets, Rise Up! riseupfeministarchive.ca; Franca Iacovetta email correspondence with Sidney Pratt, 2 and 3 June 2022 (Mantle), and with Red Berets Mariana Valverde, Ester Reiter, and Liz Martin, 10–12 December 2022.

48 Howlett later rewrote some of the lyrics for a strike at McGregor in 1988. Personal communication between Susan Howlett and Susana Miranda, 9 February 2010.

49 CAW Local 40, First Canadian Place Files, FASWOC, Susan Howlett, Cleaners' Strike Song.

50 Nettle, "Immigrant Women Clean Up!"

51 Nettle, "Immigrant Women Clean Up!"; interview with Emilia Silva by Susana Miranda, 14 July 2009..

52 "Picketing Cleaners Tackle Bay St. Giant," *Toronto Star*, 6 June 1984; "Office Cleaners' Strike Irks Tower Tenants," *Toronto Star*, 9 June 1984.

53 CAW Local 40, First Canadian Place Files, FASWOC, Rev. Eduardo Couto, President, Portuguese Pastoral Council, Archdiocese of Toronto, to Albert Reichmann, 9 July 1984.

54 CAW Local 40, First Canadian Place Files, FASWOC, NDP Caucus to Malcolm Spankie, 26 June 1984.

55 CAW Local 40, First Canadian Place Files, M. Spankie, Senior VP, Property Administration, Olympia and York Developments Ltd., to Alderman Dorothy Thomas, NDP Caucus Chairman, 3 July 1984.

56 "Four Hurt on Cleaners' Picket Line," *Globe and Mail*, 14 June 1984.

57 Both quotations (by Silva, and then Iler) in Wendy Iler, "Cleaners Strike Exposes Contracting Out Dangers," *Union Woman* 7, no. 3 (September–October 1984), Rise Up! a digital archive of feminist activism, riseupfeministarchive.ca. Silva was favourably quoted by others, including journalists who, like Rosie DiManno, had more conservative politics. See DiManno, "Strike Wins Women Better Deal," *Toronto Star*, 14 July 1984.

58 Email correspondence between Laurell Ritchie and Susana Miranda, 3 February 2005.

59 "Six-Week Strike Over: Cleaners Celebrate Win with Help of Children," *Globe and Mail*, 23 July 1984; interview with Lucia Ferreira by Susana Miranda, 20 May 2008.

60 Interview with Lucia Ferreira by Susana Miranda, 20 May 2008.

61 CAW, Local 40, First Canadian Place Files, FASWOC, Court Proceeding, Provincial Court (Criminal Division).

62 Treasury Board of Canada Secretariat, Successor Rights and Obligations, Section B, collectionscanada.gc.ca.

63 "Cleaning Jobs in Jeopardy Despite Vote," *Globe and Mail*, 16 February 1986.

64 Milkman, *L.A. Story*, 155.

65 The J4J model was imported into Vancouver in the 1990s during a period of trusteeship (a period when the union leadership strips a local of its autonomy) but was resented and abandoned by the local's personnel. It then resurfaced in 2007, when Toronto Local 204 and five other locals were merged into a mega-local of 40,000 members in Ontario. L. Aguiar and S. Ryan, "The Geographies of the Justice for Janitors," *Geoforum* 40 (2009): 949–58.

66 SEIU representative Allen Ferens (interviewed by Miranda, 16 October 2009) attributed the delay to SEIU leaders in Canada wishing to distance themselves from US-style organizing in the 1980s. On Justice for Janitors campaigns in the United States, Milkman, *L.A. Story*; Waldinger et al., "Helots No More"; Catherine L. Fisk, Daniel J.B. Mitchell, and Christopher Erickson, "Union Representation of Immigrant Janitors in Southern California: Economic and Legal Challenges," in *Organizing Immigrants: The Challenge for Unions in Contemporary California*, ed. Ruth Milkman (Ithaca: Cornell University Press, 2000), 199–224.

Chapter 7. Fighting Contracting Out in the Workplace and Political Arena

1 CTA, Joe Pantalone Fonds, 1135, Box 140194, File 7, Lino Medeiros to Brian Mulroney, Frank Miller, Bernard Ghert, Richard Thomson (14 February 1985).

2 CTA, Joe Pantalone Fonds, 1135, Box 140194, File 7, Bernard I. Ghert, Cadillac Fairview Corporation Ltd, President and CEO to Toronto City Council, Attention: Joe Pantalone, 18 February 1985.

3 A few other examples of immigrant women's activism against the state include Julie Guard, "Canadian Citizens or Dangerous Foreign Women?: Canada's Radical Consumer Movement, 1947–1950," in *Sisters or Strangers?*, ed. Epp, Iacovetta, and Swyripa; Patrias, *Relief Strike*.

4   For examples, see Pat Armstrong and Kate Laxer, "Precarious Work, Privatization, and the Health-Care Industry: The Case of Ancillary Workers," in *Precarious Employment: Understanding Labour Market Insecurity in Canada*, ed. Leah F. Vosko (Montreal/Kingston: McGill-Queen's University Press, 2005); David Camfield, "Neoliberalism and Working-Class Resistance in British Columbia: The Hospital Employees' Union Struggle, 2002–2004," *Labour / Le Travail* 57 (Spring 2006): 9–41; Stephanie Luce, "Labour Market Deregulation and the U.S. Living-Wage Movement," in *Challenging the Market: The Struggle to Regulate Work and Income*, ed. Jim Stanford and Leah F. Vosko (Montreal/Kingston: McGill-Queen's University Press, 2005). Leo Panitch and Donald Swartz's important *From Consent to Coercion: The Assault on Trade Union Freedoms*, 3rd ed. (Aurora: Garamond Press, 2003) briefly mentions it.

5   Heron, *Canadian Labour Movement*, 124–26; Barbara Cameron, "Dualism or Solidarity?: Reforming Canada's System of Labour-Market Regulation," in *Labour Pains, Labour Gains: Fifty Years of PC1003*, ed. Cy Gonick, Paul Phillips, and Jesse Vorst, Socialist Studies no. 10 (Winnipeg and Halifax, Society of Socialist Studies and Fernwood, 1996), 163–76, specifically 167.

6   LAC, Confederation of Canadian Unions Collection, R7115, Box 19, File: CCU—Cleaners Rights, "Contracting Out: How to Wipe Out Contracting Out," in *The Facts*, CUPE August/September 1978 (hereafter Contracting Out, CUPE, 1978).

7   Camfield, "Neoliberalism and Working-Class Resistance in British Columbia."

8   LLUA, SEIU Fonds, Research Department Collection Part II, Box 4, File 35, Service Employees International Union, Contracting Out: How to Fight Back and Win, 1985 (hereafter SEIU Contracting Out, 1985); Hearn, *Building a Dream*.

9   This discussion draws on several sources, including CTA, Dan Heap Fonds, Box 138425, File 23, Executive Board Statement to Labour Council of Metropolitan Toronto, 21 July 1977, Contracting Out in the Federal Public Service; Contracting Out, CUPE, 1978; SEIU, Contracting Out, 1985; Luis Aguiar, "Restructuring and Employment Insecurities: The Case of Building Cleaners," *Canadian Journal of Urban Research* 9, no. 1 (June 2000): 64–93. We thank Meg Luxton for stressing the point about the social welfare / taxpayer costs of the low-wage-and-few-or-no-benefits strategy advocated by both private sector and public sectors employers.

10 By contrast, when businesses are sold, employees retain wages and their union under the Ontario Labour Relations Act. (Ontario Ministry of Labour, July 1990, Wendy Iler Personal Files, Contract Tendering in the Contract Service Sector: Consultation Document.) See Aguiar, "Restructuring and Employment Insecurities"; Luis L.M. Aguiar, "Janitors and Sweatshop Citizenship in Canada," in *The Dirty Work of Neoliberalism*, ed. Aguiar and Herod.

11 John Howley, "Justice for Janitors: The Challenge of Organizing in Contract Services," *Labor Research Review* 9, no. 1 (1990): 65–66.

12 LLUA, SEIU Fonds, Executive Office Files: George Hardy Collection, Box 67, File 26, Hearn to George Hardy, International President, 22 July 1974 (first quotation); Box 67, File 28, Hearn to George Hardy, 21 January 1975; Box 83, File 7, Building Service and Contractors Conference of 14–15 November 1974, President Hardy Speech to Building and Service Contractors Conference (second quotation).

13 LLUA, SEIU Fonds, Executive Office Files: George Hardy Collection, Box 3, File 17, SEIU November 1983, Research Department, Report No 18: The Service

Contract Act: A Guide for Representatives; Box 84, File 25, Guide to the Service Contract Act, U.S. Department of Labor, Employment Standards Administration, Wage and Hour Division, Revised January 1978.

14 Unlike Ontario, Quebec has a Collective Agreement Decrees Act, where either party to a collective agreement may petition the Minister of Labour to apply the terms of a single collective agreement to an entire industry, trade, commerce, or occupation in the province, or in any stated region of the province. This requires that similar terms have been voluntarily entered into by a substantial percentage of employers and unions. Wendy Iler Personal Files, Contract Tendering in the Contract Service Sector: Consultation Document, Ontario Ministry of Labour, July 1990; Hearn, *Building a Dream*.

15 LLUA, SEIU Fonds, Executive Office Files: George Hardy Collection, Box 85, File 1, "Decree respecting building service employees," Montreal Region Order in Council 4400-75 of 1 October 1975, Quebec Official Gazette, 22 October 1975; File 3, "SEIU has unique pact with Quebec Government," *Building Services: A Booming Industry* (report prepared by SEIU AFL-CIO, CLC).

16 Today, SEIU Local 800 represents members from the private sector in Quebec, ues800.org.

17 AO, RG 7-22, Box 354637, File: RG 7-22-0-84, Memo: Government Tendering of Contracts and Implications for Labour Policy, 25 March 1976; Report Regarding Janitorial Work in Metropolitan Toronto, 22 March 1976.

18 On immigrants turning to their community leaders, Irene Bloemraad, *Becoming a Citizen: Incorporating Immigrants and Refugees in the United States and Canada* (Berkeley: University of California Press, 2006), 99.

19 Interview with Michelle Swenarchuk by Susana Miranda, 5 September 2007. In the 1975 Ontario election, the Progressive Conservative Party was reduced to minority status, and the NDP, which had strong support in Toronto's west end where many Portuguese and Italian immigrants lived, became the official opposition.

20 Howley, "Justice for Janitors"; Hurd and Rouse, "Progressive Union Organizing," 70–75; Fisk, Mitchell, and Erickson, "Union Representation of Immigrant Janitors," 203.

21 Swenarchuk, "Portuguese Women Organize."

22 CTA, Dan Heap Fonds, Box 138443, File 3, "Practical Politics," *The Kensington*, October 1976.

23 Hurd and Rouse, "Progressive Union Organizing," 70–75.

24 AO, RG 7-92, Box 5, File: RG 7-92-0-121, "Ontario Betrays Women Cleaners," Ontario Committee on the Status of Women (OCSW), 2 October 1975. See also Ruth Roach Pierson and Marjorie Griffin Cohen, *Canadian Women's Issues, Vol. 2: Bold Visions* (Toronto: Lorimer, 1995), 93–94, 134–135.

25 Marjorie Cohen, "Letter to the Editor," *Globe and Mail*, 19 April 1976.

26 Interview with Michelle Swenarchuk by Susana Miranda, 5 September 2007. Swenarchuk and Laurell Ritchie met with NAC president Lorna Marsden to ask for a statement of support.

27 AO, RG 7-1, Box 220763, File: Ontario Government—Government Services, Queen's Park Janitorial Services 1977–1979, Albert G. Hearn, SEIU International Vice President to Bette Stephenson M.D., Minister of Labour, 5 August 1977, Re: Cleaning Contractors, Hepburn Block and Queens Park Block.

Chapter 7

28 "97 Cleaners Lose Jobs Tonight, Government Says Hands Are Tied," *Toronto Star*, 3 October 1975; "Governo nada fez pelas mulheres de limpeza," *Comunidade*, year 1, no. 4 (October 1975; interview with Sidney Pratt by Susana Miranda, 18 June 2007.

29 OCSW, "Ontario Betrays Women Cleaners."

30 "97 Cleaners Lose Jobs Tonight," *Toronto Star*.

31 Tania Das Gupta, "The Politics of Multiculturalism: Immigrant Women and the Canadian State," in *Scratching the Surface: Canadian Anti-Racist Feminist Thought*, ed. Enakshi Dua and Angela Robertson (Toronto: Canadian Scholars Press, 1999), 193.

32 Robert Menzies, Robert Adamoski, and Dorothy E. Chunn, "Rethinking the Citizen in Canadian Social History," in *Contesting Canadian Citizenship: Historical Readings*, ed. Robert Adamoski, Dorothy E. Chunn, and Robert Menzies (Toronto: University of Toronto Press, 2002), 16.

33 Swenarchuk, "Portuguese Women Organize."

34 "97 Dismissed Cleaners Hired by New Company," *Globe and Mail*, 7 October 1975; "Raise Is Raw Deal, Cleaning Women Say," *Globe and Mail*, 7 February 1976.

35 "Queen's Park to Require Going Wage in Cleaning Contracts: No Help to 97 Who Are Losing Jobs," *Globe and Mail*, 3 October 1975; AO, RG 7-1, Box 220763, File: Ontario Government—Government Services, Queen's Park Janitorial Services 1977–1979, Robert G. Elgie MD, Minister of Labour to Lorne Henderson, Minister of Government Services, Queen's Park Re: Janitorial Contract—Queen's Park Extension Office, 10 August 1979 (hereafter Elgie to Henderson, 1979); "Governo nada fez pelas mulheres de limpeza," *Comunidade*, year 1, no. 4 (October 1975).

36 Elgie to Henderson, 1979.

37 Interview with Allen Ferens by Susana Miranda, 16 October 2009.

38 CTA, Metro Toronto Council Minutes 1966, Vol. 1, Report No. 10 of Executive Committee, Clause 22 Purchase of 590 Jarvis Street for Police Headquarters; CTA, Joe Pantalone Fonds, Box 138887, File 14, Metro Toronto Council Minutes 1974, Vol. 1, Report No. 3 of Executive Committee Clause 39; *City Hall Newsletter*, no. 2, 18 January 1977; "Tenders Called for Cleaning," *Toronto Star*, 9 March 1977.

39 CTA, Dan Heap Fonds, Box 138425, File 22, Dan Heap to Wally Majesky, President Labour Council of Metro Toronto, Les Kovacsi, President CUPE Local 43, and Dave Johnson, Manager Building Trade Council, 20 March 1980.

40 Interview with Arminda de Sousa by Susana Miranda, 15 April 2008.

41 CTA, Reference Collection, Metro Toronto Council Minutes, 1977, Report No. 3 of MEC Clause 42 Contract for Cleaning of Police Headquarters.

42 CTA, Reference Collection, Metro Toronto Council Minutes, 1977, Report No. 3 of MEC Clause 42 Contract for Cleaning of Police Headquarters.

43 Interview with Arminda de Sousa by Susana Miranda, 15 April 2008; "Tenders Called for Cleaning," *Toronto Star*; CTA, Joe Pantalone Fonds, Box 138887, File 14, *City Hall Newsletter*, no. 6, 15 March 1977.

44 CTA, St. Christopher House Fonds, Box 137057, File: Adult Services 1977–1978, Sidney Pratt, Coordinator, Services to Portuguese, St. Christopher House to Members of Metropolitan Executive Committee regarding the cleaning services at 590 Jarvis St., 27 May 1977 (hereafter Pratt to MMEC, 1977).

45 CTA, St. Christopher House Fonds, Box 137057, File: Adult Services 1977–1978, Statement of Mrs. Arminda de Sousa to Metropolitan Executive Committee, 27 May 1977.

46   Interview with Arminda de Sousa by Susana Miranda, 15 April 2008.
47   CTA, Joe Pantalone Fonds, Box 138887, File 14, *City Hall Newsletter*, no. 12, 8 June 1977; Dan Heap Fonds, Box 138425, File 23, Report of Municipality of Metropolitan Toronto, Property Department: Contract Cleaning 590 Jarvis St., 16 September 1977.
48   "Police Cleaner Sees Dirty Deal," *Toronto Star*, 28 May 1977.
49   Pratt to MMEC, 1977.
50   LLUA, SEIU Records, Executive Office Files: George Hardy Collection, Box 63, File 44, Transcript of Dan Heap speech to Proceeding of the 29th Annual Convention, SEIU Ontario Provincial Joint Council No. 22, City of Toronto, 16–19 January 1979.
51   CTA, Joe Pantalone Fonds, Box 141043, File 1, Statement from Joe Pantalone and Ross McClellan to NDP Members, 4 July 1982; File 2, Proposed Portuguese Community Political Action Plan. On the NDP's history of appealing to immigrant workers such as Italians, Robert Storey, "Their Only Power Was Moral: The Injured Workers' Movement in Toronto, 1970–1985," *Histoire sociale / Social History* 41, no. 81 (2008): 99–131.
52   Interview with Arminda de Sousa by Susana Miranda, 15 April 2008.
53   CTA, St. Christopher House Fonds, Box 137060, File 53, St. Chris Review Committee, Adult Services, Minutes of Meeting, 12 February 1979.
54   "Cleaners' Jobs May Be Tender Issue," *Globe and Mail*, 19 February 1985.
55   CTA, Joe Pantalone Fonds, Box 140194, File 7: Petition to Brian Mulroney et al., 14 February 1985.
56   CTA, Joe Pantalone Fonds, Box 140194, File 8, Flyer to tenants at TD Centre entitled "Help Save our Jobs."
57   CTA, Joe Pantalone Fonds, Box 140194, File 8, Flyer to tenants at TD Centre entitled "Help Save our Jobs."
58   CTA, Joe Pantalone Fonds, Box 140194, File 8, Mayor Art Eggleton to Bernard Ghert, 19 February 1985.
59   "Aldermen Fear Tenders Could Cost Cleaning Jobs," *Toronto Star*, 19 February 1985.
60   "TD Centre Cleaners May Lose Their Jobs as Contract Tendered," *Toronto Star*, 9 February 1985.
61   "Eggleton Intervenes on Cleaners' Behalf," *Globe and Mail*, 20 February 1985.
62   CTA, Joe Pantalone Fonds, Box 140194, File 8, Bernard I. Ghert, President and CEO Cadillac Fairview Corporation Ltd. to Toronto City Council's Attention, 18 February 1985.
63   "TD Centre Cleaners May Lose Their Jobs as Contract Tendered," *Toronto Star*.
64   CAW Local 40, First Canadian Place Files, FASWOC, Judy Darcy, "TD Cleaners Fight for Their Jobs," *CUPE Metro News*, Spring 1985.
65   Cited in Darcy, "TD Cleaners Fight for Their Jobs."
66   "250 Skyscraper Cleaners Keep Jobs and Contract," *Toronto Star*, 24 February 1986.
67   Wendy Iler Personal Files, M.G. Spankie, Senior VP Property Administration O&Y to Mr. Luyt VP Corporate Finance, Corporate and Government Banking, Bank of Montreal, FCP Tower, 20 February 1986.
68   Wendy Iler Personal Files, Tenant letter to Malcolm Spankie, 6 February 1986.
69   Hansard, Legislative Assembly of Ontario (LAO), 7 February 1986.

Chapter 7

70 "Firms Must Offer Jobs to Unionized Cleaners," *Globe and Mail*, 8 February 1986.
71 "Cleaning Jobs in Jeopardy Despite Vote," *Globe and Mail*, 16 February 1986.
72 Wendy Iler Personal Files, Committee for Cleaners' Rights (CFCR): Notes for Meeting with Hon. William Wrye, Minister of Labour, Ontario, 27 April 1987.
73 "Grant Special Rights to Cleaners, Unionist Urges," *Toronto Star*, 12 January 1987.
74 *Toronto Star*, 6 February 1986; LLUA, SEIU Fonds, William McFedtridge Collection, Box 54, File: Canadian Service Employee SEIU–CLC and AFL-CIO (1972–1987), "SEIU Continues Fight for Successor Rights," *204 Reporter* (SEIU) 11, no. 3 (September 1986).
75 Wendy Iler Personal Files, CFCR: Notes for Meeting with Wrye, Minister of Labour, 27 April 1987.
76 "Cleaners Lobby Queen's Park for Job Security," *Toronto Star*, 20 November 1986.
77 "Cleaners Fight for Rights Most Take for Granted," *Toronto Star*, 11 March 1986; Wendy Iler Personal Files, Minutes from Meeting CFCR, 9 May 1986 and CFCR flyer, "Cleaners Need Legal Rights" (n.d.).
78 Quotation and discussion from "NDP Seeks More Security for 'Vulnerable' Cleaners," *Toronto Star*, 11 July 1986.
79 "Fight for Cleaners' Rights," *204 Reporter* (SEIU) 12, no. 1 (March 1987).
80 Hansard, LAO, 27 November 1986.
81 Luis L.M. Aguiar, "Restructuring and Employment Insecurities: The Case of Building Cleaners," *Canadian Journal of Urban Research* 9, no.1 (2000): 64–93.
82 "Bill 7 Shuts Out Queen's Park Cleaners," *204 Reporter* (SEIU) 21, no. 1 (March 1996).
83 Aguiar, "Restructuring and Employment Insecurities."

Epilogue

1 "About," Vhils: Alexandre Farto, vhils.com; David Ganhão, "Scratching the Surface: Vhils," *Luso Life* (blog), lusolife.ca; quotation from "Vhils," Urban Nation: Museum for Urban Contemporary Art, urban-nation.com.
2 Susana Miranda personal communication with AnaBela Taborda, 14 July 2022.
3 "Expanding Roots," Vimeo, vimeo.com.
4 "Portuguese Canadian History Project | Projeto de História Luso Canadiana," Robarts Centre for Canadian Studies, York University, pchp-phlc.ca.
5 "History Matters Podcast: Susana Miranda on Portuguese Women in Toronto's Cleaning Industry, 1970–1990," Active History, 3 November 2010, activehistory.ca.
6 "File Name #130–Cleaner's Action | What Does It Mean?," *Department of Public Memory*, departmentofpublicmemory.com.
7 Susana Miranda personal communication with Marcie Ponte, 26 July 2022.
8 "Here to Stay," *Toronto Star*, 10 September 1992, 1–8.
9 Craig Heron, "The Labour Historian and Public History," *Labour / Le Travail* 45 (Spring 2000): 171–97; Stephanie Yuhl, "Sculpted Radicals: The Problem of Sacco and Vanzetti in Boston's Memory," *Public Historian* 32, no. 9 (May 2010): 9–30 (quotation, 9–10).
10 "Movimento das mulhers de limpeza portuguesas no Canada e legado para geracoes de emigrantes," cmjornal.pt, 21 November 2021; Fernandes, *This Pilgrim Nation*, 67–74, 322–24.
11 David Ganhão, "Scratching the Surface: Vhils," *Luso Life* (blog), lusolife.ca.
12 Franca Iacovetta personal communication with Marcie Ponte, 25 October 2022.

13　Susana Miranda personal communication with Marcie Ponte, 26 July 2022.

14　Ganhão, "Scratching the Surface: Vhils."

15　Ruth Milkman and Kent Wong, "Organizing Immigrant Workers: Case Studies from Southern California," in *Rekindling the Movement: Labor's Quest for Relevance in the 21st Century*, ed. Lowell Turner, Harry C. Katz, and Richard W. Hurd (Ithaca: ILR Press, 2001); on the film, see, for example, *Bread and Roses* (2000), dir. Ken Loach, Pioneer Valley Labour Film Festival Guide, University of Massachusetts Labor Center, umass.edu.

16　Milkman and Wong, "Organizing Immigrant Workers"; Howley, "Justice for Janitors"; Richard W. Hurd and William Rouse, "Progressive Union Organizing: The SEIU Justice for Janitors Campaign," *Review of Radical Political Economics* 21, no. 3 (1989).

17　Interview with Allen Ferens by Susana Miranda, 16 October 2009; Justice for Janitors, SEIU Local 2, justiceforjanitors.ca.

18　Lee Gilchrist, "Justice for Janitors Forges Ahead in Toronto and Vancouver," *Rank and File*, 3 May 2022, rankandfile.ca; Diego Mendez, "Janitors in Ottawa Agree to New Deal, Win Their Largest Increases Ever," Justice for Janitors, 12 July 2022, justiceforjanitors.ca.

19　Leah F. Vosko, "Representing Informal Economy Workers: Emerging Global Strategies and their Lessons for North American Unions," in *The Sex of Class: Women Transforming American Labor*, ed. Dorothy Sue Cobble (Cornell: ILR Press, 2007).

20　"Maid to Order: House Cleaning Services Have Gone from Discretionary Luxury to Essential Service," *National Post*, 10 January 2004.

21　On Jan Wong's five-part series on her experiences in the *Globe and Mail*, see "Coming Clean," 1 April 2006; "Dirty Secrets," 8 April 2006; "Cinder Sam and Benderella," 15 April 2006; "Maggie and Me," 22 April 2006; and "Goodbye to All That," 29 April 2006; Barbara Ehrenreich, *Nickel and Dimed: On (Not) Getting By in America* (New York: Metropolitan Books, 2001).

22　The quotation from "Working at Molly Maid Canada: Employee Reviews," can be found at ca.indeed.com, 19 October 2022.

23　This discussion draws on more recent conversations as well as interviews with elderly cleaners by Susana Miranda.

Epilogue

Index

Page numbers in italics represent photos and charts.

abortion, 11, 90–1
Abrigo, 107
accidents, 73, 76, 143, 161
Action Committee for Garment Workers (CATV), 225n3
activism. *See* radical activism
AFL-CIO, 113
Afonso, Elena, 118, 120
agencies, 26, 27, 31–2, 34. *See also* social services; *specific agencies*
agency of women: alliance with activists, 82, 119–20; altering managerial practices, 74; Caribbeans refusing domestic work, 52; customizing aid, 34–5; decertifying SEIU at TD Centre, 123–6; with domestic employers, 53, 57, 62–9; and domestic violence, 106–7; ESL class rejection, 33–4; hiding cash, 78; live-in work rejection, 30; and lunches, 57, 64; picket-line behaviour, 144, 145; PISEM's ideas, 94; rejection of bourgeois code, 34; rejection of union advice, 119–20; skills and methods of domestic cleaning, 68–9; at St. Stephen's Community House, 40–1. *See also* labour organizing; radical activism; strikes
Alinsky, Saul, 83–4, 92
Almeida, Elisabete, 57

American unions, 125, 127, 129, 158. *See also* Justice for Janitors
Ana (survivor), 107
anti-abortion, 90–1
assimilation. *See* socialization
assumptions of character. *See* stereotypes/assumptions
Azevedo, Idalina: about, xv–xvi, 1; commemoration ceremony/mural, 186, 190–1; employer gifts, 74; in mural, 186; with Pimentel, *121*; in Portugal, 17, 20; and stinking garbage, 109–10, 116; successor rights bill, 182; and wildcat strike, 110, 116–17
Azorean islanders (general), xix–xx, 50–1, 112, 132–3, 136, 140, 187

Babbington, Andria, 188–9
Bailão, Ana, 185, 190
Barlow, William, 183
Barrett, James, 115
Batista, Mariana, 14–15, 22, 31, 38, 72, 77
Belchior, Jose, 138
benefits, 49, 163
Bettencourt, Sofia, 20, 22, 58
Bird Dance, 144–5
Black people, 86, 216n8. *See also* Caribbean workers
bodies. *See* health
book overview, xvii–xviii, xx–xxiv, 198
Bread and Roses (film), 193
breadwinners, xvi, 122, 138, 139, 161
Brettell, Caroline, 13, 17

237

Cabral, Goretti, 129
Cadillac Fairview. *See* Toronto-Dominion Centre
Caetano, Marcello, 2
Câmara, Dom Hélder, 91
Canada Employment Centre for Students, 147
Canadian Anglican Church, 91
Canadian experience, 66
Canadian Food and Associated Services Union (CFASU), 127, *130–1*, 145. *See also* Food and Service Workers of Canada
Canadian Textile and Chemical Union, 128
Canadian Union of Public Employees (CUPE): and Committee for Cleaner's Rights, 180; at Metro Police Headquarters, 172–3, 175; solidarity at First Canadian Place, 149; at TD Centre, 102, 126–7, 176, 177–8
Canadianization: overview, 83; activism, 108, 137; ESL textbooks, 98; and food, 41; unions, 115, 120. *See also* socialization
Caribbean workers, 28, 52, 63, 86
Carnation Revolution, 9–11, 187
Carvalho, Elsa, 32
Castro, Gabriela, 97
Catholicism, 2–3, 11, 84, 90–3, 96, 144
Centre for Spanish Speaking Peoples, 104
chaperones, 29
childbirths, 35
children: daycare, 37–41, 50; discipline, 40–1; and domestic work, 49; at First Canadian Place strike, 142–3, 153–5, 155; foster care, 36; and live-in work, 30; meeting employers, 72; and social services, 35; socialization, 36; St. Veronica's school, 94–5; at union meetings, *130*; and work schedules, 31, 38; working teens, 42–3; writing letters, 161
chiropractors, 75
Christian left, 81, 84–5, 91–3, 96. *See also* St. Christopher House
churches, 27
citizenship, 33, 141

Clarke, Edith, 32
class: in Brazil, 96; in Canada, 6; and domestic skills, 66–7; and employers' lunches, 57, 64; and employers' relationships, 72; and ESL textbooks, 97–8, 99; and femininity, 54; and feminism, 85; and free time, 77; and gender roles, 33; house cleaning as "natural," 48; and housework, 51; and labour organizing history, 111; and migration, 8–9, 28; in Portugal, 5–6, 7, 8–9, 13, 15–16, 20–1; rejection of bourgeois code, 34
Cleaners' Action: overview, xx, 99–103; and Canadianization, 108; cartoon from, *102*; commemoration ceremony/mural, 191; at Commerce Court, 127–8; Domestic Violence Group Project, 106; and legal aid, 104; logo of, *101*; at McGregor Hosiery Mills, 128; songwriting, 80, 81–2; TD Centre union choice, 125; vs. unions, 102–3, 119, 124–5
Cleaners' Action mural, xv, 185–92
Cleaner's Action (newsletter), 101–2, *101–2*, 106, 186
cleaning companies (home), 195–6
cleaning products, 67–8, 74–5, 77
clothing repair, 16
Coalition for Abortion Rights, 91
Collective Agreement Decrees Act, 231n14
collective bargaining model, 165, 231n14
colonization, 4, 6, 11
commemoration ceremony/mural, xv, 185–92
Commerce Court, 127–8
Committee for Cleaners' Rights, 180–3
Comunidade (newspaper), 44–5, 83
Concorde Maintenance Ltd., *61*
Confederation of Canadian Unions (CCU), 82, 89, 113, 126–8
Consolidated Maintenance Services, *61*, 123, 168, 170
construction jobs, 35
contraception/abortion, 11, 90–1
contracting out: overview, xviii, 162–6; clauses in collective agreements,

238

Cleaning Up

163; Committee for Cleaners' Rights, 180–3; contracts up for tender, 161–2, 165, 178–9 (*see also* successor rights); corruption of, 164; First Canadian Place, 178–80; as keeping wages low, 56; and layoffs, 168, 170; Metro Police Headquarters, 171–5; of Metro Toronto, 172 (*see also* Metro Police Headquarters); Queen's Park, 166–71; and shaming building owners, 168; successor rights, 157, 178, 181–3, 192; TD Centre, 175–8; as undermining workers' power, 162–3, 198; and unions, 113, 114; and wages, 60, 62, 164–6; and welfare state, 76; work hours and pay, 69. *See also* First Canadian Place; Queen's Park; Toronto-Dominion Centre

contracts, 56–7, 62, 71, 76, 92, 120, 161
control. *See* workplace control
Convention 100, 212n43
Correia, Fernanda, 20
Correia, Margarida, 139
corruption, 164
Costa, Lina, 105–6, 107
Council of Canadian Unions. *See* Confederation of Canadian Unions
Couto, Maria, 115
Cruz, Maria, 141, 143
cultural sensitivity, 86
CUPW, 180

Davis, Bill, 167–8
de Almeida, Isabel, 90, 92–3
de Sousa, Arminda, 55, 172–4, 173
Department of Labour, 69–70
Department of Manpower, 31
Department of Public Memory, 187, 191
desertion, 36
direct action, 84, 101, 145
domestic violence, 105–7
Domestic Violence Group Project, 106–7
domestic workers: overview, xv, xviii, 51; agency of, 53, 57, 62–9; and benefits, 49; and cleaning companies, 195–6; and cleaning products, 67–8, 74–5; control, 48, 62, 63–9, 71, 73; donations to, 58; early recruitments, 27; and

employers' relationships, 53–4, 57, 62, 64, 71–3, 196; ethnicities and jobs, 51–2; and gay families, 79; and gender discrimination, 54; health of, 74–7 (*see also* health); and independence, 49, 64; and kin networks, 52, 57–8, 65; live-in, 29–30, 52, 62, 63, 71; lunches, 57, 64; and maternity leave, 57; vs. office cleaners, xvi, 48–51, 56; and own housework (*see* housework (at home)); in Portugal, 29; and pregnancy, 54; private vs. government programs, xv; recruitment requests, 29; and regional origin, 50–1; as "servants," 48, 52; skills, 66–8; as sojourners, 51; standardization, 65; and taxes, 49; and unions, 49–50, 195; wages, 56, 57–8; wages and factory work, 49; work as strenuous, 54; work ethic/pride, 71, 77–8

Duncombe, Brenda, 41, 96, 104, 108
Dzerowicz, Julie, 188

economies in Portugal, 6–7, 13
education: drop out rates, 43; ESL (*see* ESL classes); and gender, 31; in Portugal, 1, 5, 20, 21; of radical activism and strikes, 140; St. Veronica's school, 94–5; and streaming migrant children, 43; vs. working, 42–3
Eggleton, Art, 177, 180
elderly cleaners looking back, 197
Elgie, Robert, 171
Emigration Junta, 9
Empire Building Maintenance, 61, 178
employer relations: and domestic workers, 53–4, 62, 71–3, 196; and office cleaners, 71–3, 73–4. *See also* labour organizing; radical activism
Employment Standards Branch, 88–9
Equal Pay Coalition of Ontario, 60
ESL (English as a second language) classes: critiquing, 97–8; Freirean curriculum, 85; and gender, 31; gender roles in, 34; literacy as tool, 97; out of van, 108; PISEM involvement in, 95; at Queen's Park, 99, 100; song writing, 80–2, 80; *Starting from Nina* (film),

98–9; at TD Centre, 124; vs. working, 33–4, 87–8

ESL Core Group, 95–6

ESL-in-the-Workplace Task Force, 96

Estado Novo, 3–9, 11–12, 28, 29

Estrela, Maria, 139

factory work, 49

Fair Wage Officer, 173

Family Life project, 41

family organization, 14, 77–8

family support, xix, 25–6, 37–8, 50, 142–3

Faria family, 25–6

farm work in Canada, 28

farming, 7–8, 9–10, 12, 14–15, 16–17, 19

Farto, Alexandre, xv, 185–6, 190, 192

FASWOC, 70, 127, 129–31, 130, 180. See also First Canadian Place strike

Federated Building Maintenance. See First Canadian Place

Feitor, Maria, 148

femininity/masculinity, 54, 58–9, 111. See also gender discrimination; gender roles

feminism: and FASWOC, 129; and immigrant women, 105–6, 107; in labor movement, 85–6; labour history, 111; of PISEM, 93; support for Queen's Park crisis, 168–9

Ferguson, Edith, 33, 42–3

Fernandes, Gilberto, 185, 187

Fernandes, Maria, 38

Ferraro, Rick, 182–3

Ferreira, Lucia: about, xvi–xvii; on cleaners per floor, 69; First Canadian Place strike, 136, 143, 145, 156; office work vs. domestic work, 72; on resentment of supervisor, 128; sewing clothes, 16; time restraints, 70; union party, 155

Ferreira, Virgínia, 12

festivals, 27

Filipe, Celia, 17, 22, 49, 77–8

Filipina workers, 63

First Canadian Place: overview, xvi–xvii, 127, 135; CFASU in, 127; computer-controlled lights, 73; contracting-out crisis, 178–80; FASWOC in, 129–31; garbage salvaging, 70; getting work at, 31; LiUNA in, 157–8; managerial systems, 73–4; after 1984 strike, 156–8; unfair supervisor, 128–9; union drive, 128–31, 130–1; wages at, 61, 138; work amount at, 69; workplace dangers, 76

First Canadian Place strike (1984): overview, 135, 136; challenging stereotypes, 140–1, 146–7; children and husbands, 142–3, 153–5, 155; first day of strike, 136; history of, 138–40; insulted workers, 142; media attention, 136–7, 139, 141, 146–7; party, 155–6, 155; picket-line behaviour/ culture, 144–9; picket-line photos, 152; picket-line tensions, 147–9; sharing stories, 140–1; solidarity, 145–6, 149–52; strikebreakers, 147–8, 151, 156; tenants support for, 145, 151, 179; vote for strike, 139; wins and losses, 152, 155, 156–7

fishing industry, 17

food, 41–2, 57, 64, 79

Food and Service Workers of Canada (FASWOC), 70, 127, 129–31, 130, 180. See also First Canadian Place strike

Foster Day Care Project, 38–9

Free Interpreter Service, 90, 104

Freire, Paulo/Freirean radical pedagogy, 84–5, 92, 98–9

garbage salvaging, 70

garbage stinking, 109–10, 115–17

Gaspar, Fernanda, 87, 88–9, 119

gatekeepers, 26

gay families, 79

gender discrimination: at home, 34, 44; of office cleaning duties, 58–62, 61, 123, 124; and radicalization, 118; strike support, 151; and unions, 123, 124; wages at Queen's Park, 88–9

gender roles: overview, 44; and children, 38; and class, 33; in ESL classes, 34; heavy vs. light cleaning, 58–62, 61

Ghert, Bernard, 161, 177

Giles, Wenona, xviii, 30

240   Cleaning Up

Gluck, Sherna Berger, xxii
Gomes, Joaquina: about, xvi, 15, 19–20; on class of employers, 77; on cleaning products, 68; on employer relations, 72; on recommendations, 78; rejection of dangerous work, 76; shipments home, 58; working nights, 21
Gouveia, Maria, 141
The Grail, 93
grandmothers, 38
grassroots activists. *See* radical activism
Greek women, recruited, 27
Guard, Julie, 111
guerilla street theatre, 158

Hardy, George, 165
Harris, Mike, 183
health: allergies, 76; body pains, 75; and cleaning products, 74–5, 77; damaged eyesight, 143; lung conditions, 76; onsite committees for, 77; vs. productivity, 70; psychological symptoms, 76–7; and shortened lives, xvii; and workers' compensation, 76. *See also* injuries at workplace
health and safety committees, 77
Heap, Dan: and Committee for Cleaner's Rights, 180, 181; and First Canadian Place strike, 151, 154; and Modern's assistant manager, 124; and police headquarters workers, 172–3, 174, 175; and Pratt, 92; and Queen's Park workers, 168; and TD Centre strike, 110–11, 116
Hearn, Albert, 114, 165, 169
heavy vs. light cleaning, 58–62, 61, 117
Heron, Craig, 189
hidden labour, xv, 47, 135
Hobbs, May, 92, 100, 101
home cleaning companies, 195–6
homeownership, 26, 42, 43
Hondagneu-Sotelo, Pierrette, 71
hospitals, 35–6, 50, 113–14, 163
hotels, 50
House of Reconciliation, 91
housewife, as term, 13–14
housework (at home): and body pains, 75; in Canada, 44; in Portugal, 13–14, 17; vs. time with children, 38; value of, 72; values transferred, 76
Howlett, Susan, 80–1, 150

Iacovetta, Franca, xxi–xxii
Iler, Wendy, 128, 147, 178–9
illiteracy, 28, 93, 97. *See also* ESL classes
Immigrant Women's Centre, 90
immigrant women's movement, 103–5
inflation, 135, 138
injuries at workplace, 42, 139, 143
insider/outsider status, 202n26
intelligence, 28
INTERCEDE (International Coalition to End Domestics' Exploitation), 63
International Institute of Metropolitan Toronto: overview, 27, 36–7; and better job options, 32–3; describing families, 25; and mental health of clients, 35; worker preferences, 54; and working teens, 42–3
International Labour Organization, 212n43
International Ladies Garment Workers Union (ILGWU), 225n3
International Women's Day Committee, 149
international unions, 128
interpreting/translation, 90, 123
interview interpretations, xxiii–xxiv
invisibility of labour, xv, 47, 135
Italian women, 27, 52, 90, 145

janitorial workers. *See* office/institution cleaners
job searches, 31–4, 36–7, 52–3, 55–6
Johnson, Michelle, 53
Jordan, Joe, 116
Justice for Janitors (J4J), 158, 168, 183–4, 193–4, 229n65

labour organizing: overview, xviii, xxi; American unions, 125, 127, 129, 158; and Azorean islanders, 132–3, 136, 140; children at strikes, 142–3, 153–5, 155; commemoration ceremony/mural, xv, 185–92; and contracting out, 163–5 (*see also* contracting out); and

Epilogue   241 domestic work, 49–50, 195; employer intimidation, 118–20, 122; and gender, 112; gender discrimination, 123, 124; vs. higher wages, 127–8; history, 111–15; and Hobbs, 92; increasing, 110–12; international unions, 128; and kin networks, 118; in Portugal, 4; productivity and exploitation, 69; at Queen's Park (*see* Queen's Park); and radical coalitions, 192; successor rights, 157; "Sweep and Say Union" (song), *80*, 81, *81–2*; at TD Centre (*see* Toronto-Dominion Centre); union complacency, 113, 123–6; union drives, 100, 101–2, 112–13, 117–19, *122*, 128–31, *130–1*; wages, 62, 120–3; workplace dangers, 76. *See also* Cleaners' Action; First Canadian Place strike; Justice for Janitors; radical activism; strikes; *specific unions*

Labourers' International Union of North America (LiUNA), 157–8, 180

Lancia-Bravo, 137, 145

landed immigrant status, 28, 63

language. *See* interpreting/translation

language barriers: and better paying work, 33–4, 41, 87–8, 98; and Canadianization, 41; and childbirth, 35–6; current cleaners' languages, 194; and domestic work, 67, 79; Federated at OLRB hearing, 131; and formal complaints, 172; and government jobs, 174–5; and hotel work, 50; and job performance, 174–5; legal strike activities, 157; posts in unions, 157; and rights, 141, 174; and stinking garbage at TD Centre, 116; and union drives, 129, 131; and Y&R wages, 174

Lastman, Mel, 175

laundry, 64, 66–7

layoffs, 168, 170, 176, 180

letter campaign, 177

Lewis, Stephen, 60

LGBTQ+, 79

liberation theology, 84–5

literacy, 5. *See also* ESL classes

Literacy: Charitable Enterprise or Political Right? (pamphlet), 97

Literacy Working Group, 97–8

LiUNA (Labourers' International Union of North America), 157–8, 180

live-in workers, 29–30, 52, 62, 63, 71

lives cut short, xvii

Local Initiatives Program, 90

Lopes family, 25–6

Lourdes (migrant), 35–6

low pay/skilled jobs, 31, 32, 49

lunches, 57, 64

Lundie, Pat, 168–9

Luxton, Meg, 85

Machado, Diamantino P., 4, 13

Mackenzie, Robert, 181, 182

Manpower Services, 86

Mantle, Arlene, 150

Martins, Maria, 17, 21

Marxism, 85

masculinity/femininity, 54, 58–9, 111. *See also* gender discrimination; gender roles

Mata, Belmira, 36

maternalism, 56–7, 58, 71, 72–3

maternity leave, 57

McCallum, Taman, 104

McClellan, Ross, 175, 182

McFarlane, W. S., 109–10, 116

McGregor Hosiery Mills, 128

Medeiros, João, 82–3, 95–6, 98–9, 108

Medeiros, Lino, 161

Medeiros, Maria, 148, 161

media coverage, 136–7, 139, 141, 146–7, 167, 169–70

men: and child care, 37, 50; deserting family, 36; disinterest in office cleaners struggles, 167; domestic violence, 105–7; and education, 31; as heavy duty cleaners, 58–9, 117; and mental health, 35, 36; migration, 21–2, 27–9; recession and unemployment, 138; and strike breaking women, 148; strike support, 142–3; and unions, 112, 123, 124; wages, 58–9, 60, 117, 223n31; and wives working, 32–3

Mendes, José Carneiro, 190

mental health, 35–6

mentorship, 104–5

242

Cleaning Up

Metro Council Executive, 172–5
Metro Police Headquarters, 171–5
migration: overview, 21–3; and class, 8–9, 28; "disappearing" to cities, 28–9; early domestics, 29; early migrants and community, 26–7; men, 21–2, 27–9; number in 1981, 26; preferred destinations, 9, 10; Portugal passports, 29; ratio in countries, 204n34; reasons for, 1, 2, 4, 9–10, 14, 22; as recruited, 27–8; sacrifices, 140–2; second thoughts, 197. *See also* Canadianization; settling in; socialization
minimum wage, *61*, 114, 120, 166, 170–1, 196. *See also* wages
Ministry of Government Services, 166–7
Ministry of Labour, 88–9
Mior, Michelina, 137, 145
Miranda, Susana P., xxi–xxii, 185, 187, 202n26
Modern Building Cleaning, 59. *See also* Queen's Park; Toronto-Dominion Centre
Modistas Unidas, 105
Molly Maid, 195–6
morality, 29
Moreira, Rosa, 19, 72
multiculturalism, 107–8, 137
murals, xv, 185–92

National Action Committee on the Status of Women (NAC), 169, 180
National Employment Service, 31
NDP, 151–2, 162, 175, 181–3, 231n19
neoliberalism, xviii
Nettle, Mary Ellen, 80–1, 96, 104, 108
the New Left, 83
night work, other, 31
nighttime office cleaners vs. private day cleaners, xvi, 48–51, 56. *See also* domestic workers; office/institution cleaners
nurses, 35–6

odours, 54, 109–10, 115–17, 116
office/institution cleaners:

overview, xviii–xix, 54–5; amount of Portuguese people, 56; and child care, 37, 38, 50; cleaning products, 74–5, 77; Committee for Cleaners' Rights, 180–3; contractors at TD Centre, 161–2; control, 69–71, 73; and CUPE, 126–7; decertifying SEIU at TD Centre, 123–6; vs. domestic workers, xvi, 48–51, 56; gender discrimination, 58–62, 123, 124; health of, 74–7 (*see also* health); and history of immigrants, 55; informal resistance, 70–1; and kin networks, 50, 55–6; and literacy, 50; managerial systems, 73–4; OLRB compensation, 119–20; recruitment for, 56; and regional origin, 50; salvaging, 70; SEIU at TD Centre, 114–15, 123–6; stinking garbage at TD Centre, 109–10, 115–17; strikes (*see* strikes); surveillance of, 73; union drives, 100, 101–2, 112–13, 117–19, *122*, 128–31, *130–1*; wages (*see* wages); work amount and hours, 69; work ethic/pride, 70, 77–8, 176–7; and Workers' Compensation Board, 76. *See also* Cleaners' Action; contracting out; First Canadian Place strike; *specific buildings*
Oliveira, Fernanda, 34
Olympia & York. *See* First Canadian Place
Ontario Committee on the Status of Women (OCSW), 168–9
Ontario Human Rights Commission (OHRC), 86, 88–9
Ontario Labour Relations Act, 112
Ontario Labour Relations Board, 110
Ontario Labour Relations Board (OLRB), 119–20, 125, 129, 131
oral histories, xxii–xxiv
Organized Working Women, 150

Pacheco, Ana, 122
Pacheco, Manuela, 37
Pacheco, Maria, 122
Pais, Sidónio, 3
Pantalone, Joe, 175, 180, 181
Parent, Madeleine, 89, 129
part time work, 60

Epilogue

243

"*Passarinhos a Bailar*," 144–5
Passerini, Luisa, xxii, 15
paternalism, 72–3
patriarchy, 11–13, 87
Pay Equity Act, 62, 212n49
Pedagogy of the Oppressed (Freire), 85
Pedro, Emiliana, 115
Pereira, Carmina, 88
Pereira, Josefa, 53–4
personalism, 71–2, 77
Peterson, David, 179
PIDE (Polícia Internacional e de Defesa do Estado), 3, 12
Pimentel, Leopoldina, 100, 101–2, 119, 121, 137
Pinto, António Costa, 2
Pinto, Beatrice, 48
police, 116, 147–8, 150, 157
Ponte, Marcie, 100–1, 104–5, 190–1
Portugal: overview, 1–2; Carnation Revolution, 9–11, 187; class in, 5–6, 7, 8–9, 13, 15–16, 20–1; economy in, 6–9, 13; education in, 5, 20, 21; laundry routines, 66–7; living conditions vs. Toronto, 14–15; local reasons for migration, 9–10; patriarchy in, 11–13; politics of, 2–4; returning to, 22, 51, 197; socialist governments, 188; strikes to help family in, 139; wages, 12–13; women working, 11–14, 16–20, 23
Portuguese Canadian History Project, 186–7
Portuguese Interagency Network, 180
Portuguese West of Bathurst Project (PISEM), 92–7, 99, 100, 104, 108
Portuguese Women's Group, 105
poverty, 6, 7, 25, 28, 66–7
Pratt, Sidney: about, 82, 91–3; and Alinsky, 218n34; and Cleaners' Action, 100–1 (*see also* Cleaners' Action); commemoration ceremony/mural, 191; Commerce Court organizing, 127–8; curriculum writing, 98; door-to-door visits, 124; and Duncombe, 96; and Hearn, 169; multiculturalism criticism, 107–8; and PISEM, 93–4 (*see also* Portuguese West of Bathurst

Project); and police headquarters contracting-out, 172, 174, 175; and Queen's Park workers, 122, 170; and unions, 102–3; in WWIW, 104
pregnancy, 54
pride. *See* work ethic/pride
private contractors. *See* contracting out
professional workers migrating, 28
Protestants, 84, 91

Queen's Park: overview, 117; contracting-out crisis, 166–71; ESL classes, 99, 100; hours reduction, 69; personalism, 77; successor rights, 157, 178, 181–3, 192; union drive, 100, 101–2, 117–19, 122; wages at, 61, 88–9, 117, 120–1

racial tensions, 86
racism, 52, 86. *See also* stereotypes/assumptions
radical activism: overview, xx, xxi, 44–5, 82–3; commemoration ceremony/mural, xv, 185–92; ESL classes, 96–9; ideas into practice, 86–9; immigrant women's movement, 103–5; influences of cleaners' actions, 83–6, 140; mentorship, 104–5; and unions, 192. *See also* Cleaners' Action; labour organizing; Portuguese West of Bathurst Project; Services for Working People; St. Christopher House
Rae, Bob, 151, 175, 180, 181, 183
rags, 67, 68, 76
Ramirez, Judith, 90
Ramos, Rita, 9–10, 17, 66–7
recession, 138
recruitment, 27–8, 29, 56
Red Berets, 150
Reichmann family. *See* First Canadian Place
Ribeiro, Evangelina, 33
Ribeiro, Martha, 115
Richard, Claire, 92–3
Riegelhaupt, Joyce, 13
Rise Up! (digital archive), xxii
Ritchie, Laurell, 129, 156
Rocchia, Fatima, 137, 225n3
Rocha family, 32, 39

Romero, Mary, 71
Rowley, Kent, 89
rural living, 7–8, 9–10, 12, 14–15, 16–17, 19. *See also* Azorean islanders
Ryerson Polytechnical Institute, 115

Saez, Isabel, 145
Salazar, António, 2, 3, 5, 203n7
salvaging, 70
scabs, 147–8, 151, 156
schedules and children, 31
School of Social Work (University of Toronto), 88
self worth, xvi
Serafin, Maria, 147
Service Contract Act, 166
Service Employees International Union (SEIU): about, 113; and Canadianization, 115; and Cleaners' Action, 103, 124–5; and Committee for Cleaner's Rights, 180; and contracting out, 163–4, 165–6; and CUPE, 126; currently, 194; decertifying at TD Centre, 123–6; gender discrimination, 123, 124; and health and safety, 77; history in Toronto, 123; and men as cleaners, 59; and Pratt, 102; at Queen's Park, 119, 120–1, 169; revitalization of, 192–3; siding with Modern, 124. *See also* Justice for Janitors
Services for Working People (SFWP), 82, 86–7, 119
settling in: overview, 43–5; daycare, 37–41; donations, 25–6; job searches, 31–4, 36–7, 52–3, 55–6; live-in work opportunities, 29–30; and social services, 34–6; sponsorship, 25; working teens, 42–3
Sewell, John, 174
sewing, 16
sexual harassment/assault, 50
shame, 77
Silva, Emilia: about, 19; as FASWOC president, 141–2; First Canadian Place strike, 145, 153, 154; on gifts for supervisors, 74; as heroine, 156; job searches, 31, 55; joining union, 128
Silva, Mario, 47

Silva, Piedade, 50, 122, 169–70
single mothers, 30
single women, 29, 30
Snow, James, 168, 170
Soares, Carolina: Canada as modern, 66; as confident with employers, 65; and employers' families, 72; and employers' lunches, 64; as farm worker, 17; at fish-canning factory, 18–19; as long-time worker, 1; work expectation in Canada, 23
Soares, Joana: on cleaning tools, 68; and employers' lunches, 64; as farm worker, 17; at fish-canning factory, 18–19; indoor plumbing in Portugal, 15–16; as professional, 77
social movements, 82–4
social services: overview, 27, 34–6; changing approach, 82, 83; customizing aid, 27; and domestic violence, 105; in Portugal, 8; power of, 34; and status quo, 82. *See also* agencies; *specific agencies*
socialization, 36, 39, 40, 86, 108, 187–8. *See also* Canadianization
songs, *80*, 81–2, 144–5, 150–1
Sousa, Irene, 53
Sousa, John, 176, 178
Sousa Tavares, Rita, 185, 190
sponsorship, 25–6, 29
St. Christopher House: overview, 27, 89–90; and Canadianization, 37; child care, 38–9; and Committee for Cleaner's Rights, 180, 181; domestic violence help, 106–7; food, 41; Free Interpreter Service, 90, 104; hiring Pratt, 91, 92; leaflet campaigns, 101; and Portuguese language, 32; stereotypes of migrant women, 41. *See also* Cleaners' Action; Portuguese West of Bathurst Project
St. Stephen's Community House, 39–41
St. Veronica's school, 94–5
Starting from Nina (film), 98–9
Steedman, Mercedes, 123
stereotypes/assumptions: challenging, 140–1, 146–7 (*see also* agency of women); of cleaning as "dirty," 77;

Epilogue   245 education streaming, 43; ESL class rejection, 33–4, 87–8; ethnicities and jobs, 47; during First Canadian Place strike, 142; hands and type of work, 54; house cleaning as "natural," 48; and lack of English, 65; by officials, 28; Portuguese as cleaners, 47; and pride, 77–8; and radicalization, 118; of Snow, 170; and strike support, xix; and working teens, 42–3. *See also* racism

stigmas, 71, 77. *See also* stereotypes/assumptions

Stiles, Marit, 188

strikebreakers, 147–8, 151, 156

strikes: and family support, xix, 142–3; to help family in Portugal, 139; Lancia-Bravo, 137, 145; Montreal garment workers, 137; in Portugal, 4, 11; Ryerson Polytechnic Institute, 115; TD Centre, 115–17; wildcat, 109–10, 115–17. *See also* First Canadian Place strike

successor rights, 157, 178, 181–3, 192

supervisors, 73–4, 128–9

surveillance, 73

Sweeney, John, 192

"Sweep and Say Union" (song), *80*, 81–2

Swenarchuk, Michelle: about, 82; and Cleaners' Action, 103; cleaners vs. First Canadian Place, 131; Employment Standards Branch case, 88–9; OLRB compensation, 100, 119–20; and Queen's Park crisis, 170; SEIU at TD Centre, 126; on workers' power, 121

Taborda, AnaBela, 185

Tavares, Vitor and Marina, 185

taxes and domestic work, 49

technology, 66–9, 73, 213n73

temporary work visas, 28, 63

theft, 70–1

Toronto Metropolitan University, 115

Toronto-Dominion Centre (TD Centre): overview, 109; contracts up for tender, 161–2, 175–8; decertifying SEIU, 123–6;

as second home, 176; stinking garbage, 109–10, 115–17; strikes at, 109–10, 115–17; union drive, 114; unions at, 102; wages at, *61*, 176

trade jobs, 29, 35

transit, 31, 53, 57

translation, 90, 123

Travassos, Germana, 169

Unda, Jean Connon, 97, 186

unemployment, 138

União Nacional, 3

unions. *See* labour organizing; *specific unions*

United Appeal, 25, 39

University of Toronto, 88, 123

Vasconcelos, Maria, 5

Vatican II, 84, 93

Vhils, xv, 185–6, 190, 192

victimization, 87

Vilela, Natalia, 19, 67

virtue, 29

wages: biggest increase, 194; chart of different employers/years, *61*; and Committee for Cleaners' Rights, 183; and contracting out, 164–6; and contracts, 56–7; factory vs. domestic work, 49; Fair Wage Officer, 173; at First Canadian Place, *61*, 135, 138, 152; and gender discrimination, 58, 59, 60, *61*, 88–9, 117; hospital work, 49; hourly vs. flat rate, 56–7; and inflation, 138; and kin networks, 57–8; at Metro Police Headquarters, 171, 171–4, 172; minimum wage, 56, *61*, 114, 120, 166, 170–1, 196; Modern vs. Ontario government, 117; at Molly Maid, 196; office vs. domestic, 56; in Portugal, 12–13; at Queen's Park, *61*, 88, 117, 120–1; after Queen's Park union drive, 120–3; and size of houses, 57; at TD Centre, *61*, 176; vs. unions, 127–8; women as breadwinners, 122, 138, 139, 161. *See also* low pay/skilled jobs

Walhrave, Cecilia, 92
war, 6–7, 11
weekend work, 50
West End YMCA, 96, 98, 108
widows, 30
wildcat strikes, 109–10, 115–17. *See also* strikes
Willems, Emilio, 13
women as breadwinners, xvi, 122, 138, 139, 161
Women Working with Immigrant Women (WWIW), 103–4
Women's Bureau, 49, 87–8
Women's Press, 102
women's rights in Portugal, 11–13
Wong, Jan, 195–6
Wood, Neil, 124
work ethic/pride, 70, 71, 77–8, 176–7
Workers' Compensation Board, 76
Working Women Community Centre (WWCC), 104–5
workplace control, 48, 62, 63–71, 73, 76
worm picking, 31

Y&R Properties. *See* Metro Police Headquarters
Yuhl, Stephanie, 189

SUSANA P. MIRANDA is an independent scholar with a PhD in history from York University. The author of scholarly articles on Portuguese cleaners in Toronto, she currently works for the Ontario Ministry of Education and the Ministry of Colleges and Universities. A public historian, she is co-founder of the Portuguese Canadian History Project, which collects, preserves, and disseminates material related to the Portuguese in Canada. She lives in Toronto.

FRANCA IACOVETTA is professor emerita of history at the University of Toronto, and a past president of the Berkshire Conference of Women Historians. A historian of women/gender, migration, and transnational radicals, she has published eleven books, including *Before Official Multiculturalism: Women's Pluralism in Toronto, 1950s-1970s*. Award-winning books include *Gatekeepers: Reshaping Immigrant Lives in Cold War Canada* and the co-edited *Beyond Women's Words*. She lives in Toronto.